1998
Environment
Scarce.
$22
A

ISSUES&OPTIONS
The Clean Development Mechanism

Editor

José Goldemberg

Contributors

Paige Brown
Benjamin Dessus
Raúl A. Estrada-Oyuela
Gylvan Meira Filho
Alessandra Goria
Robert Hamwey
Paul Hassing
Stephen Humphreys
Josef Janssen
Nancy Kete
Robert Livernash

Matthew S. Mendis
Mark Mwandosya
Rajendra K. Pachauri
Theodore Panayotou
Domenico Siniscalco
Youba Sokona
Björn Stigson
Franciso Szekely
Jean-Philippe Thomas
Farhana Yamin

United Nations Development Programme

United Nations Publications

UN Sales No. E.99.III.B.3
ISBN: 92-1-126106-6

ACKNOWLEDGEMENTS

This report, initiated by Professor Thomas B. Johansson, Director, Energy and Atmosphere Programme (EAP), is a product of the co-operation and commitment of an extensive group of distinguished scientists, energy analysts, and some of the key negotiators who participated in the 1997 Kyoto Conference on Climate Change. The United Nations Development Programme (UNDP) is very grateful to the contributors who agreed to prepare their contributions within tight deadlines, and who provided substantial suggestions and information on the whole manuscript.

UNDP extends its sincere thanks to all those who have made this publication possible. Most importantly, UNDP is greatly indebted to Professor José Goldemberg, editor of the publication, for his leadership and commitment in pulling it all together. UNDP applauds Paul Boyd and Janet Jensen, technical editors of the publication, for their flexibility and excellent and timely work. UNDP is also grateful to Maureen Lynch of the Division of Public Affairs for her guidance and wisdom throughout all stages of print preparation, and Julia Ptasznik, Associated Print Productions, for her page layout and graphic design. Caitlin Allen-Sanchez and Annie Roncerel, were the project co-ordinators for this EAP effort, under the leadership of Thomas B. Johansson.

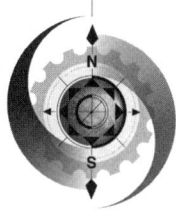

ISSUES&OPTIONS
The Clean
Development
Mechanism

TABLE OF CONTENTS

ISSUES&OPTIONS
The Clean
Development
Mechanism

LIST OF ABBREVIATIONS

LIST OF ACRONYMS

AIJ	Activities Implemented Jointly
AOSIS	Alliance of Small Island States
AGBM	Ad hoc Group on the Berlin Mandate
CDM	Clean Development Mechanism
CER	Certified emission reductions
CERUs	Certified emission reduction units
COP	Conference of the Parties to the UNFCCC
EB	Executive Board
ER	Emissions Reductions
EIT	Economies in Transition
EU	European Union
FDI	Foreign Direct Investment
FFEM	Fonds Français pour l'Environnement Mondial
GEF	Global Environment Facility
GDP	Gross Domestic Product
GWP	Global Warming Potential
HDI	Human Development Index
IBACC	International Business Action on Climate Change
IDB	Inter-American Development Bank
IPCC	Intergovernmental Panel on Climate Change
LDC	Least Developed Countries
MOP	Meeting of the Parties to the Kyoto Protocol
NGO	Non-Governmental Organisation
ODA	Official development assistance
OECD	Organisation for Economic Co-operation and Development
QELRCs	Quantified emission limitation and reduction commitments
QELROs	Quantified emission limitation and reduction obligations
SBI	Subsidiary Body for Implementation
SBSTA	Subsidiary Body for Scientific and Technological Advice
USIJI	US Initiative on Joint Implementation
UNFCCC (or FCCC)	United Nations Framework Convention on Climate Change
WEC	World Energy Council - represents the energy industries of 100 countries
WRI	World Resources Institute
WBCSD	World Business Council for Sustainable Development

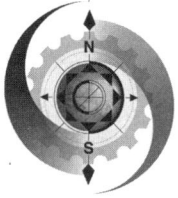

ISSUES&OPTIONS

The Clean
Development
Mechanism

GREENHOUSE GASES (GHGs) AND THEIR PRECURSORS

As defined under the United Nations Framework Convention on Climate Change, "Greenhouse gases" means those gaseous constituents of the atmosphere, both natural and anthropogenic (human-induced). The six greenhouse gases addressed by the Kyoto Protocol include:

CH_4	Methane
CO_2	Carbon dioxide
HFCs	Hydrofluorocarbons
N_2O	Nitrous oxide
PFCs	Perfluorocarbons
SF_6	Sulphur hexafluoride

In addition, the following gases, some of which are precursors to greenhouse gases, also contribute to global warming, and may be reported by countries in their national greenhouse gas emission inventories.

NMVOC	Non-methane volatile organic compounds
NO_x	Nitrogen oxides
CO	Carbon monoxide

The following greenhouse gas units of measurement were mentioned in this paper.

MtC	Million tons of carbon
TCE	Ton of carbon equivalent
Tg	Tera gram (10^{12})
g	gram

ISSUES&OPTIONS
The Clean
Development
Mechanism

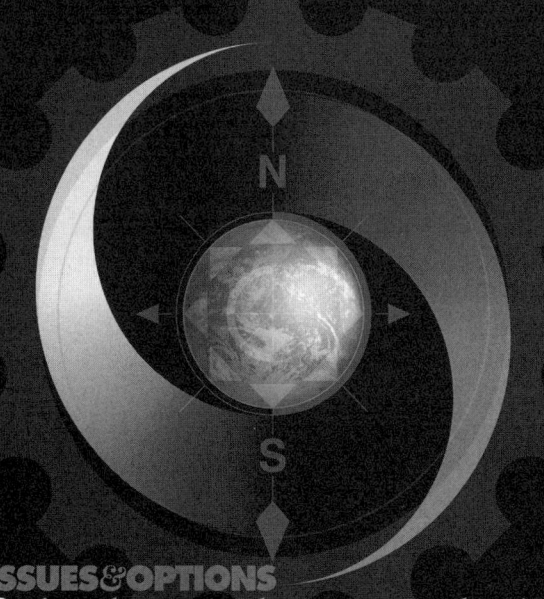

ISSUES & OPTIONS
The Clean Development Mechanism

Introduction

FOREWORD

Introduction

The agreement to create a Clean Development Mechanism (CDM) is an important component of the Kyoto Protocol adopted in December 1997 by the Conference of Parties (COP) to the United Nations Framework Convention on Climate Change (UNFCCC). A main purpose of this new cooperative mechanism – to assist developing countries in achieving sustainable development – is precisely a central objective of the United Nations Development Programme. Thus, there are significant synergies between UNDP activities and the objectives of the Convention and Protocol.

For this reason, we have engaged in exploring issues and options involved in defining the CDM's structure, operations, and project activities. Such advance thinking and timely preparation could feed into the next COP meeting in Buenos Aires, which is charged with seeking agreements that could enable the CDM to be launched. The result is the present report prepared by UNDP's Energy and Atmosphere Programme. It is based on contributions from distinguished scientists, energy analysts, and some of the key negotiators who participated in the Kyoto Conference. Professor José Goldemberg of the University of São Paulo in Brazil served as the editor.

It is clear that a series of steps remain to be taken for getting the CDM into operation – political consultations, technical and economic assessments, financial and administrative planning, and constitutional and structural preparations. Perhaps the first level of shared effort is for developed and developing countries to jointly review their respective purposes, priorities, and expectations in the creation of a CDM. Clarifying motivations and interests could improve mutual understandings, identify areas of common concern, help discover possible trade-offs, and nourish a jointly conceived framework for accommodating the range of needs of the various Parties.

A second level of work and fundamental task is to go back to the Kyoto Protocol text concerning the CDM. Starting with the intents expressed, deliberations conducted, compromises reached, and unresolved issues left at Kyoto can spark realistic ideas about how to build on those foundations.

To build on these analyses and arrive at a realistic and workable conclusion, a third level of work is to brainstorm new possibilities, develop and analyse options, and construct and test alternative scenarios for the development and operation of the CDM. The target of this creative process would be progressively to narrow the zones of disparity, unclarity and uncertainty, and

ISSUES&OPTIONS

The Clean
Development
Mechanism

dynamically to expand the areas of realistic future thinking and sound international consensus. Helpful contributions can be provided by other interested groups – for example, from the private sector, non-governmental organisations, academic and research institutions.

This book tries to cover all three levels of work as an aid to the international community in the broad next steps to be taken in creating the CDM. Speaking for UNDP, which cooperates in policy analysis and practical action in many environment and development fields, I believe that the numerous insights these authors have assembled can impart strength and substance to the planning for the CDM. And I hope that this source material will prove directly useful to negotiators and decision-makers from all concerned countries – developed and developing alike – as they give more precise shape to this innovative mechanism.

James Gustave Speth
Administrator
United Nations Development Programme
New York, September 1998

ISSUES&OPTIONS

The Clean
Development
Mechanism

OVERVIEW

Professor José Goldemberg, Editor
University of São Paulo
São Paulo, Brazil

Summary: This chapter surveys the issues and options covered by the contributors in their individual chapters and brings key points together for ease of reference. The topics covered are as follows:

- Origin of CDM
- The competition between "flexibility" mechanisms
- Governance: the Executive Board
- CDM "modus operandi"
- The certification process
- The question of baselines
- Equity
- Share of proceeds
- Project eligibility and sustainable development
- Land use changes

The Clean Development Mechanism (CDM) defined by the Kyoto Protocol (Article 12) is a new cooperative mechanism involving developing countries. Through the CDM, certified emission reductions accruing from sustainable development projects in developing countries can be used by developed countries to meet part of their reduction commitments as specified in Annex B of the Protocol.

CDM is one of four "flexibility" mechanisms for emission reductions that were adopted in the Kyoto Protocol. The other three, which can be used exclusively among Annex I countries to the United Nations Framework Convention on Climate Change (UNFCCC) are:

- Bubbles (Article 4)
- Joint Implementation (Article 6)
- Emissions trading (Article 17).

Immediately after the Kyoto Conference, the United Nations Development Programme (UNDP) recognised that the CDM could be an important instrument to further sustainable human development. With this in mind, the Administrator of UNDP, James Gustave Speth, convened a meeting in New York in early January 1998 with his Senior Advisers and a few external experts. They strongly endorsed a proposition from Professor Thomas B. Johansson, Director of UNDP's Energy and Atmosphere Programme that UNDP would commission a publication on the "issues and options" surrounding the CDM. The publication would serve as an input to the preparatory process leading to the Fourth Conference of the Parties (COP-4), in November 1998 in Buenos Aires, and beyond.

To fulfil that objective, UNDP invited a number of specialists to prepare papers on different aspects of the new mechanism. The authors include distinguished scientists, energy analysts and some key negotiators who took part in the Kyoto Conference in December 1997, which was the Third Conference of the Parties (COP-3) to the UNFCCC.

This overview attempts to capture the essence of the discussions that took place among the authors. It is not intended to represent a consensual

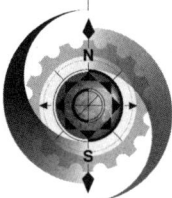

ISSUES&OPTIONS
The Clean
Development
Mechanism

position. Rather, it attempts to flesh out the key issues, to give a balanced view of different perspectives, and to point to the types of decisions that will have to be considered by future sessions of the Conference of the Parties to the Climate Change Convention (COP) or the Meeting of the Parties to the Kyoto Protocol (MOP).

What this offers the reader is a collection of contrasting approaches to a largely common group of issues. The authors bring insights and ideas from a variety of origins, disciplines, and viewpoints – North and South; legal, environmental, political, and academic; governmental, non-governmental, and business. All chapter authors are either participants of the Kyoto and post-Kyoto process, and/or active analysts of its many dimensions.

In shaping this overview, I have drawn on the work of the individual authors without attribution, since their full contributions are contained in the following chapters, which they wrote. Their viewpoints are presented in their personal capacities. The publication as a whole does not reflect a UNDP position on the issues and options facing the CDM.

ORIGIN OF THE CDM

The original proposal of Brazil that led to the CDM envisaged a "Clean Development Fund." Its financing was to come from non-compliance fees from Annex I countries that exceeded their assigned amounts of greenhouse gas emissions in a given budget period. The punitive nature of the proposal was modified after intensive negotiations involving many delegations.

The final result was Article 12 of the Kyoto Protocol, which defined the CDM. The objectives of this new mechanism are to:

- assist Parties not included in Annex I in achieving sustainable development and in contributing to the ultimate objective of the Convention

- assist Annex I countries in achieving compliance with their quantified emission limitation and reduction commitments.

The main characteristics of the CDM are:

- Non-Annex I Parties will benefit from "project activities resulting in certified emission reductions (CERs)."

- An Executive Board will be created.

- "Operational entities" will provide certification that the projects involved voluntary participation by the Parties, that real, measurable, long-term benefits are coming from the mitigation, and that reductions are additional to any that would occur in the absence of the certified project activity.

- A share of the proceeds from project activities shall be used to cover "administrative expenses" and costs of adaptation to climate change in the most vulnerable countries.

- Private entities may be involved.

- CER's obtained from the year 2000 up to 2008 can be used in achieving compliance in the first commitment period (2008-2012).

Article 12 was the result of a political compromise. It conciliated two sharply opposing views that almost wrecked the Kyoto Protocol. For some countries, an essential element for the Kyoto Protocol was emission trading based on adoption of mandatory reduction commitments by all countries. This feature was contained in a United States Senate resolution, but was unacceptable to the Group of 77 and China. One approach for solving this problem envisaged voluntary commitments from non-Annex I countries; but the idea was not accepted for fear that funding agencies would discriminate against countries not making such commitments. The creation of the CDM emerged as the solution. While the Protocol indicates that mitigation is one of the main purposes of the CDM, some attention was given also to adaptation (Article 12.8).

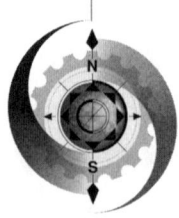

Perceptions by industrialised countries and developing countries while creating the CDM in Kyoto were clearly different:

◆ Industrialised countries saw CDM as an additional mechanism for emission reductions through a form of Joint Implementation. It could achieve reductions in developing countries at potentially lower costs than for domestic action.

◆ Developing countries saw CDM as a new channel for financial assistance, investments to promote sustainable development, technology transfer, and promotion of equity. These results, going beyond emission reductions, would reflect the more general and holistic objectives of the Climate Change Convention.

COMPETITION AMONG THE "FLEXIBILITY" MECHANISMS

In Annex I countries, there will be competition among the several mechanisms defined in the Kyoto Protocol to meet emission reduction requirements. The portion of resources allotted to each of them will prove to be an important internal problem to be resolved. The Kyoto Protocol left undefined what part of the emission reduction commitments could be met outside national borders through use of the flexibility mechanisms of the Kyoto Protocol. A small percentage would encourage domestic action in Annex I countries, reducing the financial flow to developing countries. A larger one would discourage domestic actions and eventually tend to lead to an inordinate increase of emissions in Annex I countries. In all likelihood, the share for the CDM compared with other mechanisms will be determined by the market, unless the COP/MOP establishes its share as foreseen in Article 12.3 (b) of the Protocol.

Under the CDM, emission reductions can be counted towards compliance as of the year 2000, while for the other mechanisms no similar provision exists. This will probably favour investments through the CDM in many countries. However, the CDM will be burdened by devoting a share of the proceeds to cover costs of administration and adaptation, and this could make it less attractive.

Suppose that strong preference is given to the CDM compared with emissions trading, Joint Implementation with other developed countries, and domestic actions. Under these circumstances, can we make any estimate of what might be the maximum use of the CDM? Take the United States as an example. In the Protocol, the target commitment for the US is to reduce its emissions to a level 7 per cent below the 1990 base year. To comply, the US will have to reduce its emissions in the year 2010 by 25 per cent from the level projected for that year. The reason for that large reduction is that US emissions have been growing at one per cent a year since 1990. This means that 300 megatons of CO_2 equivalents per year will be reduced in the US. On average, each AIJ pilot project now underway is reducing 1 megaton per year of CO_2 equivalent emissions. By dividing total emission reductions required (300 megatons) by the average emission reduction per project (1 megaton), we might estimate that the maximum number of CDM projects (US investor country) in the year of 2010 would be in the order of a few hundred, assuming all emission reductions would occur through CDM projects. With domestic action and other mechanisms in place, the number would likely be much smaller.

GOVERNANCE: THE EXECUTIVE BOARD

The institutional design of the CDM will be the key factor determining its performance. Early decisions are needed from the Conference of the Parties covering:

◆ the powers and composition of the Executive Board and its relation to the COP/MOP

◆ the nature and role of the "operational entities" which will undertake certification, independent auditing, and verification of project activities

◆ the basis for private and/or public entities' participation in CDM activities

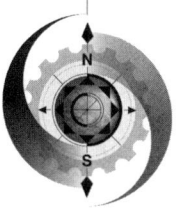

ISSUES&OPTIONS

The Clean
Development
Mechanism

◆ the nature and role of the administrative support needed for the Executive Board.

Clearly, one of the main responsibilities of the Executive Board under the authority and guidance of the COP will be to define the nature of the projects to be accepted and/or review lists of project activities for which CERs can be issued.

Although we are still in an early stage of negotiation, suggestions have been made for the Executive Board to be located in the Climate Change Secretariat.

THE CDM MODUS OPERANDI

One approach is to use existing organisations for CDM purposes, similar to the way that is was done for the Global Environment Facility (GEF). Several proposals would delegate the authority of the Executive Board to existing channels such as the GEF, and its implementing agencies the World Bank, UNDP and UNEP.

An alternative view stresses the need for an independent COP-based body in which developing countries could play a more significant role than they are perceived to play in existing institutions. Still another idea is for the Executive Board to manage an international emissions registry within the Climate Change Secretariat to certify and register emission reduction activities and transactions under the CDM and work with each country's national emissions registry. All other services could then be left to private sector entities, duly regulated or supervised. Emission offset and validation auditing could be performed by accredited independent professional auditing or accounting individuals or firms for a fee. Intermediation between suppliers/sellers and demanders/buyers of emissions offsets would be performed by independent private brokers and traders. UNDP, with its country offices and strong mandate on capacity building, could be entrusted with an important role to help developing criteria and endogenous capacity relevant to CDM projects.

There are two approaches for the operation of the CDM and exchanges of CERs:

A bilateral approach: Under this option, countries or private entities would negotiate agreements among themselves. Together, they would set criteria and rules for crediting, akin to the arrangements contemplated under Article 6 of the Kyoto Protocol for Joint Implementation.

A multilateral approach: Under this option, also called the "portfolio" option, non-Annex I countries would offer projects for emission reductions to the CDM to be picked up by the highest bidder in Annex I countries. Interested developing countries could each present a portfolio of projects and seek financial and technical support for their implementation. Developing countries could issue certificates and present them to the Executive Board for placement in the "market". They might even be offered through CDM postings on an Internet World Wide Web site. The corresponding value for each CER unit would be determined solely by the market. The Executive Board would have a fiduciary role, as it would be trying to obtain the best price for developing countries' CERs.

Politically, such an approach would remove some of the criticisms of the Joint Implementation method based on bilaterally agreed projects. Some Parties considered it unacceptable because it was seen as interfering with their sovereign choices.

One concern about the multilateral approach arises from experience with sulphur dioxide emissions (SO_2) in the United States. A significant proportion of projects to reduce these emissions takes place among branches of the same company, rather than through an open market mechanism for purchase of SO_2 reductions. Transnational enterprises might do the same with greenhouse gas emissions, acting bilaterally with their subsidiaries in developing countries. In that case, the portfolio approach would lose some of its attractiveness for developing countries.

The bilateral option will be preferred by large private investors who could view an international clearinghouse "portfolio approach" as an obstacle that will increase transaction costs. Small

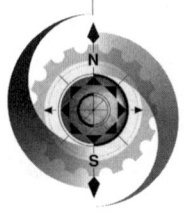

investors have no resources to develop bilateral projects and will prefer the portfolio approach. In practice, the "bilateral" and the "portfolio approach" could coexist and national governments would establish rules to be followed in their countries.

THE CERTIFICATION PROCESS

Only "certified emission reductions" can count towards compliance by Annex I Parties. For this reason, there is a clear incentive on the part of all concerned parties to achieve emission reductions. However, that incentive could lead investors (countries or companies) in the CDM projects to seek maximum emissions reductions to be used as credit towards meeting their commitments; it could also lead recipients to overstate the emission reductions to make them attractive. This reinforces the importance of having agreed ways of objectively managing the certification process and achieving credible results.

Therefore, "auditing, verification, and certification" of the projects is essential. Certification is an accepted ingredient of everyday business activities such as commodities trading (to assure quality and delivery to the buyer as agreed) and in goods shipping (to assure goods are delivered according to contracts). One could therefore view the CDM as a mechanism which establishes CER units as a new commodity to be issued and eventually traded among parties or businesses.

Submission of certificates could come through public and/or private entities. In any case, the voluntary character of the projects agreed upon by different parties would be preserved, subject to guidelines established by the Executive Board.

Considerable international experience in setting standards already resides within the International Standardisation Organisation (ISO). Their "ISO-Series" covers standards in many areas of industrial and business actions. Compliance with such standards is assessed by a variety of national institutions and possibly similar procedures could be adopted by the Parties for the CDM.

Monitoring of projects as they are executed also seems essential. This raises the issue of the lifetime, or duration, of the credits generated. A very long lifetime would bring a project's effectiveness into question; within that period, it could have been replaced by other up-to-date options. If the lifetime is too short, the incentive to conduct is reduced.

This suggests two types of certification activities:

◆ Certification of the *prospective* reductions resulting, for example, from an energy conservation project. In reality, this will be a "pre-certification" before project activities start.

◆ Periodic monitoring of *realised* emission reductions after the project is implemented. This will be an ongoing follow-up activity, particularly for projects with a long time frame.

The establishment of a certification process may lead to the establishment of an insurance system to protect investors. Since CERs, such as carbon emission offsets, will have values determined by the market and could change over time, it might be convenient to issue such certificates in carbon units and not in monetary terms. Failure or non-compliance in a given project would be insured against emission reductions in another project. Innovative insurance companies may step in and offer their services.

THE QUESTION OF BASELINES

Emission reductions can be certified if, and only if, the reductions are "additional to any that would occur in the absence of the certified project activity" (Article 12.5 (c)). In addition to that, emission reduction types of projects should achieve "real, measurable and yield long-

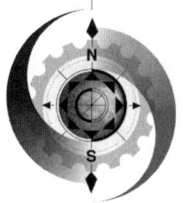

ISSUES&OPTIONS
The Clean
Development
Mechanism

term benefits related to the mitigation of climate change" (Article 12.5 (b)). Assessment of whether CDM projects fulfil these criteria involves comparing the expected emission reductions against a baseline, which is a construct that may never actually happen.

The definition of baselines will most likely become a crucial ingredient of the CDM since, as pointed out above, there will be a strong perverse incentive to overstate reductions or start from inflated baselines. An inflated baseline would create CER units for a project that would have taken place also in absence of the CDM.

Although some experience exists in establishing baselines in the AIJ pilot phase, these baselines were agreed bilaterally. For the CDM, a common methodology will have to be established. Baselines based on macroeconomic forecasts of economic development, population growth, and other factors are possible but difficult to establish in a reliable way. Project-based baselines seem to be the most realistic since they could incorporate the technological development and state-of-the-art activities that would be done in the absence of the CDM.

However, project-specific baseline scenarios do not take indirect effects into account. These can arise, for example, when a project uses goods whose production caused greenhouse gas emissions.

Emissions can also be influenced by price effects, which would provide an incentive for greater use of carbon-rich fuels and lead to an increase in greenhouse gas emissions. Another problem is subsidy effects: if the host country distorts fuel and electricity markets by granting production or consumption subsidies, these would change a country-related baseline, and a project-related baseline cannot take it into account.

Despite these problems, baselines on a project-by-project basis will probably be adopted initially, as was the case in the AIJ pilot phase, until more experience is gained. In that case, a "dynamic baseline approach" should be adopted since any new project that leads to emission reduction lowers the baseline for subsequent projects or subsequent years. Dynamic baselines could, however, lead to uncertainty on the investor's part, as the credited emission reduction would depend on the adjustments of the baseline.

The implementation of a large number of CDM projects under market conditions will help solve a longstanding problem among energy analysts: the real cost of emission reductions. According to a "top down" macroeconomics approach, these costs are high; according to the "bottom up" approach, these costs are low and even negative in some cases. Experience will tell which is the more realistic approach.

EQUITY

Because rapidly industrialising countries have better infrastructure, lower risk, and the largest greenhouse gas saving potential, the CDM might generate financial flows directed toward those countries which are already receiving the bulk of private capital flows from industrialised countries. The point has therefore been made that, in the interest of equity of access to the mechanisms under the

Climate Change Convention, programmes and projects must be fairly distributed among regions. This could be avoided by introducing a quota-based system – for example, one-third of the effort is to be implemented on the African continent. Obviously, non-African countries, such as the small islands, should also be considered if such a mechanism is adopted. A criterion based on income per capita could be considered.

SHARE OF PROCEEDS

ISSUES&OPTIONS
The Clean
Development
Mechanism

Article 12.8 establishes that a share of proceeds from CERs is to be used to cover administrative expenses, as well as to meet costs of adaptation

of developing countries that are particularly vulnerable to climate change. What this means is that two charges will be imposed on the proceeds of CDM projects:

◆ The share for administrative expenses will cover necessary services in support of the Executive Board. Based on similar activities, it will be reasonable to set a ceiling on this share, such as 3 per cent of the market value of CERs.

◆ The share to cover costs of adaptation as mandated by Article 12.8 will probably be much more difficult to establish. "Adaptation" to climate change is particularly important for small island states, but many larger developing countries such as China and India recently drew attention to their own vulner-abilities. Although a figure of 10 per cent of the market value of CERs has been often mentioned, it is not clear what is the basis for such a choice. In any case, this surcharge will disadvantage CDM projects compared with the other flexibility mechanisms (emissions trading and Joint Implementation) and domestic measures. To level the playing field among the mechanisms, the same surcharge could be applied to all of them.

Costs of certification and monitoring could be included in the projects themselves. The lower the charges, the more transactions are likely to go through the CDM; a higher fee will reduce the number of transactions.

PROJECT ELIGIBILITY AND SUSTAINABLE DEVELOPMENT

Not all projects that result in emission reductions are eligible for trading under the CDM. In order to qualify, projects will need to have several general characteristics which are explicit or implicit in the Kyoto Protocol. Projects should:

◆ provide real, measurable, and certifiable reductions, i.e. strong "additionality"
◆ assist in sustainable development

Restricting acceptable projects to well-defined types that have these characteristics would go a long way toward minimising "leakage"[1] and associated "hot air"[2] projects.

To illustrate the range of available options, Table 4 in Chapter 12 presents a list of GHG offsets options and ranks their probable contributions toward meeting the above criteria.

Questions might arise as to whether adequate capacity presently exists to identify, develop, assess, certify, and monitor a diverse range of activities worldwide. For this reason, it might be useful to think in terms of a three- or four-year period when certain types of projects would be preferred over others that could perhaps be taken up in the second phase starting, let us say, in the year 2004 or so.

Some authors emphasised the need to give greater attention to social components of projects to be accepted, and to include technology transfer as an integral part of the projects and discourage projects with low technological content. Others agreed that such questions are very relevant, but that it should be left to sovereign national governments to decide what is best in each case, subject to general rules established by the Executive Board on the nature of projects to be accepted.

Since some projects might not fully meet sustainable development criteria, one could introduce additional costs to them or limit their acceptance in time so as to reduce their attractiveness.

The COP/MOP ultimately will have either to decide which projects qualify under the CDM or to entrust the Executive Board with such a task.

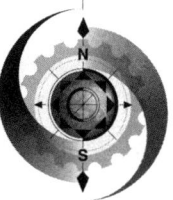

---

[1] *Leakage refers to lower-than-anticipated total greenhouse gas emissions resulting from flexibility mechanisms due to the displacement of activities leading to carbon emissions. For example, a reduced impact logging project may lower timber output in one area causing increased harvests in another.*

[2] *A term coined by some observers to describe inflated greenhouse gas budgets (as compared to 1990 levels), which may lead to increased emissions if traded internationally.*

There is disagreement over the extent to which forest and land use change projects will be allowed under the CDM. Different parts of the Kyoto Protocol give differing treatment to the issue. In Article 6, there is explicit language about "enhancing anthropogenic removals by sinks" and counting the sequestration so achieved towards fulfilment of emission reductions. However, these points are not mentioned in Article 12 on the CDM where it covers "emission reduction" or "certified emission reductions" (as in Article 12.3 (a)). The reasons for such differences in dealing with sinks are not clear, but apparently the lack of time in the final hours of discussions at Kyoto prevented full consideration of the issue.

Therefore, there are four options for dealing with sinks under the CDM:

◆ to construe the Article 12 text literally and exclude all sinks projects under the CDM

◆ to interpret Article 12 in the light of Article 3 which allows Annex I Parties to include a limited category of sinks in achieving their emission reductions

◆ to design a new regime for sinks that is specific to the CDM

◆ to exclude sinks altogether from the Protocol, using specific language to that effect.

To resolve the problem of sinks, new negotiations will be necessary at COP-4 or beyond.

CONCLUSIONS

While many countries are keen to secure early operation of the CDM, important roadblocks still stand in the way of an effective mechanism for implementation. On the one hand, some countries face ratification challenges. On the other hand, some countries want more time to evaluate the implications of what was agreed in Kyoto before engaging in so potentially powerful a new economic instrument as the CDM. As the CDM offers important sustainable development opportunities, it is important to solve these questions and transform it into an effective mechanism. ■

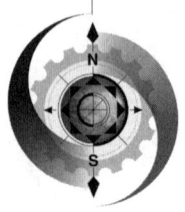

ISSUES&OPTIONS

The Clean
Development
Mechanism

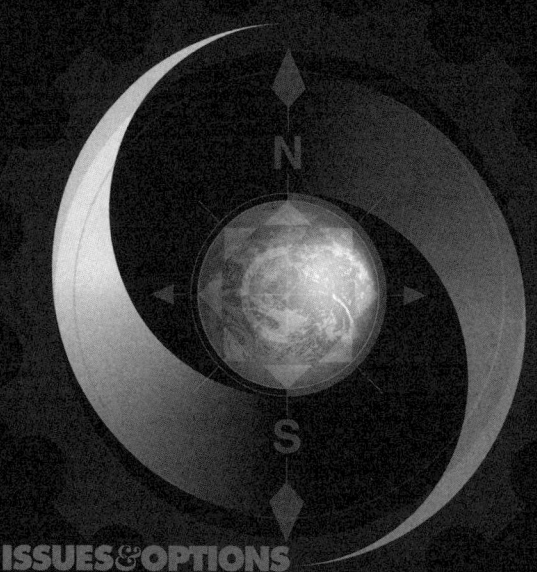

ISSUES & OPTIONS
The Clean Development Mechanism

First Steps

FIRST APPROACHES AND UNANSWERED QUESTIONS

Ambassador Raúl A. Estrada-Oyuela
Buenos Aires, Argentina

The Clean Development Mechanism (CDM) was called the surprise of Kyoto. But actually it can be considered a hybrid of two earlier ideas: the new development fund proposed by the Group of 77 and China, and the Joint Implementation plan involving developed and developing countries, as proposed by some developed countries and Costa Rica.

Whether a surprise, a hybrid, or both, it was a relatively late proposal. It came just days before the deadline of 1 June 1997 when the "seeds" of all possible features of the Kyoto Protocol had to be communicated to all Parties. The United Nations Framework Convention on Climate Change (UNFCCC) requires the Secretariat to make such texts available at least six months before a Conference of the Parties (COP) is to consider a Protocol – and the Kyoto COP was set for December 1997.

The concept of a Clean Development Fund was introduced by Brazil on 28 May 1997, during the seventh session of the Ad Hoc Group on the Berlin Mandate (AGBM), established by the first Conference (COP-1) in Berlin in April 1995.

The idea had several roots. The concept of a fund for sustainable development had been jointly raised by Argentina and Brazil during preparations for the 1992 UN Conference on Environment and Development. Since the Climate Change Convention was adopted in 1992, the possibility of reducing emissions in developing countries instead of doing it domestically has been on the agenda of the Annex I countries. The idea had not been accepted because many developing countries were reluctant to give credits to developed countries for emission reductions performed in developing countries. Debate on that matter during COP-1 in 1995 instead lead to the creation of a pilot phase of "Activities Implemented Jointly" (AIJ), which ends in the year 2000. The CDM has been presented as the way to use Joint Implementation with credits from the year 2000.

HISTORY OF THE CDM

The proposal introduced by Brazil on 28 May 1997 called for a Green Development Fund as a new element of the financial mechanism established by the UNFCCC. The Brazilian proposal took a totally different approach to the whole Protocol, with two features relevant to this analysis: a new approach to the definition of the mitigation commitments, and the punitive meaning of contributions to the Fund.

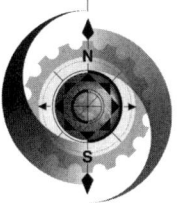

ISSUES&OPTIONS

The Clean
Development
Mechanism

Mitigation commitments in the Brazilian proposal took more closely into consideration the real increase in mean temperature, computing also the contribution to concentrations of greenhouse gases in the atmosphere. The idea was intellectually attractive and perhaps much fairer, since regulating future emissions only, as the Kyoto Protocol does, does not take into account historic responsibilities. In spite of the efforts made by Brazil to explain its proposal to all interested parties, end of May 1997 was too late in the process of negotiation to introduce a change in a basic criterion already in use by everybody. It was so understood by Brazil, whose delegation, in presenting the new proposal during the seventh session of the AGBM, suggested its analysis by the subsidiary bodies of the Conference after the meeting in Kyoto.

The Green Development Fund was to be funded with contributions from those Annex I Parties which exceeded their assigned amounts of greenhouse gases emissions. The Fund was explained on the basis of the "polluter pays" principle, in such a way that Parties in non-compliance should contribute (or pay a fine) of US$10 per ton of carbon. Guidelines for distribution of the financial resources were drafted as giving most of them to the major developing countries, but up to 10 per cent could be used in adaptation projects. In all cases projects were to be proposed by the developing countries (non-Annex I countries).

Since the Brazilian delegation suggested a post-Kyoto analysis of its proposal, none of its elements were included in the negotiating text I presented in October 1997 to the Eighth Session of AGBM in Bonn. During the session, however, the Group of 77 and China took up the idea and moved to incorporate the Clean Development Fund in the texts going forward to the Kyoto Conference. This was done in Article 3, paragraph 18. The text, which follows the Brazilian proposal, said that contributions to the fund shall be made by "Parties in non-compliance" and also admits voluntary contributions. Location and wording accurately show the punitive nature of the proposal at that time.

The Japanese Government, host of the forth-coming Kyoto Conference, was very concerned about the need to foster understanding between delegations and groups of delegations. So it organised advance meetings in Tokyo to exchange views and explore possible agreements that could emerge at the Kyoto Conference. The last meeting was held in November 1997, with almost all elements of the negotiations on the table. On this occasion, the United States delegation was headed by then Under Secretary of State for Global Affairs Tim Wirth – his last intervention in climate negotiations. Also participating for the United States were Rafe Pomerance and Mark Hambley, among other very experienced negotiators. The delegation of Brazil was formed by Antonio Dayrell de Lima and Gylvan Meira Filho. In an exchange of views between these two delegations, in front of the others, the possibility arose of moving away from a system of paying fines for non-compliance, as in the Brazilian proposal. In its place came the idea of buying some kind of license to exceed the assigned amount of greenhouse gas emissions.

It is not clear whether the United States delegates had been considering this possibility before the meeting, or the idea surged as the talks developed. A similar idea had been reflected in a previous United States proposal to "borrow" emissions in one commitment period from a future commitment period in order to exceed the assigned amount. But that idea did not "fly" because very few people believed that a debt of this kind would ever be paid. In the case of the CDM, the United States delegation also favoured a solution in which the "financial contribution" or payment could be made by private entities. That would avoid a repetition of the difficulties the Congress has imposed on the Executive Branch to fulfil the United States commitments to the Global Environment Facility (GEF).

These fresh ideas on the CDM were introduced to other delegations at the beginning of the Kyoto Conference. That was exactly the purpose of the informal consultations held in periods between negotiating sessions: a group of delegations exchanging views could envision new possibilities. It was not for them to negotiate or to decide on anything, but just

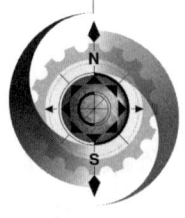

ISSUES&OPTIONS
The Clean
Development
Mechanism

to find fresh ideas to be brought to the negotiation by all participants.

As with many other points, we created a negotiating group open to all delegations for action on the Brazilian proposal and subsequent ideas. I asked Gylvan Meira Filho (Brazil) to lead the work as Chairman. He was very well known and respected by all sectors. He could provide the best account of the work of the group, but the results can be seen in the numerous differences between Article 3.18 of document FCCC/CP/1997/2 as presented to the Kyoto Conference, and the present Article 12 of the Protocol that emerged from Kyoto. Eight differences can be mentioned:

- From a "fund" we moved to a "mechanism."

- The original idea of contributions or fines related to "non-compliance" was replaced by the concept of assisting Annex I Parties in achieving compliance with their commitments.

- Non-Annex I Parties would benefit from "project activities resulting in certified emission reductions" and Annex I Parties would benefit from "certified emission reductions."

- An "Executive Board" was created.

- "Operational entities" will certify emission reductions, with voluntary participation of Parties concerned, with real, measurable, long-term benefits for mitigation, provided that reductions are additional to ones that would occur otherwise.

- "A share of the proceeds" shall be used to cover "administrative expenses" and to meet costs of adaptation.

- Private entities may be involved.

- The system will start working in the year 2000 with credits to be used in the commitment period 2008/2012.

I did not like the proposal, but it got wide support and I facilitated its approval. Many sectors were interested in it. Of course, Annex I Parties found a way for a different form of "Joint Implementation" with non-Annex I. The Alliance of Small Island States (AOSIS) got concrete reference to resources for adaptation. Perhaps a number of delegates saw new possibilities in the "Executive Board."

Though I facilitated approval of this proposal, I did not like it. My reservation was that the CDM is considered a form of Joint Implementation, but I do not understand how commitments can be implemented jointly if only one of the Parties involved is committed to limit or reduce emissions and the other Party is free from the quantitative point of view. Such a case can be called "extraterritorial implementation" or "off-shore implementation" but not "Joint Implementation." On the contrary, the Joint Implementation case is clear if both parties are committed to limit or reduce emissions as in Article 6 of the Protocol. This problem will become serious if baselines for individual CDM projects are set without regard to the total emissions of greenhouse gases in the country where the project is located. The hypothesis that mitigation costs are lower in developing countries is true only if market distortions of values are adjusted, because otherwise everything is cheaper in developing countries, including labour and natural resources. That disparity has been at the root of every colonisation since the time of the Greeks.

During the negotiations driving to the adoption of the Protocol, the Argentine delegation proposed that developing countries could undertake quantitative voluntary commitments on reductions or limitations of emissions and after that, participate in Joint Implementation and emissions trading. That possibility could create a third category of countries, with differentiated commitments, contributing to the global mitigation efforts whose participation in Joint Implementation would have a solid base. The proposal was not accepted: developed countries attached conditions to the voluntary commitments heavier than those established for the so-called "economies in transition"; and developing countries, taking into account their experiences, were concerned by the possibility of being forced into "voluntary" commitments.

25

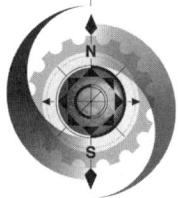

ISSUES&OPTIONS

The Clean Development Mechanism

The CDM is part of the Kyoto Protocol which nearly forty Parties to the UNFCCC signed within ten weeks after it was open for signature. The signatories represented one-third of the total CO_2 emissions of Annex I Parties in 1990. A number of governments rely on the CDM as a critical feature in implementing the Protocol. The challenge now is to make it work.

> A number of governments rely on the CDM as a critical feature in implementing the Protocol. The challenge now is to make it work.

In order to implement the CDM, a number of questions have to be answered by governments. Some questions relate only to the CDM. Others – like monitoring and verification – are also relevant for other "flexibility mechanisms" of the Protocol. All questions are going to be decided by the political will of governments, and trying to prejudge what they should do would be an act of arrogance. Following are brief treatments of six questions which need discussion and decision.

Portfolio or project-by-project?

One main question is whether the CDM will be a system with a portfolio of projects designed by developing countries to satisfy their needs and waiting to be implemented with the financial and technical support of developed country Parties, or an accumulation of bilaterally agreed projects. The first option looks like a mostly governmental approach, almost a way to replace the GEF. It seems difficult to imagine private entities providing financial resources unless they have a relevant role in defining projects that involve their action. The future of climate projects in the GEF is also an open question. Developing countries in general are not totally satisfied with GEF and some developed countries will prefer a system with contributions paid by private entities. The World Bank, somewhat the initial patron of GEF, indicated that it wants to operate in the field of the CDM. The Interamerican Development Bank has already announced a similar intention, and other regional development banks may also want to participate.

It may be presumed that, in prioritising projects, developing countries will prefer development-oriented alternatives, and developed countries or their private sectors will prefer mitigation-oriented alternatives. It is also reasonable to assume that the developed side will be mostly in favour of a bilateral, project-by-project approach, in spite of higher transaction costs, whilst there are indications that developing countries are working on the idea of a portfolio under the authority of the Executive Board. In addition, some developed countries will invite and encourage the participation of the private sector in the CDM. This is particularly so for the United States, the major contributor in any cooperative programme and the country with the biggest reduction commitment in absolute terms. It is hard to imagine utilities, for example, providing resources for a portfolio of mitigation projects.

Most probably the CDM will end up being a hybrid of both things, but this is going to be discussed perhaps for long time. In the original Brazilian text, developing countries had to propose the projects, and Parties making contributions to pay for non-compliance had nothing to say; but the structure of Article 12 is different and most probably the source of financing would like to be hear because that will relate with reduction's marginal cost.

Advance implementation

In accordance with Article 12.10 of the Protocol, advance implementation means that certified emission reductions obtained from the year 2000 onwards can be used in order to achieve compliance in the first commitment period from 2008 to 2012. However, by the year 2000 the Protocol most probably will not yet be in force; only when it is in effect can a Meeting of the Parties (MOP) be held to decide on the modalities and procedures of CDM. Modalities and procedures need decisions, and the doubts listed below also need to be

resolved. For emissions trading, the situation is different because under Article 17 it is the Conference of the Parties (COP) to the Convention, which is already functioning, that shall define principles, modalities, rules, and guidelines. Nevertheless, there is always the possibility that a political understanding on how to implement Article 12.10 can be reached at an earlier, political stage, even with difficulties from the point of view of legal formalities.

The rationale behind "advance implementation" is that the concentration of greenhouse gases in the atmosphere will be influenced by any reduction of emissions, including reduction of emissions occurring even prior to the commitment period. Besides, Article 3.2 requires that each Party included in Annex I shall have made demonstrable progress in achieving its limitation or reduction commitments by the year 2005, and Article 12.10 can help to demonstrate progress.

> **If at the end of the process this "share of proceeds" looks like a tax, a number of governments can be very reluctant to agree.**

Carbon sequestration

Another strategic question has already been tabled: are carbon sequestration projects a matter for the CDM? Article 6 on Joint Implementation includes both reduction of greenhouse gases emissions and removals of greenhouse gases; it explicitly refers to "projects aimed at reducing anthropogenic emissions by sources or enhancing anthropogenic removals by sinks." However, Article 12 on the CDM instead only refers to reduction of emissions of greenhouse gases and says nothing about removals of greenhouse gases. It is only logical to conclude that different wording reflects different meaning, and it is against any legal methodological interpretation to hold that different wordings in the same legal text have equal meaning. It has been suggested that there was an understanding among negotiators to make the texts of Articles 6 and 12 uniform on this point. That was never brought to my knowledge, neither during the negotiations

nor after the negotiations in the Committee of the Whole and before formal approval by the Conference. Delegates involved in the negotiations were well-experienced diplomats, scientists, and professional staff, and nobody should be induced to error. If a negotiation ends with "we'll revisit this text later" and that "later" never comes, it is because the will to revisit the text did not exist. At the end, in this as in other matters, the only real truth is the political will of governments, and sequestration will be included in the CDM or not according that will.

The other side of the same coin relates to forest management to reduce emissions which, without management, would be generated by deforestation. A couple of developing country governments are offering "carbon certificates" for a price in exchange for sustainable management of areas in risk of deforestation. Since binding commitments on forest protection do not exist and agreement on them does not seem possible in the near future, it is difficult to understand how the baseline on such projects can be defined. In fact, thousands of square kilometres of rain forest are at risk of deforestation and, if that happens, millions of tons of CO_2 will be emitted. Providing "carbon certificates" on an endless hypothetical deforestation would be the best way to insure that CO_2 emissions from developed countries will continue – that means "business as usual" and perhaps worse. Should that be considered an admissible political behaviour? Is it not part of the normal responsibility of governments to protect their own natural resources?

Baselines and certification

Determining the baseline for the CDM is a complex question because an emission reduction can be certified if, and only if, the reduction is "additional to any that would occur in the absence of the certified project activity." Complexity is greater since similar wording is used in Article 6 for Joint

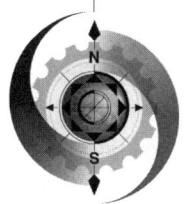

Implementation, where both Parties have quantified limitation or reduction commitments. Should the same standard be implemented in both cases? Or should the quantitative commitment of the "recipient" Party in Article 6 call for a higher standard for what would have occurred in the absence of the project?

Certification also requires approval by the governments involved, as well as "real, measurable long-term benefits" related to the mitigation of climate change. Approval by governments should be easy to verify, in spite of possible difficulties in identifying the competent organ of each government to express the conformity. But "real, measurable long-term benefits" requires careful attention. That phrase reinforces the interpretation that sequestration projects should be excluded from the CDM, since sequestration by definition implies a possible return of carbon to the atmosphere, sometimes before any possible "long-term" period has passed.

Annex I Parties can benefit from Article 12 in order to fulfil "in part" their limitation or reduction commitments. Should this be understood as having the same meaning that the "supplemental" nature established by Joint Implementation by Article 6 or trading by Article 17? Again if the wording is different, solid reasons are needed to justify equal meaning, but I see a tendency in favour of simplification.

"Certified emission reductions" must be expressed in some unit. The original Brazilian proposal had a "carbon ton equivalent" unit that most probably will be used for the CDM and also for Joint Implementation and trading. The equivalencies to carbon are determined by the global warming potential (GWP) of each gas compared with CO_2. The problem is that GWP can change with the advance of research, but any revision of GWP shall apply only to commitment periods adopted after such revision (Article 5.3).

The certification by "operational entities" should take into account different degrees of certainty in the estimation of emissions of different gases and also the different degrees of certainty according to the sources of emissions. It seems advisable to exert great precaution in selecting entities for this purpose. Transaction costs are always relevant. It has been said that the CDM may help to reduce transaction costs that could be higher in bilateral project negotiations.

However, before assessing the possibilities created by the CDM, it would be necessary to clarify the concept of "proceeds" used in Article 12.8. The Brazilian proposal and the G77 proposal refer to contributions from Parties in non-compliance, and the Brazilian proposal allowed up to 10 per cent of those contributions to be allocated for adaptation. Article 12 is not explicit, to say the least. A "certified project" will include resources from both Parties, the Annex I Party and the non-Annex I Party. Will both contributions be deemed "proceeds"? Will the transfers of "know how," for instance, be included in the proceeds? Or will only financial contributions be deemed "proceeds"? Or will only financial contributions from the Annex I Party be deemed "proceeds"? Perhaps the use of the word "proceeds" is not the happiest selection. Once the meaning of the concept is agreed, it will be necessary to establish which percentage will go for "adaptation" and which "to cover administrative expenses." Only after those points are clarified will it be possible to estimate transaction costs and compare different options. If at the end of the process this "share of the proceeds" looks like a tax, a number of governments can be very reluctant to agree.

> The CDM opens a universe of possible cooperation for mitigation of climate change and development, aims which are not always easy to conciliate. A great effort of imagination and compromise is required for successful implementation of the CDM.

Private sector

The private sector has different functions to perform in the CDM.

 Article 12.9 foresees that private entities may participate in the CDM, including in

project activities resulting in certified emission reductions. As pointed out above, that feature is a great attraction for countries planning to allocate their "assigned amounts" among private entities which, in turn, will be able to exceed their part of the "assigned amount" using certified emission reductions under Article 12 of the Protocol.

◆ The other function of private entities could be certifying emission reductions, as foreseen in Article 12.5. In both cases, guidelines will be needed.

◆ Finally, independent auditing and verification of project activities may also be commissioned to private entities, including nongovernmental organisations.

In order to organise the participation of the private sector, principles and guidelines are required.

Executive Board

Article 12.4 also calls for the creation of an "Executive Board" to supervise the CDM. According to "inter-agency" recommendations to be submitted to the Latin American Ministers of Environment, the board should have no more than 9 members. Little more is known about that board. Will it be a permanent body (Executive Board) or a body with periodic meetings? How will members be elected? Will they represent constituencies as in GEF? Will this supervision be coordinated with the required auditing and verification? If so, how?

The CDM opens a universe of possible cooperation for mitigation of climate change and development, aims which in many opportunities are not easy to conciliate. A great effort of imagination and compromise is required for the successful implementation of the CDM. ■

ISSUES&OPTIONS

The Clean
Development
Mechanism

FROM ORIGINS
TOWARDS OPERATIONS

Professor Mark J. Mwandosya
Centre for Energy, Environment,
   Science and Technology (CEEST)
Dar-es-Salaam, Tanzania

Summary: As Chairman of the Group of 77 and China for the United Republic of Tanzania at the time of the Kyoto Conference, Mr. Mwandosya is able to offer insights into the genesis of the Clean Development Mechanism (CDM) from its roots in an innovative Brazilian proposal. He further clarifies the basic principles and objectives of the CDM, which are consistent with the Climate Change Convention itself. Eligibility criteria and implementation and governance issues are explored as well.

EMERGENCE: BONN AND KYOTO

The Clean Development Mechanism (CDM) was defined in Kyoto during the Third Conference of the Parties (COP-3) to the United Nations Framework Convention on Climate Change. The Kyoto Protocol to Convention defined the CDM as an instrument to foster cooperation between Annex I Parties to the Convention (developed country Parties) and non-Annex I Parties (developing country Parties) in working towards sustainable development and in meeting the ultimate objective of the Convention.

Before analysing how the mechanism is defined in Article 12 of the Kyoto Protocol and what attributes the CDM should have, we may ask what was the genesis of the mechanism? It is the ultimate product of a proposal made by Brazil. That proposal suggested elements for inclusion in a Protocol or other legal instrument that would strengthen the emission reduction commitments of Annex I Parties to the Convention, as contained in Article 4.2 (a) and (b) of the Convention.

The Brazilian Proposal

Brazil submitted its proposal on 28 May 1997 for consideration by the Ad hoc Group on the Berlin Mandate (AGBM). The proposal was for consideration by the group at its Seventh Session in July 1997 (document FCCC/AGBM/1997/Misc./Add.3).

The proposal contained two key elements – one to measure climate change and assess responsibility for it, and the other to "penalise" countries not meeting their emission reduction targets:

Measurements: The proposal sought to use the change in global mean surface temperature as an indicator of climate change. It would assess the origins of this change, focusing on anthropogenic emissions by sources and

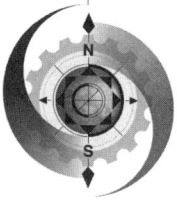

ISSUES&OPTIONS
The Clean
Development
Mechanism

removal by sinks of greenhouse gases not controlled by the Montreal Protocol. Then it would weigh the relative responsibilities of individual parties as contributors to the change in global mean temperature. Using this objective criterion, the burden would be shared among Annex I Parties, with the most burden for those contributing the most to climate change.

The Brazilian proposal contained two key elements – one to measure climate change and assess responsibility for it, and the other to "penalise" countries not meeting their emission reduction targets.

the atmosphere at a level that would minimise further dangerous anthropogenic interference with the climate system. That level should be achieved quickly enough to allow ecosystems to adapt naturally to climate change, to ensure that food production is not threatened, and to enable economic development to proceed in a sustainable manner.

Penalties: In order to promote compliance or, conversely, penalise non-compliance with agreed targets for emission reduction, Brazil proposed that parties failing to meet the required target be obliged to contribute to a Clean Development Fund to be used in non-Annex I countries.

As proposed by Brazil, the Fund would have the following characteristics:

◆ It would promote precautionary measures in non-Annex I Parties.

◆ It would be managed by the financial mechanism of the Convention.

◆ Its resources would be distributed to reflect the relative contributions of individual non-Annex I Parties to climate change.

◆ The Conference of the Parties (COP) would approve appropriate regulations on application and disbursement of funds.

◆ A small portion (not exceeding 10 per cent) of resources would be assigned to climate change adaptation programmes.

◆ The large portion of the resources would be assigned to mitigation programmes.

Brazil argued that the Fund would get non-Annex I Parties to engage constructively in the implementing the Convention. Thus, they would contribute to the ultimate objective of stabilising greenhouse gas concentrations in

Adoption by the Group of 77 and China

Almost all the negotiators in Bonn during AGBM-7 appreciated that Brazil had put forward a novel proposal. It called for a system of burden sharing and allocation of emission responsibility based on the contribution of individual parties to temperature increase and a clean development fund linked to non-compliance. At the time they recognised that the proposal had come in rather late in the negotiation process. Its two main elements are complex and their full consideration would require ample time.

The second part of the Brazilian proposal on the Clean Development Fund was discussed in the Group of 77 and China as it was preparing the Group position on quantified emission limitation and reduction objectives (QELROS). The Group decided to adopt the Brazilian proposal and forward it as a Group of 77 and China submission. In submitting its proposal on QELROS on 23rd October 1997, the Group of 77 and China suggested the following paragraph for inclusion in the Protocol:

"A Clean Development Fund shall be established by the Conference of the Parties to assist the developing country Parties to achieve sustainable development and contribute to the ultimate objective of the Convention. The Clean Development Fund will receive contributions from those Annex I Parties found to be in non-compliance with its QELROs under the Protocol. The Clean Development Fund will

also be open for voluntary contributions from Annex I Parties." (Document FCCC/AGBM/1997/Misc.1/Add.6)

This paragraph found its way into the final negotiating text of the Protocol. It became the basis of negotiations which resulted in the definition of the CDM appearing in Article 12 of the Kyoto Protocol.

In response to the Brazilian proposal concerning measurement of climate change and assessing its origins, the Kyoto Conference decided on 5 December 1997 to request consideration of the methodological and scientific aspects by the Subsidiary Body for Scientific and Technological Advice (SBSTA). Its findings are to be given to the COP at its fourth session in Buenos Aires, Argentina, in November 1998.

Objective and principles

The CDM is one of the cooperative implementation instruments under the Kyoto Protocol, which in turn seeks the ultimate objective stated in Article 2 of the Convention. By definition, therefore, the CDM, the Protocol, and the Convention have the same objective and should have the same principles. Furthermore, the Protocol is guided by Article 3 of the Convention.

> **The CDM must be guided by the need to protect the climate system for the benefit of the present and future generations.**

The CDM must therefore be guided by the need to:

◆ protect the climate system for the benefit of the present and future generations

◆ be based on equity

◆ be based on common but differentiated responsibilities and respective capacities of the Parties

◆ address specific needs and special circumstances of developing countries

◆ take precautionary measures

◆ promote sustainable development.

In defining the CDM, the Kyoto Protocol stated that its purpose is to assist Parties not included in Annex I in achieving sustainable development and contributing to the ultimate objective of the Convention, and to assist Parties included in Annex I in achieving compliance with their commitments under Article 3 of the Protocol.

Outputs or expected benefits

Article 12.3 specifies that developing countries will benefit from project activities and developed countries from certified emission reductions generated by specific CDM projects in non-Annex I parties. Article 3.12 of the Protocol provides for certified emission reductions from a non-Annex I Party to be credited to an Annex I Party

The benefits to developed country Parties are clear and specific and can be measured in terms of certified emission reductions. However, those accruing to developing countries are less clear. It is perhaps assumed that before certification, project results will have to show the extent to which a project has contributed to sustainable development. Clear measures or indices of sustainable development need to be agreed upon between the investor and the host country. The indices must indicate the additionality to sustainable development over and above that which would have been obtained without the project.

Acquisition of credit for certified emission reductions (CERs) is explicitly provided in the Protocol for Annex I Parties. Equity will demand that CERs arising from a CDM project be shared between the investor and the host in proportions to be determined by the COP. In the Protocol and the Convention, developing countries have no quantified commitments for emission reduction. Nevertheless, CERs from CDM projects would serve to highlight the role of developing countries in stabilising emission

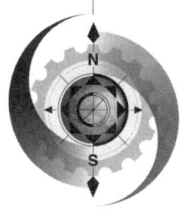

ISSUES&OPTIONS

The Clean
Development
Mechanism

concentrations and could be covered in their national communication reports.

Environmental additionality

The principle of additionality poses some requirements on CDM projects if CERs are to be acquired and transferred:

◆ Real, measurable and long-term climate change benefits arise from the transfers.

◆ Reductions in emissions are additional to those that would otherwise have occurred.

This principle of additionality is embodied in Article 12.5 of the Protocol. To ascertain additionality requires detailed understanding and clear establishment of the net environmental benefits arising out of a CDM project compared with the baseline scenario established during the project inception.

ELABORATION: TOWARDS BUENOS AIRES

Methodological and implementation issues

The CDM is new and will require further elaboration before coming into being. Careful definition is particularly important since the CDM will involve "offshore" implementation by Annex I Parties, voluntary participation by host countries, and the offsetting of assigned emission amounts. This definition should include the following as attributes of the CDM:

◆ It facilitates projects that are environmentally effective.

◆ The mechanism and project implementation must be efficient.

◆ Monitoring, reporting, and verification must be done in a way that enhances the credibility and transparency of the CDM.

◆ Rules, methodologies, and modalities for implementation must be simple and effective.

◆ Project baselines must be clearly defined.

◆ Roles and participation of all stakeholders must be clarified.

◆ The developmental benefits of a CDM-based project should be clear.

In line with these attributes and in order to preserve the credibility of the CDM, all of its systems for regulation, accounting, and other functions must be just as efficient in the investors' countries of origin as in the host countries.

Governance

Article 12 of the Kyoto Protocol merely defines a broad framework for establishing the CDM, its structure, its rules and regulations, and its relationship with other instruments of the Convention and the Protocol. These tasks are entrusted to the COP and the COP serving as the meeting of the Parties to the Protocol (COP/MOP).

Article 12 identifies the following institutions or organs that relate to the CDM.

The COP/MOP is responsible to:

◆ determine how certified emission reductions accruing from project activities will contribute to compliance with part of the commitments of Annex I Parties of the Convention (Article 12.3 (b))

◆ exercise overall authority and give guidance to the CDM (Article 12.4)

◆ designate operational entities to certify emission reduction resulting from project activity (Article 12.5)

◆ elaborate modalities and procedures to ensure transparency, efficiency, and

accounting through independent auditing and verification (Article 12.7)

◆ ensure that a share of the proceeds from certified project activities is used to cover administrative expenses and adaptation costs of vulnerable developing countries (Article 12.8).

The Executive Board has been given the function of providing overall supervision of the CDM (Article 12.9), as well as guidance on participation by private and/or public entities.

> **Standards must be set and oversight provided to ensure that a unit of certified emission reduction in one country is the same as in another country.**

Operational entities have the function of certifying the emissions reduction resulting from each project (Article 12.5). They are not defined, and presumably could be national or multinational, as the COP/MOP will deem fit.

Private or public entities of investor and host nations may participate in project activities resulting in certified emission reductions and in the acquisition of such reductions (Article 12.9). Standards must be set and oversight provided to ensure that a unit of certified emission reduction in one country is the same as in another country. It is also important to ensure that the oversight mechanisms in the investor country are as effective as those in the host country.

Possible CDM structure

Developed countries have been enthusiastic about the CDM, perhaps for different reasons than developing countries. Developed countries see it as another form of Joint Implementation between developed and developing countries, with associated credits. Their main criterion for involvement will be the maximisation of certified emission reductions and their transfer under Article 3 of the Protocol. On the other hand, developing countries view the CDM as an additional channel for new technology and funding to further their objective of sustainable development. This view will guide their choice of projects. The structure of the CDM will ultimately be determined by taking into account these two seemingly divergent but perhaps complementary criteria.

The CDM could also include a clean development fund to finance all clearinghouse functions for projects from host states and provide information and training costs for project activities. It could receive funds from developed countries and the private sector of investor states.

The policy framework for the CDM will clearly lie with the COP/MOP. The oversight function will be carried out by the Executive Board. The Board could follow the lines of the Executive Committee of the Multilateral Fund of the Montreal Protocol and consist of representatives from developed countries and developing countries. The exact composition should be determined by COP/MOP. ■

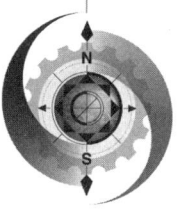

ISSUES&OPTIONS
The Clean
Development
Mechanism

ISSUES&OPTIONS
The Clean Development Mechanism

Next Steps

IDEAS FOR IMPLEMENTATION

Luiz Gylvan Meira Filho
President, Brazilian Space Agency
Brasilia, Brazil

Summary: From his perspective as the Chairman of the Contact Group that negotiated the inclusion of the Clean Development Mechanism (CDM) in the Kyoto Protocol, this author considers the historical evolution of the CDM and examines it in terms of the broader goals of the United Nations Framework Convention on Climate Change (UNFCCC). He then offers specific guidelines and practical steps for successfully implementing the CDM.

HISTORICAL EVOLUTION

The idea of promoting cooperation between industrialised and developing countries to assist the latter grow along a "cleaner" or, to be more precise, a more carbon-free path, has early been recognised as a "win-win" exercise. This is based on the fact that avoiding emissions night be less costly in countries where the infrastructure in the greenhouse-gas-related sectors has yet to be built It incorporates the notion of technological "leap-frogging" — that development of the energy-related infrastructure in developing countries should occur in such a way as to leap over emission-intensive steps that have been taken by industrialised countries. Much has been written on these concepts, in general finding no fault with them.

Early attempts to translate these ideas into practice fall into two major categories, with minor and, for the purposes of this note, negligible variations. The first is the concept of "incremental cost" adopted by the Global Environmental Facility, together with the provision of the Convention that non-Annex I Parties could voluntarily participate in the effort to mitigate climate change. The incremental cost of such actions would be covered by Annex I Parties through the financial mechanism of the United Nations Framework Convention on Climate Change.

The second was the experiment made with the so-called "Joint Implementation with credit," involving Annex I and non-Annex I Parties, and the associated interim solution of "Activities Implemented Jointly" (AIJ) and its pilot phase. The basis for those efforts was an extension of the provision of Article 4.2 of the Climate Change Convention on specific commitments by Annex I Parties to reduce their net emissions in line with the general commitments of all Parties, included in Article 4.1.

The successful negotiation of the Kyoto Protocol introduced into the climate negotiations a regulatory element with legally binding, quantitative emission limitations and reductions by Annex I Parties. The basis for this is the agreement in the Climate Change Convention that industrialised countries must take the lead in decreasing their emissions, because the present concentrations of greenhouse gases are mostly due to their actions.

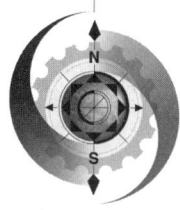

ISSUES&OPTIONS
The Clean
Development
Mechanism

This transition to a regulatory approach in dealing with climate change naturally brought into the spotlight the fundamental question of how to share the burden of mitigating climate change among the countries.

> There seems to be an opportunity now to effectively change the trend of global warming in a manner that is consistent with the Convention and in a way that it will be advantageous to all Parties involved.

climate change, weighed against the perceived burden on countries that will result from limiting or reducing emissions. The second issue is apportioning this burden among countries, within the principles agreed to in the Convention.

My personal view of the Climate Change Convention is that there are only two central issues to be negotiated regarding the mitigation of climate change. The first issue is the consensus decision, to be reviewed periodically, on how much the global emissions are to be reduced in the near future. This decision will depend on the perceived importance of avoiding or limiting

It is in within this new framework that the implementation of the Clean Development Mechanism (CDM) must be analysed. There seems to be an opportunity now to effectively change the trend of global warming in a manner that is consistent with the Climate Change Convention and in a way that will be advantageous to all Parties involved.

GUIDELINES FOR THE IMPLEMENTATION OF THE CDM

The following are, in my personal view, conditions that must be fulfilled as necessary conditions for the successful implementation of the CDM.

The governance of the CDM, through the Executive Board, must be efficient. Therefore the Executive Board should be relatively small, while maintaining the necessary representativeness of the different interests at stake.

The categories of projects certifiable under the CDM must, by general consensus, result in real reduction of emissions. Since it is impossible to determine the baseline against which the emission reduction is to be counted on purely technical grounds, and there may be controversy as to whether a baseline is appropriate or not, it is the "representativeness" of the Executive Board

that will guarantee that the credits for emission reductions under the CDM will be accepted towards compliance of the quantified emission limitation and reduction commitments (QELRCs).

The selection of the subcategories of projects that will be accepted for submission to certification and the approval of individual projects must be left to individual non-Annex I countries. They can then adapt their decisions to national development priorities.

For the sake of efficiency, the actual certification of projects must be distributed among existing institutions working under the strict guidance and supervision of the Executive Board. The feedback only achievable through a regulatory and auditing process is an essential part of the guidance and supervision.

OTHER ACTIONS RELEVANT TO THE SUCCESS OF THE CDM

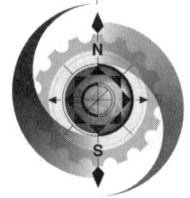

It is often said that one of the reasons the concept of AIJ never produced satisfactory results was that there were no credits in its pilot phase. In my opinion, a similar argument

applies for the CDM. Even though a credit is clearly associated with the CDM – to the extent emission reduction certificates will be accepted towards a demonstration of compliance with QELRCs of Annex I Parties – there will be no real incentive for its use until the Annex I Parties clearly establish national regulations limiting their emissions. There will be a real incentive to acquire such emission reduction certificates only when Annex I governments and/or private entities – depending on their particular choice of economic management tools – are faced with the clear alternative of: (a) reducing their emissions; or (b) paying a significant penalty; or (c) acquiring a CDM emission reduction certificate.

In other words, I believe that the effective functioning of the CDM absolutely depends on the effective implementation by Annex I Parties of national measures towards respecting their agreed emission limitation and reduction objectives.

A second overall condition that must be fulfilled in order for the CDM to have success is the realisation that there is a fundamental difference between the CDM and other so-called flexibility mechanisms.

The success of emissions trading in the case of urban pollutants is a case in point. This example is often cited to show the advantages of the market forces in dealing with an emissions problem. It is important to notice, however, that this kind of emissions trading regime works because there is a limitation imposed. A limited number of emission permits are available in the market, and the only other alternative to reducing emissions or purchasing emission certificates is the payment of a high penalty for non-compliance.

In the case of the CDM, it is thus important to establish strong non-compliance mechanisms, so that Annex I Parties will be prompted either to acquire CDM emission reduction certificates or, if they prefer, to establish national regulations

that would encourage the private sector to do so. The governments would accept those certificates in demonstration of compliance with the domestic limits, and use them, in turn, to demonstrate international compliance.

Another important difference between the CDM and either the emission permits regime or the other so-called flexibility mechanisms under the Kyoto Protocol is the fact that the CDM offers no emission entitlement or permit. Rather, Parties have an obligation to limit or reduce emissions. The difference may be non-existent from a mathematical point of view to the extent that the difference between a national baseline and a limitation or reduction objective is actually a ceiling. But from the point of view of compliance with the Climate Chance Convention, the difference is essential.

Moreover, both the emission trading regime among Annex I Parties and the project-based approach allowed by the Kyoto Protocol have the same effect – that of a "bubble." A "bubble," in my view, is simply permission for QELRCs compliance to be achieved jointly, rather than individually, by Annex I Parties, a point that was agreed upon in the Convention itself. Except for the format aspects and allocation of responsibility for non-compliance among the participating Parties in the "bubble" scheme, the question of the exchanges that take place among them is, in a sense, irrelevant for the objectives of the Convention provided that, with the agreement of the Parties involved, the national inventories of emissions include additions and subtraction that add up to zero.

The CDM, on the other hand, is based on a completely different concept in its international organisation, even though Annex I Parties will correctly view it as one additional flexibility mechanism.

PRACTICAL STEPS IN THE IMPLEMENTATION OF THE CDM

In my opinion, the implementation of the CDM should start sooner rather than late, because of the provision in the Kyoto Protocol that the emission credits may accrue as of the year 2000. In order to accomplish this, attention should be focused on the establish-

ment of the Executive Board, the negotiation of its terms of reference, and the guidelines under which it is to operate.

The following are some preliminary ideas on relevant aspects of these tasks, based on a

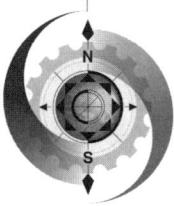

ISSUES&OPTIONS

The Clean
Development
Mechanism

series of discussions with Professor José Goldemberg over the first half of 1998.

The Conference of the Parties to the Convention must establish the Executive Board of the Clean Development Mechanism - EB/CDM.

> **The roster of certifiable projects must be dynamic, starting with those for which there is more certainty about the emission reductions and less controversy about their inclusion.**

- The EB/CDM is to be composed of a group of nine representatives of Parties to the Protocol, selected on the basis of parity among the regions of the world and representing an adequate balanced of Annex I and non-Annex I Parties.

- The EB/CDM shall follow the guidelines established periodically by the COP and have the mandate suggested below.

- The EB/CDM shall be supported by the Secretary of the Convention/Protocol, which will act as the Secretariat of the CDM and receive a fee for these services.

- The EB/CDM shall meet three times a year and report annually to the COP.

The following are suggested initial guidelines for the CDM.

- The reduction of emissions obtained in specific projects to be certified under the CDM shall be computed against a baseline that takes into account the projection, on a sector-by-sector basis, of the emissions for each country.

- The International Standard Organisation (ISO) will be requested to establish the detailed methodology for the definition of certifiable baselines and reductions and to use its system of accreditation of certifying organisations, for the purposes of issuing the emissions reduction certificates.

- Certificates of emissions reductions may be presented by non-Annex I Parties (see next item on the procedure) to the Secretariat of the CDM, for placement in the market.

- Each non-Annex I Party shall establish national mechanisms to regulate the submission of requests by any Party for certification for projects in its territory, which may vary from a requirement that each request be processed and submitted by the government itself to a general authorisation for the Secretariat to receive project proposals and to inform the government.

- The total credit for each Annex I Party that may be obtained through CDM certificates shall be limited in such a way that their national emissions do not exceed the 1990 level plus 2.5 per cent.

- The emission reduction certificates shall state the number of tons of carbon to which it refers, The corresponding value shall be determined by market mechanisms, avoiding the concept of incremental costs.

- The share of the proceeds of the CDM devoted to adaptation projects shall not exceed three per cent of the total.

- The share of the proceeds of the CDM devoted to administrative costs shall not exceed three per cent of the total.

The following are suggested terms of reference of the Executive Board of the CDM.

- To accredit organisations – governmental or otherwise – to systematically offer to the highest bidder the certificates of emissions reductions available at the Climate Change Secretariat, without prejudice to an open negotiation by anyone else.

- To accredit, through the ISO, organisations – governmental or otherwise – to pre-certify the emissions reductions as requested by non-Annex I Parties.

- To verify periodically, through accredited organisations, the correspondence between the pre-certified and the realised emissions reductions, and to issue the corresponding certificates of emission reductions.

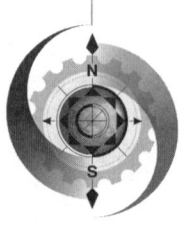

◆ To establish and periodically review the list of project activities for which emission reduction certificates may be issued. This global list should take into account exclusively the aspects related to the establishment of a credible baseline, leaving to governments the authority to establish their own list of eligible projects, taken from the former list. The national list will take into account, additionally, the sustainable development priorities.

In defining baselines on a sector-by-sector basis, the Executive Board shall consider, among other factors, the introduction of new technologies that will create new baselines. The technological impacts should be incorporated into the respective sectors, with a consequent review of the baselines.

In addition, the emission reductions to be certified must be agreed upon by both the donor and host governments.

The key to the successful implementation of the CDM lies with the establishment of baselines for certifiable emission reductions on a sector-by-sector basis for individual countries. It is essential that this process occur in such a manner that the emission reductions are comparable, according to the best available technical knowledge and to the political agreement of parties, through the Executive Board.

The roster of certifiable projects must be dynamic, starting with those for which there is more certainty about the emission reductions and less controversy about their inclusion Such a list is to be progressively expanded to include other types of projects as they meet the above criteria. ■

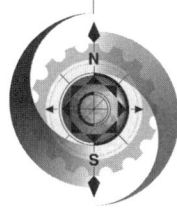

ISSUES&OPTIONS
The Clean
Development
Mechanism

Next Steps

Chapter 4

SIX QUESTIONS OF DESIGN AND GOVERNANCE

Theodore Panayotou
Harvard Institute for International Development
Cambridge, Massachusetts, USA

Summary: Whether the CDM will succeed in its ambitious objectives depends on how it is designed and governed. This paper studies six questions of design and governance: project eligibility, development impact, verification and additionality, national baselines, equity considerations, and governance and participation.

The Clean Development Mechanism (CDM) is one of the geographic-flexibility mechanisms provided under the Kyoto Protocol for efficient mitigation of greenhouse gases. The others are emissions trading, bubbles, and Joint Implementation. These four methods can be called geographically flexible because they provide for emissions reduction activities beyond the limits of a single country, involving one form or another of "trading."

Emissions trading is the more general, market-based instrument. It enables achievement of limits at least cost by taking advantage of marginal cost differentials in emissions abatement among countries. Since greenhouse gases are a uniformly mixing global pollutant, both the damages from emissions and the benefit from emission reduction are independent of their origin. In order to minimise the cost of given global emission reduction, abatement should take place where the costs are lowest. Emissions trading allows this to happen in an efficient and, one hopes, fair manner. Fairness, however, depends more on the initial allocation of reduction commitments than on emission trading itself, provided the system is properly designed. (Emissions trading is covered in Article 17 and referred to in Article 3.10 and 3.11 of the Protocol.)

Bubbles, Joint Implementation, and the CDM are all forms of restricted emissions trading:

Bubbles allow for trading within a group of countries such as the European Union who wish to jointly comply with the Kyoto commitments; "trade" is restricted to the countries within the geographically defined bubble (covered in Article 4 and referred to in Article 3.10 and 3.11 of the Protocol).

Joint Implementation limits emissions trading to developed countries that have accepted emission reduction commitments under the Kyoto Protocol, as listed in its Annex I. Countries that are certified to be below their national limits are allowed to sell greenhouse gas offsets to other Annex I countries who are above their own limits. The latter's motivation is the opportunity to meet their commitments at lower cost than through purely domestic actions (covered in Article 6, and referred to in Article 3.10 and 3.11 of the Protocol).

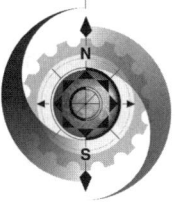

The Clean Development Mechanism, on the other hand, is an instrument for joint action on emissions reduction (and therefore trading) between the "developed" countries listed in Annex I of the Kyoto Protocol and "developing" countries, which are not listed in Annex I. It essentially allows joint implementation activities between countries in these two categories (covered in Article 12 and referred to in Article 3.12 of the Protocol).

But there are important differences. First, since non-Annex I countries have no quantitative commitments under the Kyoto Protocol, they lack national emissions baselines against which surplus reductions can be established and traded. This opens the possibility of project-by-project "additionality" of Annex I commitments. Alternatively, emissions baselines for developing countries (perhaps based on projections under a business-as-usual scenario) must be established before full-fledged emissions trading among Annex I and non-Annex I countries is allowed. Since national scenarios are both technically and politically problematic at this early stage, the CDM offers a modest first step in the direction through a bilateral or multinational (project portfolio) approach to "trading" on a project-by-project basis. However, precisely because of the absence of national baselines, CDM projects would require significantly more effort to ensure that they are "real," "measurable," "additional," and "long-term." Those are the criteria they need to meet to qualify for crediting, as would Joint Implementation projects.

Like Joint Implementation, the CDM does not allow for unlimited trading among eligible countries. Rather, it limits trading to a fraction of Annex I reduction commitments, although the precise fraction is not specified. Limitation in the scope of emissions trading, of course, imposes costs and reduces the gains from trade. The "benefits" that are usually invoked to justify such limits are technological evolution in terms of the development of cleaner technologies, and behavioural change in terms of more efficient energy use domestically. Whether these are real benefits and large enough to justify the cost of limits on otherwise allowable trades has not been demonstrated. In any case, it is not possible to know what the optimal limit is without analysing the corresponding marginal benefits and costs.

But the CDM is not just an instrument for restricted trading between Annex I and non-Annex I countries, and hence an investment option for emission reductions by Annex I countries. It is much more than that. It is designed to help developing countries achieve sustainable development while contributing to the objectives of the Convention. It offers a way to engage developing countries in the global efforts to control greenhouse gas emissions without constraining their development prospects. If anything, it aims to hasten development so that non-Annex I countries can begin to assume their own emission reduction commitments. Ideally, the CDM will induce additional capital flows to developing countries, accelerate technology transfer and enable developing countries to leapfrog to cleaner technologies, while helping developed countries achieve their emission reduction commitments, at a lower cost.

In so doing, the CDM is an effort to reconcile and integrate global environmental protection and local economic development – not unlike the Global Environment Facility (GEF). The CDM, however, is explicitly a mechanism, not a fund. The CDM also attempts to address developing country concerns about the distribution of benefits from emissions trading and joint implementation and about possible effects of carbon offset projects on their development priorities. It stresses the "fair" sharing of the benefits and compatibility of CDM projects with national development priorities.

> **Ideally the CDM will induce additional capital flows to developing countries, accelerate technology transfer and enable developing countries to leapfrog to cleaner technologies, while helping developed countries achieve their emission reduction commitments, at a lower cost.**

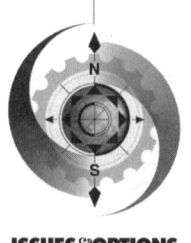

ISSUES&OPTIONS

The Clean
Development
Mechanism

Finally, the CDM recognises that despite global efforts, some climate change is inevitable and that the poorest countries are among the most vulnerable; for example, small island states are disadvantaged by their geography and the difficulty of adapting to rising ocean levels. Thus, it provides for a share of the proceeds from certified projects to be used to assist poor countries that are particularly vulnerable to climate change.

Whether the CDM will succeed in its ambitious objectives depends critically on how it is designed and governed. The Kyoto Protocol left both the design and the governance questions of the CDM and the other flexibility mechanisms unanswered and referred them to subsequent meetings of the Conference of the Parties to resolve. To operationalize the CDM, the following six questions need to be answered:

Project eligibility: What types of projects will be eligible for the CDM and what criteria will be used to determine acceptability?

Development impact: How to evaluate the development impact of CDM projects and ensure that they contribute to sustainable development?

Verification and additionality: How to verify emissions reductions and assess "additionality"?

National baselines: Should the CDM require non-Annex I countries to establish national baselines before they can sell credits, and if so, how should the baselines be set?

Equity considerations: How are equity concerns to be addressed, and how are the benefits to be divided between investing and host countries?

Governance and participation: How should the Executive Board be organised and which would be the operational entities domestically and internationally? In this regard, what should be the role of the public sector, and how much can be left to the private sector?

The ultimate challenge is to structure the CDM in such a way as to channel private investments and efficient technologies towards globally efficient mitigation projects consistent with the development priorities of the host countries.

PROJECT ELIGIBILITY

Not all projects that result in emissions reductions are eligible for trading under the CDM. The following general criteria, which are explicit or implicit in the Kyoto Protocol,

> **CDM should set clear eligibility and selection criteria, allow open competition for projects, and encourage experimentation with new project concepts.**

would limit qualifying, eligible projects to those which:

◆ are developed in a non-Annex I country with assistance (funding, technology transfer) from an Annex I country.

◆ result in real, measurable, and long-term emissions reductions that are additional to what would have occurred under a baseline situation, i.e. emission reductions that would not have occurred without the project. This clearly requires a "with and without" project

analysis, not a "before and after" accounting.

◆ result in sustainable development benefits for the host country. While the letter of the Protocol is not as explicit on development benefits as it is on emissions reductions, the spirit of the Protocol is quite clear: development benefits need to be as real, measurable, and additional as the emissions reductions. This raises three difficult questions: (a) How is sustainable development to be defined? (b) How are development benefits to be measured? and (c) Should carbon offset certifications await the generation and documentation of sustainable development benefits?

Beyond these general eligibility criteria, the Protocol is silent on both the types of projects

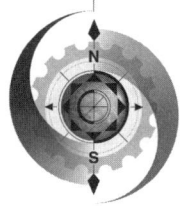

that qualify and the criteria for selection among them. Are projects aimed at enhancement of sinks as eligible for the CDM as projects aimed at mitigation of sources? In principle, both types of projects should be eligible. In practice, mitigation of sources, especially in the energy sector, is much easier to audit and document (using a mass balance accounting) than enhancement of sinks or mitigation of non-energy sources such as deforestation, agriculture, and land use change. However, exclusion of the latter group from the CDM would clearly contradict the sustainable development objective of the CDM. A two-step compromise could be envisaged. Begin with easily verifiable energy projects as test cases for developing the operational principles and accounting procedures of the CDM, and subsequently extend them to land use projects. It is important, however, that trading and crediting should be available for reforestation and other land use projects that fully meet the CDM criteria starting in the year 2000 or soon thereafter.

Should a list of acceptable projects be drawn up, or should private and legal entities be free to submit any project for consideration? The CDM should avoid the temptation of picking winners, an approach that only limits competition and stifles inventiveness. The CDM should set clear eligibility and selection criteria, allow open competition for projects, and encourage experimentation with new project concepts.

However, the lack of sectoral or, better, national baselines introduces uncertainty regarding true additionality. To minimise the leakages (the so-called "hot air"), it would be necessary for the Executive Board of the CDM to define a limited list of types of projects with strong additionality features that would be eligible for the CDM. At the same time, allow a broader set of projects (sector-wide) for countries that voluntarily establish and negotiate sectoral baselines, and even a wider set of projects (no restrictions, except certifiability) for countries that establish and negotiate national baselines. Such a system will act as an incentive for countries to graduate into increasing responsibility as they are prepared to do so, in the context of common but differentiated responsibilities.

DEVELOPMENT IMPACT

If only projects that contribute to sustainable development would be eligible for the CDM, how is sustainability to be defined and development impact measured? In the absence of widely acceptable sustainability indicators, the evaluation of the development impact of CDM projects could be based on conventional social benefit/cost analysis, extended to include macro-economic and environmental externalities beyond the mitigation of sources and enhancement of sinks. A project will meet the "sustainable contribution" criteria if it can be shown to generate for the host country a positive net present value, net of the cost of negative local environmental impacts and gross of the positive ones. A positive net present value from an economy-

> The ultimate challenge for CDM is to be structured in such a way as to channel private investments and efficient technologies towards globally efficient mitigation projects consistent with the development priorities of the host countries.

wide perspective would reflect an increase in green GDP or sustainable output. However, ultimately the host countries hosting a CDM project must have the last word in verifying that the projects contribute to sustainable development.

One likely need is to assess the long-term effects of current projects or technology choices. Almost by definition, the CDM will target developing countries at a phase of heavy infrastructure development, such as transport systems, power stations, or urban development. Investment and technological choices with regard to infrastructure have a lock-in effect on both global emissions and local environmental impacts for many years to come. How can these

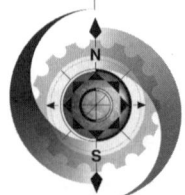

be anticipated, measured, and incorporated in the sustainability impact appraisal of CDM projects? Can the past experience of industrialised countries with investment decisions and technology choices help assess the development and environment impacts of CDM projects in the corresponding sectors?

Difficult assessment problems are also presented by projects with substantial learning, capacity building, and technology transfer benefits. These may turn out to be more important in the long-run to the aims of the CDM than capital flows and short-term benefits, yet they may not be fully captured by benefit-cost analysis.

ADDITIONALITY AND VERIFICATION

Only projects that result in verifiable, incremental emissions reductions would be eligible for crediting under the CDM. How is additionality defined and measured and how can claims to that effect be verified? At a general level, we can define two types of additionality:

Weak additionality: an emissions reduction is additional or incremental or surplus (and hence attributable to the project and creditable to the investor) if it is in excess of emission reduction requirements required by other laws and regulations. A reduction that is relied upon by the country or another buyer to comply with another law or commitment is not additional and hence not creditable.

Strong additionality: an emission reduction is additional or surplus if it would not have happened in the baseline situation (business-as-usual scenario) without the project.

Regardless of which definition of additionality is adopted – under some interpretations the two converge – it is necessary to establish a baseline against which surplus emission reductions or sink enhancements would be counted. There are many ways in which baselines can be defined. Here are four examples based on Michaelowa (1998)[1]:

Constant emissions based on historical levels. This must be discarded outright despite its low-cost appeal. It is a poor depiction of reality and tends to overstate future emissions by developed countries and understate future emissions by developing countries.

Linear extrapolation of past and recent trends – also a crude method, but somewhat more reliable.

Forecast based on economic development, population growth, and possibly other (exogenous) factors. This baseline definition gives the best depiction of reality and a more reliable prediction of future emissions (under business-as-usual scenario), provided that the growth assumptions are realistic. However, the costs of drawing up this scenario are high, as it requires careful modelling and accurate data.

Individual project-related scenarios. These ignore indirect effects,[2] as well as fail to provide a comprehensive picture of the growth of emissions over time for the country as a whole. Thus, one is not assured that the project-induced emission reductions are not offset by increases elsewhere in the country.

To avoid loopholes and "hot air" effects entirely, the use of the CDM for emissions trading must be conditional upon non-Annex I countries establishing national baselines prior to the sale of credits. This indeed could act as an incentive for developing countries to inventory, project and report their emissions, a first step in the process of engagement in the global efforts to control greenhouse gases. To facilitate this, the Convention could establish a new Annex to which both potential sellers and buyers of CDM offsets must access before they can engage in trades. Establishment of emissions baselines would then be a requirement for such accession.

---

[1] *Michaelowa, Alex. "Joint Implementation–The Baseline Issue: Economic and Political Aspects" Global Environmental Change, 1998. (Also http://perso.easynet.fr/~michaelo/baseli.htm.)*

[2] *For example, when a project uses inputs whose production generates greenhouse gases.*

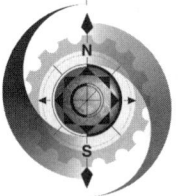

However necessary national baselines may be for preventing leakage and ensuring additionality, non-Annex I countries are neither technically nor politically prepared to establish such national baselines. Therefore, a second-best approach would assess additionality project-by-project within narrowly defined categories, and offer dynamic incentives to encourage countries voluntarily to establish and negotiate sectoral or national baselines. For example, one incentive would be to allow eligibility for a wider set of projects once a country has set baselines.

EQUITY CONSIDERATIONS

Many dimensions of equity pertain to the CDM. From a Northern perspective, equity is cast in terms of fairness in participation in emissions reduction, or at least some "meaningful participation" by all countries in global efforts to mitigate climate change. From a Southern perspective, equity is cast in terms of historical emissions, per capita emissions, right to unconstrained growth of emissions to enable rapid economic growth, or simply in terms of development and access to technology. Then there is the issue of intertemporal equity: whether it is fair for earlier generations to enrich themselves at the expense of future generations that will inherit the excessive concentrations of greenhouse gases and consequent climate change impacts. Implicit in the Kyoto agreement is emissions "trading" or "trade-offs" between generations.

The CDM introduces yet another dimension of equity: equity between emerging economies and less developed countries in terms of access to the CDM and the resources it can potentially mobilise. Because emerging economies have the better infrastructure, lower risk, and largest greenhouse gas-saving potential, there is a major risk that the CDM could generate a financial flow towards those countries that are already receiving the bulk of private capital flows from industrialised countries. One approach to resolving this equity issue is to set up regional quotas to ensure that poor regions, such as sub-Saharan Africa, receive their share of capital flows and technology transfers. Another solution might be to give extra "credit" when Annex I countries meet emissions reductions commitments through investments in CDM projects in countries with per capita incomes of less than US$1,000.

The magnitude of the allocation of CDM benefits (funds) between administrative costs and assistance to vulnerable countries would determine how this equity issue is resolved. Industrialised countries would benefit from low-cost carbon credits; emerging economies would gain additional capital flows and clean technology; less-developed countries should benefit from sharing in these benefits through the CDM "investment tax".

To address the North-South equity issue, it is necessary to start with common but differentiated responsibilities and to establish some rules of convergence, taking account of initial conditions with regard to per capita income and emissions and to development needs based on economic and population growth. These considerations should be incorporated into the baselines for non-Annex I countries beyond which CDM offsets can be traded and credited.

Another equity issue concerns the sharing of the benefits from CDM projects among investing and host countries. If the baseline of the host country is used as a benchmark, most, if not all, the benefits will come to the investing country. If, on the other hand, the baseline of the investing country is used (i.e. the domestic emission reduction that the investor would have undertaken in the absence of the CDM), most of the benefits would accrue to the host country. The CDM divides the benefits into four shares: (a) investing country; (b) host country; (c) vulnerable countries; and (d) administrative costs. The exact formula has not been worked out, but it is clear that efficiency and sustainability as well as equity need to be taken into account. The latter three are a tax on CDM projects and will tend to reduce their attractiveness to investors vis-à-vis other investment options such as domestic action and Joint Implementation.

There are good reasons for imposing an administration fee to pay for the auditing,

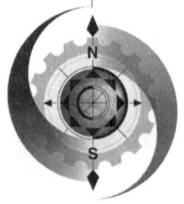

certification, and crediting of CDM offsets. It is also appropriate to provide some assistance to vulnerable, low-income countries. What is not clear is whether there should be a sharing of certified emission reduction credits between the investing and the host country. If so, should the proportions be determined by COP or left to the parties in the transaction? Furthermore, what is the value for the host country to thus become a holder of certified emission reductions, other than reporting in national communications?

Yet another equity issue is the unfairness of placing an adaptation investment tax on the CDM while Joint Implementation and emissions trading remain untaxed. Equity considerations would require that this fee or tax be applied to all flexibility mechanisms.

VALIDATION AND CREDITING PROCEDURE

The CDM validation and crediting procedures must be such that CDM projects (a) are attractive to the private sector as investment options; (b) are attractive to the host country as development opportunities and as magnets for capital flows and technology transfer; and (c) yield certified emission reductions that constitute acceptable offsets for emissions reduction obligations under the Kyoto Protocol. Given these goals, CDM procedures should aim to minimise red tape, simplify the approval process and keep administrative costs to a minimum. They should also seek to preserve the competitiveness of CDM projects vis-à-vis other flexibility instruments such as emissions trading and Joint Implementation, as well as domestic measures with Annex I countries. The criteria for auditing, verification, and crediting must be consistent and comparable, to the extent possible, with those for emissions trading and joint implementation, as well as consistent with sustainable development priorities and policies. They should also enhance the incentives for developing countries to increase their involvement in global emission control efforts and contribute to the overall efficiency of global mitigation actions.

GOVERNANCE

The Kyoto Protocol provides for an Executive Board of the CDM to provide overall supervision and guidance on the participation by private and public entities. The Executive Board could be similar to the Executive Committee of the Multilateral Fund of the Montreal Protocol, which consists of representatives from developed and developing countries. The exact composition will be determined by the COP/MOP which provides the ultimate authority and guidance for the CDM. Furthermore, the COP/MOP is to designate operational entities to certify emission reductions resulting from project activities. The operational entities are not further defined, leaving open the possibility that they may be national or international.

One view is to use existing bodies with relevant scientific knowledge and experience, such as the Global Environmental Facility (GEF) or the International Energy Agency (IEA). This is likely to be favoured by Annex I countries on the grounds that new international bureaucracy would be costly and superfluous.

An alternative view, favoured by non-Annex I countries, is that there is a need for an independent COP-based body in which developing countries could play a more significant role than they are perceived to play in existing institutions.

Yet a third view is simply to establish an international emissions registry within the Climate Change Secretariat to certify and register emission reduction activities and transactions under the CDM. The international emissions registry would then work with each country's national emissions registry to establish and monitor national emission reduction programs and to certify and register

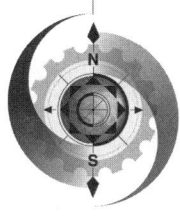

purchased or sold offsets. Such registries already exist in some countries and would be nationally appointed or set up in others. All other services could then be left to private sector entities duly regulated or supervised. Emission offset and validation auditing could be performed by accredited independent professional auditing or accounting individuals or firms for a fee. Intermediation between suppliers/sellers and demanders/buyers of emissions offsets would be performed by independent private brokers and traders.

The advantage of this decentralised operating system is that these international emissions registries would set the rules (to be applied by the private firms) and would limit themselves to an oversight role similar to that of securities exchange commissions. They would not carry out detailed assessments or be involved in the transactions, but would ensure that private auditors and national registries are complying with set rules and standards through reporting requirements, random inspections, and disqualification in case of non-compliance. This is a decentralised market-based approach that minimises international bureaucracy. It favours the CDM as a bilateral-based mechanism acting as a small and efficient project clearing-house in which private and public finance for the CDM passes directly from investors to recipients.

An alternative view favours a multilateral fund with centralised project identification, selection, and funding. While there are some merits to such an arrangement, especially in terms of mobilising funds for poor countries that are unlikely to receive them through the market, the need to provide strong incentives to both investing and host countries to fund and implement projects favours the decentralised approach. ■

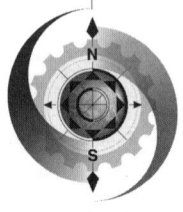

OPERATIONAL AND INSTITUTIONAL CHALLENGES

Farhana Yamin[1]
**Foundation for International Environmental
   Law and Development (FIELD)**
London, UK

Summary: Some fundamental aspects of the Clean Development Mechanism (CDM) have yet to be resolved. Much of the Protocol text is compromise language crafted to paper over differences of views that seemed unresolvable during the Kyoto Conference. This paper seeks to pave the way for future negotiations by highlighting gaps and ambiguities in the Protocol text, examining critical issues the Parties must address to make the CDM work as intended, and weighing options, where possible, for achieving functional answers to pending questions.

   Part I sets out the basic provisions of Article 12. It describes the bilateral and the multilateral approach to designing the CDM and summarises the key issues that need to be examined in detail. The various sections in Part II address each of these issues in turn. Part III deals with the complex governance and institutional issues involved in the early operation of the CDM.

INTRODUCTION

The Clean Development Mechanism (CDM) is perhaps the most innovative feature of the Kyoto Protocol. It allows Annex I Parties to invest in projects in developing countries that promote sustainable development and contribute to the ultimate objective of the Convention. In so doing, Annex I Parties can fulfil an as yet undefined "part" of their quantified emission limitation and reduction commitments (QELRCs) through "certified emissions reductions" (CERs) generated by such projects. The CDM is intended to help channel private sector investment towards climate-friendly projects. It is also intended to generate a surplus that can be used to assist Parties particularly vulnerable to the adverse impacts of climate change. The CDM has the potential to become highly efficient in promoting cost-effectiveness through the achievement of win-win options worldwide. But from an environmentalist standpoint, it is also the riskiest of the "flexibility mechanisms" in the Kyoto Protocol. Its operation could "blow open" the cap on Annex I Parties' emissions mandated by Article 3, rendering ineffectual the constraints imposed by the Protocol.

No Party's proposals resemble the CDM. Before Kyoto there were no published papers about it. The CDM is very much a creation of political necessity, drawing on the Brazilian proposal concerning the Clean Development Fund and various proposals concerning Joint Implementation. Its details were worked out in informal contact groups in the last few days of Kyoto, spearheaded by the Brazilian delegation with United States support. Its final inclusion in the Protocol is intimately linked to trade-offs and deals struck between countries over apparently unrelated issues. And much of the

---

[1] *Farhana Yamin is Director of the Foundation for International Environmental Law and Development (FIELD). She runs FIELD's climate change programme. This chapter draws on her contribution to a book she is writing on the history and analysis of the Kyoto Protocol (with S. Oberthur and H. Ott) to be published in 1999 by Cambridge University Press. Ms. Yamin has participated in the UNFCCC process as legal advisor to Samoa. The views expressed in this article are made in her personal capacity.*

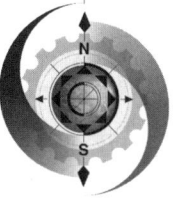

ISSUES&OPTIONS
The Clean
Development
Mechanism

detail of how it will work has been left to future negotiations at COP-4 and beyond.

This paper seeks to facilitate such negotiations by examining the key issues which Parties must address to make the CDM operational. It examines Parties' underlying approaches to the CDM. In particular, it highlights gaps and ambiguities contained in the Protocol text, much of which is compromise language crafted to paper over what appeared in Kyoto to be unresolvable differences of views. Where possible, it examines options for dealing with key unresolved issues.

PART I: PURPOSE AND SCOPE

Article 12 of the Kyoto Protocol

The purpose of the CDM, as defined in Article 12 of the Kyoto Protocol, is to assist Parties not included in Annex I in achieving sustainable development and in contributing to the ultimate objective of the Convention, and to assist Parties included in Annex I in achieving compliance with their quantified emission limitation and reduction commitments under Article 3. The Article specifies that this will be achieved by developing country Parties benefiting from project activities resulting in CERs, and Annex I Parties using those CERs to comply with part of their QELRCs under Article 3. How this is to be done will be determined by the Conference of Parties to the Convention as a meeting of Parties to the Protocol (COP/MOP).

The COP/MOP is to designate "operational entities" to certify project activities on the basis of:

◆ voluntary participation approved by each Party involved

◆ real, measurable and long-term benefits related to the mitigation of climate change

◆ reductions in emissions that are additional to any that would occur in the absence of the certified project activity.

The CDM is subject to the authority and guidance of the COP/MOP and is to be "supervised by an Executive Board" (Article 12.4). Participation in the CDM "may involve private and/or public entities, and is to be subject to whatever guidance may be provided by the Executive Board of the CDM." The CDM is to assist in arranging funding of certified project activities as necessary (Article 12.6). An innovative provision in Article 12.8 requires the COP/MOP to ensure that "a share of the proceeds from certified project activities is used to cover administrative expenses as well as to assist developing country Parties that are particularly vulnerable to the adverse effects of climate change to meet the costs of adaptation." The final element of the CDM relates to another innovative provision in Article 12.10 that allows CERs obtained during the period 2000 – 2007 to be used to assist in achieving compliance in the first commitment period (2008-2012). This subparagraph is explicitly referred to in the "prompt start" decision adopting the Protocol that requires the Chairman of the Convention's Subsidiary Bodies to undertake an "analysis of the implications of Article 12.10 of the Protocol."

Bilateral or portfolio approach?

Post-Kyoto discussions have revealed more clearly that Parties' views about the CDM are inspired by two contrasting approaches. The first is the bilateral approach, which stresses the similarities of the CDM with Joint Implementation under Article 6 and appears to be favoured by many Annex I Parties. The alternative portfolio approach focuses on the CDM's multilateral character and possible linkages with emissions trading, and is drawing greater attention from developing countries. These approaches are not rigidly defined, or even articulated openly, but form what might be called two mindsets around which opinions about the future evolution of the CDM appear to be emerging. Parties' views are also influenced by experience of the Activities

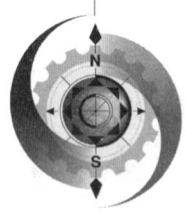

Implemented Jointly (AIJ) pilot phase, including Costa Rica's decision to issue "Certifiable Transferable Offsets,"[2] and by developments outside the Convention process such as the initiative by the World Bank to establish a prototype Carbon Fund.[3] The main elements and contrasting features of each approach are summarised in Table 1 and discussed below.

The bilateral approach to the CDM emphasises the needs of investor Parties and the interests of their private sectors. Under this approach, the CDM would define certain rules and exercise scrutiny over certification. But the development and implementation of CDM projects – and distribution issues concerning benefits and risks – would be dealt with in a contractual manner on a project-by-project basis by the Parties and entities involved in the project. The CDM would offer investor and host countries (and their respective private sectors) the maximum amount of choice to determine the nature of CDM projects, their financial contributions and the resulting sharing of CERs – with minimal interference from a centralised, international bureaucracy. The bilateral approach, therefore, favours the very minimal use of CDM institutional machinery. In essence, it need only consist of a clearinghouse mechanism that puts investors in touch with interested hosts to reduce transaction costs, and an independent certification process to generate environmental integrity and business confidence in the system.

Because of its emphasis on cost-effectiveness, the bilateral approach views the collection of proceeds for adaptation mandated by Article 12.8 as an unnecessary, additional cost; it would increase Annex I Parties' compliance costs and/or reduce project benefits accruing to host nations. And on that count, adaptation costs must be kept as low as possible. Nor can the bilateral approach clearly identify a role for the CDM for arranging funding of certified project activities mentioned in Article 12.6, as project development and finance are supposed to be driven by the market. The CDM is seen

as one of the Protocol's "flex-mexs" (flexibility mechanisms), whose purpose is to reduce Annex I Parties' compliance costs by generating cheap emission reduction "offsets" overseas. Loading additional responsibilities on to it, such as assistance in funding, may reduce its attractiveness to Annex I Parties.

The portfolio approach, by contrast, stresses the multilateral character of the CDM. The basic idea behind the portfolio approach is to "shield" host countries from direct "buying" and "selling" of CERs. Instead of approaching host countries directly, investors would buy CERs from the CDM itself, which will channel monies received to host countries that have submitted "bundles" or portfolios of projects to the CDM for certification. Financial contributions to the CDM are not mandatory but simply the receipts from CERs sold to Annex I Parties. These receipts are channelled back to the countries providing the CERs.

Advocates put forth three major advantages of such an approach. First, it would ensure CDM projects are really compatible with host country priorities. Second, it might result in higher prices for CERs because the CDM will be the sole supplier of CERs, and hence be able to negotiate a higher price than individual developing countries competing with each other on a project-by-project basis. And third, by allowing risk diversification between project types and countries, the portfolio approach might spread out the risk that is inherent in single projects under the bilateral project-by-project approach. This would attract large and small investors, which would, in turn, reduce transaction costs.

Portfolio approach proponents point out that the bilateral approach, typified by the Joint Implementation provisions of Article 6, were not acceptable to the majority of developing countries on grounds of national sovereignty. The CDM, as defined in Article 12, is acceptable precisely because it sanctions a multilateral form of Joint Implementation that respects

---

[2] *See Michaelowa and Dutschke,* Joint Implementation as Development Policy: The Case of Costa Rica, *January 1999, presented at the 1998 OECD Forum on Climate Change, Paris, France. Available upon request; e-mail: dutschke@hwwa.uni_hamburg.de.*

[3] *This would amount to a mutual fund for offsets that allows investors to pool their money to support a portfolio of projects developed and financed by the World Bank with a "green" element supported by contributions to the fund.*

Table 1. Bilateral versus Portfolio Approach to the CDM

BILATERAL APPROACH	PORTFOLIO APPROACH
Project-by-project	"Bundling" of projects in portfolios
Investor-led	Host country-led
Private sector emphasis	National sovereignty emphasis
Emphasises contributions to emission reductions	Emphasises contributions to sustainable development
Proceeds for adaptation unnecessary, seen as additional costs to achieve Article 3 compliance	Proceeds for adaptation seen as necessary to benefit all DCs and to increase global participation in Protocol
May concentrate on countries already benefiting from foreign direct investment	Could allow equity considerations to tailor portfolios to benefit all DCs' mitigation efforts
Primary purpose of CDM is clearinghouse function	Primary purpose of CDM is to obtain best price for CERs, shield hosts from undue pressure; clearinghouse function is a necessary feature

host country priorities and national sovereignty. It does so by allowing host countries to offer portfolios of projects that already form part of their sustainable development strategies, rather than devising new CDM projects they fear may be investor-led. Many developing countries are concerned that uncontrolled private sector partnerships with Annex I counterparts may lead to the introduction of inappropriate or hazardous technologies. They are also concerned that it could constrain their economic growth (by, for example, committing them to preserve forests when they may need land for growing food).

Proponents of the bilateral approach, on the other hand, are wary of establishing the CDM as a large international bureaucracy. They believe that investor choice in project selection is more efficient and desirable as it generates greater identification with the project, and, in turn, greater scrutiny over costs.

An additional point of contrast between the two approaches is treatment of equity issues. First, the portfolio approach, like the original Brazilian proposal, regards the collection of proceeds to fund the adaptation measures of Parties particularly vulnerable to climate change as an essential to ensuring that all developing countries benefit from the CDM. The emphasis on fairness and economic benefits for all Parties is based partly on the traditional solidarity of developing countries in the Group of 77, and partly on their astute

political recognition that Parties not benefiting from the CDM could block its progress. The bilateral approach regards the adaptation element as an unnecessary "surcharge" that should be minimised as much as possible. Its proponents give little recognition to the political realities of consensus-based negotiations in the UNFCCC, where lack of procedural rules on majority voting give each Party a veto on policy-making.

A final point of differentiation between the two approaches concerns the equitable distribution of CDM mitigation projects. Foreign direct investment is concentrated in a handful of developing countries that have the infrastructure, markets and government support. The bilateral approach to the CDM, as it stands now, is likely to reinforce such trends, resulting in only 10-20 developing countries benefiting from CDM projects. With its emphasis on cost-effectiveness and the primacy of markets in making the best choices, the bilateral approach has little to say about how the bulk of developing countries who stand to gain little from CDM mitigation activities (and who might even lose out if the CDM weakens the Global Environment Facility (GEF)) should be encouraged to participate in the CDM or support its early establishment. The portfolio approach offers a number of relatively straightforward options to ensure that all geographical areas benefit from the CDM, for example, through a requirement that a certain percentage of a portfolio must be based on geographically balanced production of CERs.

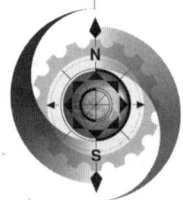

The provisions of Article 12 are general enough to accommodate the bilateral or portfolio approach or some combination of these. The key issues to putting the CDM into operation are listed below, with each analysed in more detail in Part II. They include:

◆ the nature of CDM projects

◆ environmental benefits and additionality

◆ auditing, verification, and certification

◆ financing of projects

◆ adaptation proceeds

◆ pre-commitment CER banking and supplementarity

◆ linkages with emissions trading and Joint Implementation.

Nature of CDM projects

Article 12.3 specifies that the CDM is to be *project-based*. A number of important clarifications are needed to decide:

◆ What is the definition of projects?

◆ Which projects are eligible?

◆ Who decides project eligibility, and by what criteria?

Definition of "project"

Article 12 refers to projects, but does not mention "policies," or "programmes." The former could include, for example, economic subsidy or tax policies, while programmes could encompass purely capacity-building activities. Both categories of activities may lead to a decline in greenhouse gas emissions, and may even be prerequisites for emission reductions.[4] But on their own, neither would appear to qualify as a "project activity." Strictly, therefore, these do not appear to be covered by the CDM. But as there is no definition of "project" in the Kyoto Protocol, Parties will have to decide whether to construe this term narrowly or broadly.

A wider definition covering macro-economic or sector-wide initiatives would give the CDM a very broad scope of activities. One advantage of a wide definition would be to allow Parties to generate more CERs under the CDM, benefiting investors and hosts, and covering large segments of economic activity. Provided these activities satisfy the "additionality" test discussed below, this can only be beneficial. But if the additionality test is weak or problematic (as will be the case with counter-factual baselines, discussed below), the CDM will end up covering activities that may or may not be additional. Such "gaming" may increase the volume of CDM transactions, benefiting individual investors and hosts, but would wreck the environmental credibility of the CDM.

Thus, whether one takes a bilateral or portfolio approach, the definition of a "project" needs to be agreed upon. Parties must know in advance what kind of initiatives can generate CERs. Moreover, it must be possible to devise an agreed methodology to measure the amount of CERs generated by a particular kind of activity, as the whole point of the CDM is to generate quantifiable results that can be credited to the investor's account.

One approach might be to specify a list of activities that qualify as "projects" to be included in the CDM's guidelines for project eligibility. This is the approach taken, for example, by the Multilateral Fund of the Montreal Protocol (MFMP), whose eligibility criteria are explicitly stated:

> "the term "projects" is used to describe any activity qualifying for assistance under the Fund. A project can include, *inter alia*, training, technical assistance, pre-investment studies, country program preparation, technology development or capital investment to modify or establish a manufacturing facility."[5]

Parties will need to consider carefully the range of activities considered as "projects" in the Montreal Protocol context. Two immediate

---

[4] *Article 6 also uses the term "project." In the negotiations of that Article, inclusion of "programmes" and "policies" was advocated by the some Parties but was not accepted.*

[5] *See MFMP, Criteria for Project Selection Under the Multilateral Fund.*

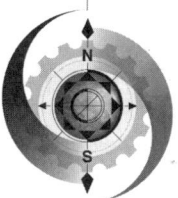

differences between the Montreal and the Kyoto Protocol need to emphasised. First, the CDM will operate *alongside* the Convention's financial mechanism operated by the GEF, which already funds a number of activities that might also be covered by the CDM. Second, the effect of activities under the CDM must be clearly demonstrable and highly measurable because, unlike the Multilateral Fund, the CDM will result in CERs – a commodity with a financial value. UNFCCC Parties' definition of "projects" will, therefore, need to be tailored to the CDM context.

Project eligibility

Article 12.2 states that the purpose of the CDM is to assist non-Annex I Parties in achieving sustainable development. Paragraphs (a) - (c) of Article 12.5 specify three criteria that projects must fulfil before their emissions reductions can be certified:

- voluntary participation and approval of projects by Parties

- production of real, measurable, and long-term mitigation benefits

- reductions "additional to any that would occur in the absence" of the project.

Parties will need to decide whether the requirement that the CDM contribute to the sustainable development of non-Annex I Parties will be used to limit the kind of projects the CDM can certify. They will also need to clarify how the project level criteria will be put into practice. A specific question thrown up by the textual ambiguities and gaps in the text of Article 12 is whether sequestration (sinks) projects are covered by the CDM. The following section looks at each issue in turn.

Sustainable development

The CDM's statement of purpose expressly refers to "achieving sustainable development" for non-Annex I Parties. This reference precedes mention of the Convention's ultimate objective. It explicitly links the CDM with the sustainable development of non-Annex I countries. In so doing, it balances the goal of mitigating climate change against other competing goals, such as social and economic

development, the alleviation of poverty, and adaptation. This developmental focus would be weakened if the reference were to the Convention's environmental objective alone. By contrast, the reference to sustainable development does not mention Annex I Parties. For them, the CDM's purpose is explicitly linked to compliance with their Article 3 commitments. This explicit linkage creates reasonable expectations on the part of Annex I Parties that the CDM will be operational within a time-frame that will allow them to make use of it.

The reference to sustainable development appears in Article 12.2, which defines the *overall purpose* of the CDM. It does not appear in Article 12.5, which lays down eligibility criteria applicable at *the project level*. This suggests that negotiators may not have intended the reference to sustainable development to act as a fourth, independent criteria that projects need to satisfy in addition to the three listed in Article 12.5, (a) – (c). As there is no internationally agreed operational definition of "sustainable development" that would allow Parties to objectively determine which projects are "sustainable" or otherwise, there are sound policy reasons for not including sustainable development as a criterion to be satisfied at the project level.

A number of practical conclusions relevant to designing the CDM follow. First, negotiators should focus their efforts on the eligibility criteria set out in Article 12.5 rather than getting bogged down in trying to define what is or is not a "sustainable development CDM project." Second, non-Annex I Parties attempting to use the reference to sustainable development to avoid international scrutiny about the kind of projects that are acceptable under the CDM (by arguing that only national authorities are competent to make decisions about what is or is not sustainable) are missing an important point. Operationalizing the project eligibility criteria set out in Article 12.5 rests with the COP/MOP, which shall designate *operational entities* to check that these are being met by each project. The eligibility process is thus already "internationalised." The issue at hand is how to make *project level* eligibility criteria promote the *broader objectives* – supporting the

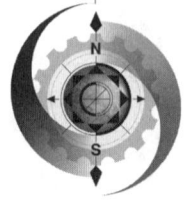

sustainable development of non-Annex I Parties and the compliance of Annex I Parties. These broader objectives may require, for example, that the CDM support projects in all sectors and all countries so that one country or one sector (e.g. forestry) does not benefit disproportionately. They may also demand that CERs generated by sectors rife with scientific uncertainties be appropriately discounted.

> **Certified emission reductions generated by sinks projects could be discounted to take into account the greater scientific and methodological uncertainties associated with them.**

Voluntary participation and approval

The first eligibility criteria specified in Article 12.5 (a) concerns the voluntary participation and approval of the Parties involved. Both of these elements are taken from the COP-1 decision establishing the AIJ pilot phase.[6] The voluntary element stresses the non-compulsory nature of AIJ activities, which no country was being "forced" to accept. The approval of each project activity by both investor and host countries was designed to ensure that both Parties agreed that the project was a (voluntary, not legally obligatory) contribution to their implementation of the Convention. Agreement by the host country is also a shorthand way of fulfilling AIJ mandates that require activities implemented jointly to be "compatible with and supportive of national environment and development priorities and strategies."[7]

During the AIJ pilot phase, governments notified the Climate Change Secretariat of their *prior* acceptance, approval or endorsement of AIJ activities. Even with the relatively small number of projects undertaken in the pilot phase, the prior approval process caused delays in communication and analysis of information. A similar CDM procedure could cause more substantial delays, as most Parties are expecting the numbers of projects to increase substantially.

The wording in Article 12.5 does not mandate "prior" approval of CDM projects by Parties involved, but does specify that approval must occur at least by the time *certification* is determined. One practical way to expedite information flows might be to provide that information about CDM projects could be sent directly by the entities involved to the Secretariat, *prior to certification*, provided they fell into a *pre-determined list* of project categories approved by the national authorities involved in the project. This would obviate the need for Parties to approve individual projects, at least until the certification process was nearing, and thus reduce the bureaucracy at earlier stages. And, provided the format and guidelines for the information could be agreed by Parties, such a process could also transfer the burden of communicating such information to the project participants (primarily the private sector). This, in turn, would release precious human and financial resources within government ministries, reduce tendencies towards micro-management of projects, and allow government officials to concentrate on broader policy issues relating to the CDM's operation.

Inclusion of sinks

Before discussing the other project eligibility criteria specified in Article 12.5 (b) and (c), it is useful to look at the specific issue of whether sequestration projects (sinks) are eligible under the CDM. Paragraph 3 (a) and the remainder of Article 12 talk about "certified emission reductions" (CERs) or about "emission reductions." There is no mention of "enhancing anthropogenic removals by sinks" and of counting the sequestration so achieved towards fulfilment of QELRCs.[8]

The negotiations on the CDM were taking place at the same time as those on the broader issue of the inclusion of sinks under Article 3.

---

[6] *Decision 5/CP.1. See Report of COP-1.*

[7] *Ibid., paragraph 1(a).*

[8] *cf. Article 6(1), which explicitly mentions anthropogenic removals by sinks and the use of emission reduction units (ERUs) obtained from sink enhancement for meeting QELRCs. See also Decision 5/CP.1 establishing the AIJ pilot phase, which explicitly stated that AIJ could cover all GHG sources, sinks and reservoirs.*

Certainly for many Parties, the inclusion of sinks was closely related to the kinds of projects they wanted to see included in the CDM or which developing countries might undertake under the article on voluntary commitments.[9] One factor in these broader sinks negotiations was that uncertainty levels relating to sinks would be magnified many fold if sinks were allowed under the CDM, or if developing countries could take on voluntary commitments. Because developing country sinks are generally not as well inventoried as those in Annex I countries, their inclusion could undermine the credibility of the Protocol by generating "low certainty credits" in place of more certain ones.

In view of these differences, delegations involved in the CDM negotiations appeared to agree that the CDM sinks issue would be revisited once the broader questions of sinks had been settled. Unfortunately, the lack of time did not allow Parties to fully reconsider this issue in the final negotiations. Therefore, the three options for sinks inclusion under the CDM are:

◆ Construe the Article 12 text literally and exclude all sinks projects under the CDM.

◆ Interpret Article 12 in the light of Article 3, which allows Annex I Parties a limited category of sinks that can be included to achieve their QELRCs.

◆ Design a new regime for sinks that is specific to the CDM.

Opinions as to what negotiators actually intended differ. The Brazilian Chairman of the CDM negotiations has suggested the second option, requiring Article 12 to be read in conjunction with Article 3. This understanding appears to be shared by the European Union (EU). Other delegations, such as the United States, are known to want a more generous category of sinks to be covered by Article 12 than is included in Article 3. Alliance of Small Island States (AOSIS) countries have formally stated that since Article 12 does not make

reference to sinks, Parties have an opportunity to reconsider whether and how sinks should be dealt with in the CDM.[10]

If the second option is chosen, inclusion of sinks under the CDM should receive the same, or stricter, levels of scrutiny as Annex I Parties using domestic sinks for emissions reductions. The inclusion of Annex I Parties' own sinks was fought over in extensive detail and is subject to stringent conditions specified in Article 3.3 and 3.4. Negotiators in the broader sinks discussions did not expect that a less stringent standard for sinks inclusion would be set for developing country sinks under the CDM. The evolution of sinks projects under the CDM should, therefore, follow the same (or higher) levels of scrutiny as those specified in Articles 3.3 and 3.4, or else be excluded altogether.

Those arguing for inclusion note that, in practice, developing countries may find it easier to report on sinks CDM projects (because of their smaller scale) than to inventory each country's entire land use change and forestry sector according to COP-approved guidelines for national communications. Furthermore, the need to attract CDM projects may also lead to more rapid improvements in non-Annex I Parties' inventory and national communications than perhaps might otherwise have taken place. Finally, CERs generated by sinks projects could be discounted to take into account the greater scientific and methodological uncertainties associated with them. This would provide an alternative to their total exclusion and at the same time motivate Parties to resolve these uncertainties so they can claim full credit.

The way in which non-Annex I Parties would have to account for sink projects based on the approach identified in Article 3 is proving problematic and will be elaborated within the on-going discussions in the Convention's subsidiary bodies. At their meetings in June 1998, Parties clarified the meaning of Article 3.3 and 3.4. They agreed to organise a workshop prior to COP-4 to consider data availability for Article 3.3 and a workshop after COP-4 for Article 3.4. In addition, the Subsidiary Body for Scientific and

---

[9] *Known as the Lost Article 10, this provision was lost in the final night of negotiations.*

[10] *Submission of Samoa (for AOSIS) to Secretariat, 23.3.98, see FCCC/SB/1998/MISC.1.*

Technological Advice (SBSTA) requested a special report from the IPCC to enable the COP to take decisions on land use and forestry projects.

This work will indirectly influence whether and how developing country sinks will be dealt under the CDM. Ultimately, it is a matter for further political negotiations.

Environmental benefits and additionality

Paragraphs (b) and (c) of Article 12.5 set out two project criteria.[11] The first requires that environmental benefits of CDM mitigation projects must be real, measurable, and long-term. The second requires that the benefits be additional. Additionality has both environmental and financial aspects. This section looks at environmental additionality. In the absence of binding targets for non-Annex I Parties, the environmental effectiveness of the CDM will hinge on the way in which emissions reductions are measured.

Assessment of whether CDM projects will fulfil these criteria requires comparing projects against a baseline, which could be static or dynamic. In any case, it is a counter-factual construct that may never actually happen. Assessing environmental benefits also requires establishing system boundaries appropriate to the scale and complexity of the project to assess "leakage." In addition, common time-frames for analysing these benefits for different kinds of projects should be determined.

Common methodologies for baselines

The AIJ pilot phase has led to useful work in identifying key baseline issues. But the weakness of AIJ is that it did not require Parties to agree on common definitions or a common methodology for determining baselines. The result is that Parties involved in AIJ projects have used different assumptions and methods, and have not reported on these in a rigorous manner.

This "let a hundred flowers bloom" approach cannot be replicated in the CDM because, in contrast to AIJ, it is intended to result in CERs which will be transferred for money between Annex I and non-Annex I Parties. An independent evaluation of the AIJ pilot phase, mandated by Decision 5/CP.1 to take place before the end of the decade, would assist the "prompt start" preparation of the decisions COP/MOP must make covering, inter alia, common definitions and methodological and reporting issues to ensure transparency and efficiency.

The evaluation of the AIJ pilot phase should seek, in particular, to illuminate the critical question of baseline construction. Baselines can be sector-specific, technology-specific or country-specific.[12] Because nearly all the baseline scenarios involve counter-factual assumptions, they cannot be empirically proved or disproved. All partners in a project stand to gain by inflating the amount of project reductions. To ensure transparency and a "level playing field" among those involved in generating CERs, Parties must agree on baseline construction methodologies.

The baseline issue involves technical aspects. But it is rooted in an irreducible element of policy that cannot be answered technically or "contracted out" to outside organisations or scientists to resolve.[13] There is no "right" or "wrong" baseline. What matters is that Parties

> **The baseline issue involves technical aspects. But it is rooted in an irreducible element of policy that cannot be answered technically or "contracted out" to outside organisations or scientists to resolve.**

---

[11] *In fact, in the decision establishing the AIJ pilot phase, these criteria were contained in a single sentence that read "activities implemented jointly should bring about real, measurable and long-term environmental benefits related to the mitigation of climate change that would not have occurred in the absence of such activities," 5/CP.1, paragraph 1(d).*

[12] *For a comprehensive assessment of the literature and specific proposals about choice of baselines and methodological issues, see http://www.unfccc.de, CC:INFO/AIJ. Note on methodological issues. See also H. Ott, Operationalizing Joint Implementation, cite.*

[13] *The IPCC has, for example, refrained from defining "anthropogenic sinks" so far as the Convention process is concerned.*

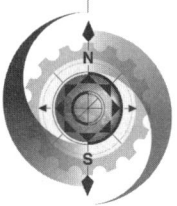

use a common framework that is open to third party scrutiny – in other words, the "independent auditing and verification" referred to in Article 12.7. This process is essential for "operational entities" in the certification process. Entities will only be able to do this job if they can ascertain that the environmental benefits and additionality criteria have been met, and that the reductions that have been claimed have actually been produced.

> There is no "right" or "wrong" baseline. What matters is that Parties use a common framework that is open to third party scrutiny.

Clarification of the methodological issues under the AIJ pilot phase has led to working definitions of terms such as "real," "measurable," and "long-term" environmental benefits that are "additional." These definitions could be considered useful starting points for implementing Article 12.5 (b) of the Protocol.[14]

The methodological work on AIJ suggests, for example, that environmental benefits related to climate change projects could be recognised as real if the actual greenhouse gas emissions or sequestration can be shown to differ from a credible and probable baseline scenario, taking leakage into account.[15]

Environmental benefits could be considered measurable if the actual level of greenhouse gas emissions of the project case and the level of greenhouse gas emissions in the baseline scenario can be established with a reasonable degree of certainty (which would have to be stated), using direct measurement for observing emissions in the project case.[16]

Benefits could be recognised as long-term if the emissions avoidance or sequestration are sustainable, that is, if they persist over an appropriate time period (agreed by Parties for different categories of projects).

Finally, environmental benefits to emission reductions could be recognised as additional if it can be demonstrated that they would not have occurred otherwise.

Common methodologies for additionality

Expert consideration has led to three methods that might be used to demonstrate additionality. They could be used in the CDM context individually or in combination:[17]

◆ measuring additionality against a credible, quantitative baseline[18]

◆ defining narrow categories of projects the emission benefits of which will *a priori* be considered additional[19]

◆ assessing additionality by evaluating whether a CDM project has overcome financial, institutional, technological or other barriers to project development.[20]

Each approach has merits and difficulties. The simplest, and probably least costly, method is the second. Limited lists, however, are difficult to agree on in consensus-based negotiations like the UNFCCC, because each Party has the right to insist that projects of interest to itself are included. In the CDM context, for example, some Parties may insist that sequestration or nuclear power projects are included, even

---

[14] *The methodological note on AIJ suggests, for example, the following. "Environmental benefits related to the mitigation of climate change would be recognized as real if the actual GHG emissions or sequestration can be shown to differ from a credible and probable baseline scenario taking leakage into account".*

[15] *Ibid.*

[16] *Ibid.*

[17] *Ibid.*

[18] *Luhmann et al. suggest, for example, that in the power sector, the average utilization ration of power plants in the host country or of the investing country, or the use of best available technology (state-of-the-art) minus some percentage could be used.* Making Joint Implementation Operational, *Wupppertal Papers No. 31, March 1995.*

[19] *See Chapter 12 in this book by Paul Hassing and Mathew Mendis*

[20] *See e.g. I. Minzter, Institutional Options and Operational Challenges in the Management of a Joint Implementation Regime, in* Criteria for Joint Implementation Under the Framework Convention on Climate Change, *ed. Ramakrishna, Woods Hole, 1994. See also Torvanger et al.* Joint Implementation under the UNFCCC: Phases, Options and Incentives, *Report 1994:6, CICERO, Oslo.*

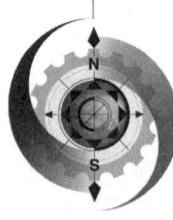

ISSUES&OPTIONS

The Clean
Development
Mechanism

though these are considered to be controversial by other Parties. To overcome these problems, Parties could aim for a two-tiered system. Projects that are indisputably climate friendly, such as renewable energy and energy conservation, could be included in a list of projects whose additionality is agreed *a priori*. Projects not on this list would have to prove additionality through the other two methods, which, of course, would have to be further refined.

Parties may wish to draw on the experience gathered by the GEF in assessing environmental additionality at the project level. The GEF has used the concept of "agreed incremental costs" to determine a baseline against which it can judge the additional value of its contribution. This requires a complex, and controversial, series of assessments as to what would have happened without GEF assistance and what investments a developing country should bear because they produce "national benefits," which are judged to be in their interest to pursue.[21]

Like the GEF, the CDM will clearly have to set some kind of environmental standards or constraints for project activities before private sector investments can be recognised as having made a contribution that is additional to what would otherwise have occurred. The policy guidance provided by the COP to the GEF on the kinds of projects and programs the GEF should fund provides one approach the CDM could examine, if only to avoid.[22]

Auditing, verification and certification

Article 12.7 mandates the first meeting of the COP/MOP "to elaborate modalities and procedures with the objective of ensuring transparency, efficiency and accountability through independent auditing and verification of project activities." Article 12.5 refers to "operational entities" designated by the COP/MOP to certify emission reductions based on the criteria discussed above.

Auditing is the examination of accounts by an authorised person or persons to check that calculations are accurate and undertaken in accordance with specified standards. Auditing is about correct bookkeeping and balancing. The "books" in the case of the CDM would comprise project level documentation collected at the national level relating to the generation, acquisition or transfer of CERs – a national registry of sorts. The international "books" would consist of data related to projects collected from Parties – including their national communications, and comprising an international register of CER transactions. All CDM projects must be subject to the same standard of auditing to ensure the financial integrity of the whole system.

Verification means checking that the emissions reductions claimed in the national and international registers or "books" have actually occurred. Verification is a "reality check" on the books. It could involve physical, on-site inspection, or, where useful, deployment of techniques such as remote sensing, or interviewing relevant personnel – in person or otherwise. Verification could occur on each and every project, or on a fraction of projects chosen randomly or selected according to some agreed-upon criteria.

Certification is an official declaration – a certificate – confirming the achievement of a specific result based on satisfactory auditing and verification. It would specify the amount of CERs achieved and provide details of the project.

Auditing, verification and certification constitute three steps that take place sequentially. All are underpinned by prior monitoring, which involves the collection of project data by direct measurement and its comparison with the baseline scenario. Monitoring is best done by those closest to the project, the project partners.

Parties need to decide who should undertake auditing, verification, and certification, according to what standards, and how adherence

---

[21] *There is no agreed definition of incremental costs. At their simplest, incremental costs are arrived at by calculating the difference between the cost of an action that a country would undertake in its own national interests (the "baseline") and that of a more expensive alternative undertaken by that country in order to implement the Convention.*

[22] *Decision 11/CP.1.*

to such standards can be ensured. Four choices present themselves: international institutions, national institutions, the private sector, or some combination of all three. The institutional issues surrounding which entities do what functions are discussed in the section on governance in Part III.

Financing CDM activities

The bilateral and portfolio approaches to the CDM were inspired by very different expectations about the financing of CDM projects. Four key financing questions arise:

◆ Should the CDM should be a public fund or a clearinghouse mechanism facilitating private investment?

◆ What will the relationship between the CDM and the GEF be?

◆ Should rules of financial additionality apply to the CDM, and, if so, which ones?

◆ How should equity issues arising from private sector investment be addressed?

Fund or Mechanism?

The Brazilian proposal, and the modified version put forward by the Group of 77, advocated the establishment of a government-backed Clean Development Fund to finance projects. Annex I Parties wanted a government-supported clearinghouse mechanism that could facilitate private sector investment.

The word "mechanism" was used in the Protocol instead of "fund" because it was clear at an early stage in the negotiations that most developed countries did not want to commit themselves to a fund for mitigation efforts in developing countries. The larger donor countries

were worried that a new fund would undermine the GEF. They were also reminded of the developing countries' pre-Earth Summit demands for the establishment of the "Green Fund," which they had managed to resist.[23] Finally, developed countries were much more influenced by various policy papers on Joint Implementation that had advocated the establishment of an international clearinghouse mechanism that would facilitate, rather than fund, private sector Joint Implementation deals.[24]

The compromise term, "mechanism," does not preclude the possibility of a fund being established as part of the CDM. But neither does it mandate one. Article 12.1 states that the CDM is "hereby defined" for much the same reason. The Group of 77 proposals stating that the CDF is hereby "established" met with resistance from some developed country delegations, particularly the EU, because they wanted to avoid any connotation of establishing a new funding institution. They wanted, in particular, to leave open the possibility of using the GEF to "operate" all or part of the CDM.[25]

The CDM and the GEF

The eventual acceptance at Kyoto that the CDM might not be a new fund was influenced by the widespread recognition that official development assistance (ODA) for sustainable development is becoming scarce and is likely to remain so. Developing country expectations of the amount of resources that would be made available through the GEF have not been met. Developing country delegates knew that the creation of another "fund" would do little to address the underlying causes of that decline. They also knew that while the role of ODA is declining, the size and flow of private sector investment has expanded exponentially.[26] Over the last ten years, net flows from private/commercial sources of funding have increased

[23] *The Green Fund concept was put forward by the Indian Prime Minister, Rajiv Ghandi, and endorsed by the South. See e.g. the Beijing Ministerial Declaration on Environment and Development, 19 June 1991. For a history of the GEF see Helen Sjoberg, The Global Environment Facility, in Werksman, ed., Greening International Institutions, Earthscan, London, 1996.*

[24] *See e.g. I. Minzter, Institutional Options and Operational Challenges in the Management of a Joint Implementation Regime, in* Criteria for Joint Implementation Under the Framework Convention on Climate Change, *ed. Ramakrishna, Woods Hole, 1994. See also Torvanger et al.* Joint Implementation under the UNFCCC: Phases, Options and Incentives, *Report 1994:6, CICERO, Oslo.*

[25] *The "defined" terminology is rooted in Article 12(1) of the Convention, which defines a financial mechanism whose operation is entrusted to one or more existing international entities (at present the GEF).*

[26] *Source: FCCC/TP/1997/1, Trends of Financial Flows and Terms and Conditions Employed by Multilateral Lending Institutions.*

from approximately US $25 billion to US $170 billion.[27] In 1990, ODA accounted for 56 per cent of the total amount of financial flows. By 1996 it was just 14 per cent. Overall financial flows have expanded by 184 per cent since 1990 due to the strong growth of private capital flows.

Resolution of the public funding versus private investment issue has a number of extremely important consequences. If CDM projects are publicly funded, the CDM will compete directly with the GEF for ODA resources. Annex I Parties will switch funding intended for the GEF to the CDM because it will earn them emission credits, not just political kudos. In that scenario, the GEF would tend to decline. That is why its supporters at Kyoto sought to find a complementary role for GEF, including as an operator for some or all of the CDM.

Negotiators appeared to recognise these problems at Kyoto. Those from developing countries regarded CDM financing as being separate from and additional to the financial obligations of the Parties included in Annex II of the Convention within the framework of its financial mechanism. They regarded it as additional to current ODA flows as well.[28] The financial provisions of the Protocol, contained in Article 11, were, in effect, extending the scope of Annex II Parties' financial obligations to the implementation by developing countries of the commitments covered by Article 10 of the Protocol. The CDM was not intended to undermine the Convention's (and the Protocol's) financial mechanism. Rather, it was intended to tap a separate source of funds: private sector investment flows. Negotiators explicitly discussed the fact that the GEF had mobilised only a very low level of private sector financing of GEF projects and negligible amounts from private financial institutions.[29] And the new mechanism they were creating was intended to reverse this shortcoming.

Financial additionality

The requirement in Article 12.5(c) that CDM projects result in emission reductions that are "additional to any that would occur in the absence" thus also refers to an element of financial additionality. Private funds are, by definition, additional to and separate from GEF contributions; thus, they would not need to "demonstrate" any additionality.[30] The question really concerns publicly-funded CDM projects. How can the additionality of these be guaranteed?

Under the Convention, the financial additionality criterion has been difficult to apply and enforce in relation to public sector flows.[31] The Overall Performance Study Report of the GEF, requested by the GEF Council in 1996, concluded that the "new and additional" requirement of GEF funds was not being met if one were to use the only operational definition of additionality: whether ODA flows had been reduced as funding was provided to the GEF.

One way to ensure additionality would be to limit the CDM to privately-funded projects, so that it would not undermine the predominantly publicly funded GEF. This must remain a thriving institution, particularly because not all developing countries may benefit from CDM activities, and because the private sector will not fund "core" activities and support technologies that are not commercially viable.

Equity and private sector flows

The rationale behind the CDM is to "green" private investment flows. These flows currently are concentrated in some 25-30 developing countries, of which just 12 have absorbed some 80 per cent of flows since 1990.[32] For the poorest

---

[27] *Barbara Bramble, note Financial Resources for the Transition to Sustainable Development, in F. Dodds, ed. The Way Forward: Beyond Agenda 21, 1997, Earthscan, London, p194.*

[28] *Decision 5/CP.1 makes this clear by explicitly stating that "the financing of activities implemented jointly overall framework of the financial mechanism as well as to current official development assistance (ODA) flows."*

[29] *Porter et al, Study of the GEF's Overall Performance. GEF, 1998.*

[30] *Assuming these investments satisfy criteria relating to environmental benefits and environmental additionality.*

[31] *See Barbara Bramble, note 27.*

[32] *For an excellent summary of the state of public and private sector flows to developing countries see the following ODI Briefing papers:* Rethinking the Role of Multilateral Development Banks *(1996/4),* The UN's Role in Grant Financed Development *(1997/2), and* New Sources of Finance for Development *(1996/1). Available from ODI (London) or from their website: www.oneworld.org/odi (as at May 1997).*

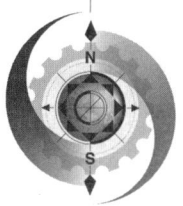

developing countries, mainly in Africa, or those lacking large markets, such as small developing country islands, access to these funds is difficult or impossible and dependence on bilateral and multilateral sources will continue to be essential.[33] Their dependence on ODA, and on the GEF for Convention activities, is likely to remain.

Given the current disparities, should the GEF attempt to skew the pattern of private sector investment to benefit countries not receiving private sector investment on the same scale as others? And if so, how? For example, CDM projects could be required to be undertaken equally in all UN regions. Or, a fixed number of CERs could be required to be generated in certain countries.[34] The original Brazilian proposal mandated a quota system of sorts, but one based on a formula favouring the biggest developing country emitters, such as India and China, in absolute terms. The proposal also stated that 90 per cent of Clean Development Fund resources should go toward mitigation projects. This may explain, in part, why the original Brazilian proposal stipulated that the other 10 per cent had to go to countries vulnerable to climate change: by and large these countries contributed little to global emissions and would not expect to benefit directly from CDF mitigation projects.

Economic efficiency certainly argues for this approach, or something similar, which will channel the biggest share of CDM resources to places where they are likely to achieve the biggest impact. But it is unlikely to pass muster with countries already disadvantaged in the world economy. These countries constitute

> The rationale of the CDM is to "green" private investment flows. But these flows remain concentrated in some 25-30 developing countries, of which just 12 have absorbed some 80 per cent of flows since 1990.

almost a majority of the 130 or so developing country Parties in the UNFCCC.[35] Equity-based reasoning argues that, while the UNFCCC and the Protocol cannot change the inequities of the global economy, they should not exacerbate existing disparities, and should certainly, if the Protocol is to be implemented swiftly, take into account the views and interests of all Parties.

Obviously, this would not set a precedent. Nationally, and internationally, "fairness" or equity considerations have led to regulatory intervention to promote opportunities for economically disadvantaged countries or regions, by constraining or channelling private sector flows in particular directions.[36] Many countries, for example, provide grants or other incentives for businesses to locate in less prosperous areas. The EU uses its structural funds to finance the development of disadvantaged regions. Moreover, under Part XI of the UN Convention on the Law of the Sea, developing and land-locked countries are given access to benefits generated by other countries and by commercial interests from their access and exploitation of the resources of the deep seabed.[37] A laissez-faire approach is unlikely to command widespread political support.

Adaptation and proceeds

Article 12.8 adds another purpose to the CDM: to generate a share of proceeds to cover administrative expenses as well as to help meet the costs of adaptation in developing countries that are particularly vulnerable to the adverse effects of climate change. This provision evolved from the original Brazilian idea that

---

[33] *This fact may explain, in part, why the original Brazilian proposal contained a set amount of funding for countries vulnerable to climate change, as by and large these are also the countries contributing little to global emissions and who would not expect to benefit directly from CDM mitigation projects.*

[34] *See for example the suggestion by Youba Sokona for region-based quotas in Chapter 9 of this publication.*

[35] *Counting the 35 AOSIS and about the same number of African Parties.*

[36] *See Principles of Burden-Sharing Relevant to the FCCC/KP, Thematic Report 1, FIELD, produced as part of the EU/UNFCCC Project (forthcoming).*

[37] *Ibid.*

the CDF would give 10 per cent of its funds to adaptation measures. As can be expected, many of the textual proposals relating to the adaptation element came from AOSIS.

Administrative expenses

AOSIS suggestions for administrative fees to be borne by the users of the CDM, with an additional surcharge levied to generate funds for adaptation, were initially resisted by some developed countries. A number of EU countries, in particular, were concerned that the concept of "user fees" and "surcharges" might set a precedent for international taxation, or be used as a model in other agreements. The compromise was that a "share of the proceeds from certified project activities" will cover administrative expenses and adaptation.

A number of issues need to be clarified. How are the "proceeds" to be determined? What transactions, what players and what rates apply? Who will administer these proceeds? Which institutions will receive the revenue raised by "proceeds"? What rules will govern how this revenue will be used? Who will exercise financial scrutiny (auditing) over the use of this revenue? And will mechanisms be required to enforce payment and penalise evasion?

Distribution of proceeds

The issue of adaptation raises many questions as well. Who can qualify for adaptation funds? The language of Article 12.8 does not limit itself to small island states. Indeed, at the most recent subsidiary body meeting, many larger developing country delegations, such as China and India, drew attention to their own vulnerabilities. Parties need to decide who is particularly vulnerable to the adverse effects of climate change. What are the "costs of adaptation" that can be funded by proceeds, when and on the basis of what information? How can the amount of adaptation funding be established? And what pre- and post-receipt of money reporting requirements and

evaluation process(es) would ensure that the proceeds are being spent in an appropriate manner?

Negotiators will also have to decide how adaptation funds raised by the CDM relate to Article 4.4 of the Convention, which requires Annex II Parties to assist developing country Parties that are particularly vulnerable to the adverse effects of climate change in meeting the costs of adaptation to those adverse effects. Likewise, any actions that may be taken by the COP/MOP to implement Articles 2.3 and 3.14 of the Protocol concerning how Annex I Parties minimise the adverse social, environmental and economic impacts on developing countries of their implementation of Article 2 (policies and measures) and Article 3 (targets) will have to be agreed.[38]

Most of these issues were not discussed in detail at Kyoto. This is unfortunate, because the CDM does mandate the creation of a *fund* to collect proceeds from certified project activities to finance the administrative costs and to assist particularly vulnerable Parties meet the costs of adaptation. Most developed country interventions were aimed at avoiding the establishment of a new fund to finance *mitigation projects* and did not express views about the structure and operation of the fund that would result from the collection of proceeds. Thus another of the key issues for future resolution is the institutional character and "home" of the CDM-generated administrative costs and adaptation fund(s). Options for handling this issue include the establishment of a new fund under the Protocol, or using existing institutions, such as the GEF, to manage funding of the adaptation activities.

Pre-commitment CER banking and supplementarity

Article 12.3(b) allows Annex I Parties to use CERs to meet "part of" their Article 3 QELRC commitments. The quantification of this "part" will be determined conclusively by the Conference of the Parties serving as the meeting of the Parties to the Protocol.[39]

---

[38] Articles 2.3 and 3.14 require the COP/MOP to consider what actions are necessary to minimize the adverse impacts of climate change and/or sponsor measures including looking at the establishment of funding, insurance and transfer of technology.

[39] Although like other matters relating to the CDM, the UNFCCC COP is not legally empowered to decide this matter. But politically, rather than legally, there is no reason to question the practical validity of a COP decision adopted by an overwhelming consensus between 170 Parties on this matter. There is a small risk that such a decision might be substantially modified by a smaller subset meeting such as the COP/MOP if there is a significant change of circumstances between the adoption of the Protocol and its entry into force.

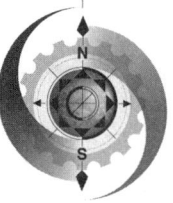

ISSUES&OPTIONS
The Clean
Development
Mechanism

Rationale

There are many reasons for including the "part of" provision in this Article. First, the term represents an attempt to limit the use of CDM-generated CERs to evade domestic action. This view was pressed strongly by the EU, which had successfully argued for a "supplementarity" provision in the other two flexibility mechanisms – trading and Joint Implementation.[40] One drawback of these supplementarity provisions is the lack of agreement about what they might mean in practice. The US and other non-EU developed countries resisted EU attempts to set a quantified limit on the use of Joint Implementation and trading. The adoption of a specific, quantifiable limit on the use of CERs from the CDM, made possible by the "part of" formulation, would represent a favourable contrast in terms of legal clarity.

A number of countries, particularly from the EU, wanted the Protocol to specify a fixed percentage in place of the "part of" provision. But the majority thought that quantification might lead to inconclusive discussions about the precise number, and hence, lead to the less specific "supplementarity" approach instead. They also favoured leaving the decision for COP/MOP, as its decisions can be reviewed and revised in the light of evolving experience, particularly as it becomes clear how much domestic effort is likely by each Party. The actual QELRCs adopted by Annex I Parties, let alone the domestic effort component, was not available to negotiators in Kyoto until all the provisions of the Protocol had been adopted.

It will be up to the COP/MOP to define "part of." What units should be used? Should it be one set figure or differentiated amounts for each Party? If so, on what basis? Should it be expressed in CO_2 equivalent tons or as a percentage of the assigned amount? And what considerations are relevant in setting the actual limit? This will depend on the amount of pre-2008 use of CERs allowed by Article 12.10, discussed below.

The pre-budget banking of CERs mentioned in Article 12.10 is an important element of the CDM. It is the only part of the Protocol that allows Parties to take credit for actions taken before the start of the first commitment period in 2008. This provision was designed to catalyse early mitigation actions that benefit all. Specifically, it was intended to help developing countries gain access to Annex I funds and technology that might otherwise flow to Annex I countries with low abatement costs (such as Economies in Transition). And finally, some delegations may have thought this provision would aid ratification, particularly by the US, by demonstrating the concurrent participation of developing countries in Article 3 mitigation commitments.

Risks

These potential benefits need to be carefully weighed against the obvious risk of "blowing the Annex I cap." In the most extreme situation, pre-commitment CER banking could thwart action in Annex I Parties because of a plentiful supply of cheap CERs available from 2000. The total availability of CERs in the 2000-2008 period is thus critically linked to the issue of domestic action. A concrete number for "part of" will depend on the availability of CERs post 2000 and Annex I Parties' preference for domestic versus offshore action.

Whether the "part of" will be determined purely by political bargaining between Parties or whether their decision could usefully be guided by some "objective information" needs to be considered carefully. An objective assessment seems to be the intent in the Protocol (see its Article 12.10, and paragraph 5(e) of Decision 1/CP.3 which adopted the Protocol). It foresees that Subsidiary Bodies supported by the Secretariat, would analyse the potential CERs that Annex 1 Parties might try to generate through the CDM. Comparing this with what they could achieve domestically or collectively with other Parties, they could make more rational decisions.

Finally, the COP/MOP must decide when to take the decision on "part of." A decision is not required during the first COP/MOP session. If

---

[40] *Article 6 requires the acquisition of ERUs to be "supplemental to domestic actions for the purposes of meeting commitments under Article 3". Article 17 states that "trading shall be supplemental to domestic actions for the purposes of meeting" Article 3 commitments.*

the Protocol enters into force by 2002, as is currently expected by the Secretariat, experience of actual projects will still be in the early stages. However, there may be pressure from Annex I Parties to fix a percentage in advance of their ratification and before the Protocol has entered into force. Parties will have to balance the interests of greater certainty for Annex I Parties against the risk that this information may reduce their domestic efforts.

Linkages with emissions trading and Joint Implementation

Property rights

The concept of CERs is central to the working of the CDM. But their legal nature is still undecided: What kind of property rights (if any) do they represent, and for how long? How can they be transferred, apportioned or appropriated? This lack of specificity is common to the other flexibility mechanisms: trading and Joint Implementation. However, these legal questions must be addressed before new "commodities" are generated and exchanged/ sold to ensure legal certainty for Parties involved in these transactions.[41]

Two questions are key. First, are CERs fully fungible? In other words, can CERs be traded by entities that had nothing to do with their initial generation? Second, can they be owned or held by non-State actors, such as the private sector or Egos? A third set of issues concerns who issues them, on what basis and at what cost.

The CDM, Joint Implementation, and emissions trading are intellectually and operationally linked.[42] Unlike emissions trading, the CDM and Joint Implementation are project-based mechanisms. All three face issues of project eligibility, monitoring, verification and certification as well as baseline issues, which are generally less problematic for Article 6 Joint Implementation.

Stepping stone for trading

The relationship between the CDM and emissions trading is more complex. The CDM can be seen as a stand-alone mechanism, or it can be seen as laying the groundwork for global emissions trading. One important issue is whether the CDM can, and should, accommodate developing countries' participation in emissions trading. In this context, Parties need to decide whether CERs generated through the CDM should be fully tradable (between third parties) or whether there should be restrictions on their fungibility. The text of Article 17 of the Protocol on trading, and the provisions on transference and acquisition in Article 3, are inconclusive. Yet Parties *must* agree on the issue of the relationship between the CDM and trading. If CERs prove plentiful and cheap, the CDM may "kill emissions trading" by robbing it of its economic rationale.[43] The same is true of Joint Implementation under Article 6. By selling CERs more cheaply than emission reduction units generated by Annex I Parties under Article 6 or "parts of assigned amounts" under emissions trading, developing countries could throttle the development of Joint Implementation and emissions trading among Annex I Parties. They have timing advantages, as CERs can come on stream from 2000 and be counted towards Article 3 compliance.

A portfolio-based approach to the CDM might promote developing country participation in emissions trading more than a bilateral approach. Except in the forest sector, individual projects tend to generate small quantities of CERs that may not "register" as significant amounts in a trading system. If countries could bundle projects together, they could garner greater interest – and more bargaining power – in the global trading system. Because developing countries are not bound by any legally binding quantitative restrictions for emitting greenhouse gases, their entry into the trading market through the indirect route of the CDM would have to be particularly carefully considered to

---

[41] *Article 6 creates the concept of "emission reduction units" while Article 3.11 speaks of trading in "parts of an assigned amount".*

[42] *These are discussed in detail in FCCC/SB/1998/2.*

[43] *This point was made by Jean Charles Hourcade in his presentation to a European Commission DGXII, sponsored workshop considering equity, efficiency and effectiveness issues relating to the Protocol, Brussels, 18-19 May, 1998.*

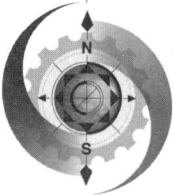

ISSUES&OPTIONS
The Clean
Development
Mechanism

ensure that the environmental objectives of the Protocol and the emission reductions it mandates are not undermined.[44]

At Kyoto, developing countries were united behind the CDM proposals that forced Annex I Parties to accept the CDM. Developing countries that were more interested in the voluntary commitments option, that would have clearly allowed them to participate in emissions trading, were either unsure about the benefits of trading or else inarticulate in pressing their case.[45] An issue for future COPs is whether this situation will continue to prevail.

PART III: GOVERNANCE AND INSTITUTIONAL ISSUES

Article 12 defines potentially sweeping actions that could impact billions of dollars of foreign aid or investment flows. Yet it provides very little detail about the institutional structures to oversee and implement this broad array of functions. The specified actors in the CDM include the COP/MOP, an Executive Board, "operational entities," and private and/or public entities. Significantly, the Article makes no mention of the Convention's financial mechanism or of its current operating entity, the GEF, or of the COP that will undertake interim work to establish the CDM.

The nascent literature on the CDM implicitly or explicitly acknowledges that the institutional design of the CDM will largely determine its success or failure. The most salient issue is whether the CDM should operate as a fund to finance projects, or as a clearinghouse mechanism to facilitate projects. Parties' views on the CDM's institutional character must begin to converge before the respective roles of the various institutions can be determined.

Needed definitions for establishing the CDM

Following is a brief listing of the key institutional issues which need definition and decision for the establishment of the CDM:

Role of its plenary body (COP/MOP). What will be the extent of its plenary versus executive role (vis-à-vis the Executive Board)? What impact will its composition, powers (functions) and voting procedures have on the CDM's operation? What is the relationship between the COP and the COP/MOP?

Nature and role of the Executive Board. What is its composition and powers? Particularly, what is the extent of its supervisory/executive function, as well as its advisory and/or administrative roles? Should it be a subsidiary body of the COP/MOP or its principal organ? Finally, what is the nature and impact of the Executive Board's voting procedures on the CDM?

Nature and role of administrative support needed for Executive Board and COP/MOP. Administrative tasks can often be decentralised. Article 12 does not specifically assign any administrative functions to the secretariat established by the Convention, which is to serve as the Secretariat to the Protocol (Article 14). Should all, some or any of the CDM's administrative tasks should be undertaken by the Secretariat? Or should they be undertaken by non-Convention/Protocol bodies, and if so, which ones? These tasks range from developing and identifying suitable CDM projects for Executive Board or COP/MOP approval, to running a website "bazaar" where Annex I Party investors are put in touch with those offering CDM projects (a sort of marketing service), and preparing policy-relevant documents on the operation of the CDM.

The nature and role of the "operational entities" that must undertake certification. What criteria should the COP/MOP use to select operational entities? What standards

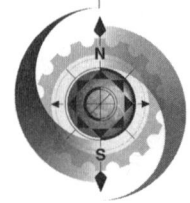
---

[44] *For example, one could envisage a restriction on participation in global trading for those developing countries that had provided information on national baselines.*

[45] *Likewise, Annex I Parties who continued to draft and redraft their proposals for Article 10 until a late stage, thus hampering wider agreement.*

should be used to guide their conduct and periodically evaluate their performance?

Financing of administrative expenses, and adaptation costs in particularly vulnerable countries. The main matters that need to be considered are (a) the budget process; (b) the exercise of internal and external control over the use of funds provided in the budget; (c) how funds are raised; and (d) in the case of operational expenditures, policies for determining eligibility. Participation in CDM activities is stated to be "voluntary," and private sector entities are not directly bound by the Protocol. Therefore, the source of the obligation to pay, in particular, needs to be considered. Under what circumstances can Parties and other participating entities withhold funds due to the CDM?

The basis for public and/or private participation in CDM activities. Parties' views on these issues will differ depending on their approach to the following: First, what is the appropriate level of regulatory action for the different functions outlined above (project, national, regional or international)? Second, should existing institutions and processes, within and outside the United Nations family, including private entities, perform some of these functions? Third, how much control should donors exercise, and how much of the CDM should be centred around private sector expectations and interests? Fourth, how much coordination should there be among existing or new sources of development finance (public and private). Fifth, what level of risk or certainty will ensure that the Protocol's overall objective and specific commitments are achieved?

Institutional functions and relationships for an effective CDM

The section below sets out the issues and options relating to the involvement of the institutional entities that will need to work together to make the CDM effective.

The role of the COP and the COP/MOP

Two issues are relevant here. First, in the short-term what decisions can the COP make to establish the CDM before the COP/MOP meets? Second, what is the longer-term role for the COP once the COP/MOP is up and running?

The COP's interim role

The CDM is "subject to the authority and guidance of the COP/MOP." The first meeting of the COP/MOP cannot take place until the Protocol has entered into force.[46] By the most optimistic estimates, it might convene in 2001 or 2002. But investors and hosts will want to see the CDM operational before 2000, particularly if they want to make use of the provisions for pre-commitment period banking from 2000 (Article 12.10).

The COP's legal mandate to make decisions about the CDM is circumscribed. The COP cannot legally make COP/MOP decisions. Furthermore, its interim work relating to the Protocol, contained in the "prompt start" Decision 1/CP.1, only gives the UNFCCC's Subsidiary Bodies a mandate to examine the implications of Article 12.10, rather than all of the questions raised in establishing the CDM.

Before the first meeting of the COP/MOP, there is nothing to stop the COP (and its Subsidiary Bodies) from assuming a larger mandate than the one contained in Decision 1/CP.1, if Parties so wish. Indeed, the first document prepared by the Secretariat on the flexibility mechanisms suggested that Parties look at all the issues raised by Article 12.[47] At the June meeting in Bonn, it became clear that while Parties respect private sector interests and their need for early decisions to influence investment decisions, CDM issues are complex and linked to other Convention and Protocol issues.[48]

If the political will exists, UNFCCC Parties could agree to establish the CDM, on an interim

---

[46] The double-trigger contained in Article 25 means that practically and politically all of the major Annex I GHG emitters, including the US and Russia, must have ratified the Protocol.

[47] FCCC/SB/1998/2.

[48] Many developing country Parties, for example, expressed disquiet at the amount of pressure from non-Parties and "outside" interests to force early agreement on the CDM. They are not keen for developments such as the World Bank Carbon Initiative to influence Convention developments.

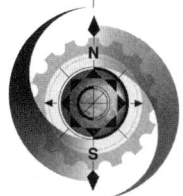

ISSUES&OPTIONS
The Clean Development Mechanism

basis, leaving the COP/MOP to confirm these arrangements as permanent. There is little reason to think that a subset of UNFCCC Parties meeting as the COP/MOP would "overturn" a consensus-based decision adopted by the COP. The private sector can cope with the legal uncertainty caused by the fact that each COP can make decisions that revise or alter earlier ones. The fact that a COP decision may be altered by the COP/MOP does not generate a higher level of legal uncertainty than the normal course of events.

What is more important to businesses is the timing. Business is keen to know when rules for the CDM will be agreed, not which body will agree on them. Work in the period before entry into force of the Protocol should aim at paving the way for the COP/MOP to confirm decisions on the CDM. Political effort should be spent on forging consensus to make that possible.

COP's longer term involvement

The COP/MOP is functionally autonomous from the COP. It is the plenary body of the CDM where all Parties to the protocol can expect to be kept informed of developments relating to the CDM. The COP/MOP will make decisions about the CDM once it begins to meet. But the COP is mandated to "keep under regular review the implementation of the Convention and any related legal instrument adopted by the COP" (emphasis added).[49] It could therefore continue to look at issues arising from the operation of the CDM, for example, on the sensitive issue of developing country commitments. The proper demarcation of the COP's review mandate, and the appropriate level of oversight it exercises over the Protocol, remain to be set.

One potential future institutional conflict between the COP and the COP/MOP stems from the mandate given to the COP by Article 17 of the Protocol on emissions trading. This provision is a rare case in which the Protocol gives the institutional authority to determine the rules and modalities of emissions trading to the COP, and not to the COP/MOP. The elaboration of these rules, and any continuing

oversight the COP retains over the implementation and further development, could have a significant impact on the market for CERs generated by the CDM. The reverse is also true. Unless the COP and the COP/MOP make concerted efforts to avoid conflicts, it will be difficult to discuss the linkages and impacts of the CDM and emissions trading holistically.

The Executive Board

Notwithstanding their desire to not create new institutions, Annex I Parties had to agree to the establishment of one new institution: the Executive Board of the CDM, an idea put forward by developing countries at Kyoto. Article 12.3 states the CDM is to be subject to the authority of the COP/MOP and "be supervised by an Executive Board."

Functions

The Executive Board's functions hinge on whether the CDM is a fund or a clearinghouse mechanism. The character, role, and powers of an executive board of a financial institution can be expected to be very different from that of a clearinghouse.

An executive board supervising a financial institution has a fiduciary duty to its shareholders to make the most of its assets. This involves safeguarding assets, obtaining the best prices and conditions for investments, minimising risks through portfolio management and diversification, being a market player, generating demand for goods or services. If the Executive Board of the CDM were to be supplier of CERs, it would need to engage in marketing, make contracts with buyers, collect monies and distribute them to suppliers. All these are executive, rather than administrative functions, and ones that existing UNFCCC institutions, like its subsidiary bodies or the Secretariat are ill suited for.

An Executive Board supervising a clearinghouse mechanism, on the other hand, would need to anticipate the needs of buyers and sellers and provide services to facilitate trade between them. It could do this by organising a "bazaar"

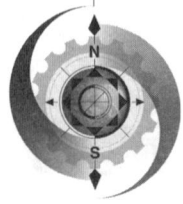

---

[49] *Article 7, UNFCCC.*

site on the World Wide Web, maintaining a CDM opportunities bulletin board, publishing details of projects for dissemination, and/or trying to match donors with suitable projects or visa versa. These activities would fulfil the provisions of Article 12.6, which specify that the CDM "shall assist in arranging funding of certified project activities as necessary." These are essentially administrative tasks that could be undertaken by a competent administrative body, such as the Secretariat.[50]

Subsidiary or principal organ?

The institutional design of the CDM will have to clarify the extent of authority the Executive Board is given, the amount of freedom it has to undertake the functions clearly assigned to it under the Protocol, and the level of scrutiny the COP/MOP exercises over its day-to-day supervision of the CDM. Does the Executive Board "sign off" on a range of issues which have been defined as being within its functions? Or does it provide advice to the COP/MOP to take these decisions? In legal terms, the distinction involves determining whether the Executive Board is a subsidiary body or a principal organ to order to assess what degree of control can be exercised over it by the plenary organ, the COP/MOP. The hierarchical or parallel relationship between the COP/MOP and the Executive Board is not an arcane legal matter. It goes to the practical heart of how the Executive Board might work.

In international law, a subsidiary body is subordinate to its plenary organ. There is a clear hierarchy between the subsidiary body and the plenary organ, in which the latter delegates some of its authority to the former.[51] A *principal body*, by contrast, may have a relationship which is hierarchical, parallel or a mixture of both. A principal body may, for example, have some functions it is mandated to fulfil which the plenary organ is not entitled to take away or whose exercise it cannot control.

The plenary body may have some functions that cannot be delegated.

This non-hierarchical relationship between the plenary organ and the principal body is, in fact, typical of international financial institutions.[52] Their executive boards (or the equivalent) are not just subsidiary bodies, but more substantive institutions with specific mandates the plenary body cannot take over. This fact underpins their day-to-day work by allowing the smaller, limited membership body to work in an efficient manner.

Article 12 is not clear about the relationship between the COP/MOP and the Executive Board.[53] It gives the COP/MOP the following functions:

◆ to determine how much the CDM can contribute to Article 3 commitments

◆ to designate "operational entities" to certify emission reductions

◆ to elaborate modalities and procedures for, inter alia, independent auditing and verification

◆ to ensure a share of the proceeds from projects covers adaptation and administrative expenses.

Apart from its supervisory role, the Executive Board is given one specific, but highly critical, function: to determine participation in the CDM. The term "participation" could be read to cover both the participation of non-Annex I Parties in project activities (Article 12.3 (a)) as well as guidance for the participation of public and/or private entities in CDM projects and the acquisition of CERs (Article 12.9). No specific body is charged with assisting in arranging funding of certified project activities referred to in Article 12.6.

[50] *The Secretariat is already engaged in some of these activities to support the AIJ pilot phase.*

[51] *C. F. Amersinghe,* Principles of the Institutional Law of International Organizations, *Cambridge University Press, 1996.*

[52] *Ibid. The World Bank, for example, has a plenary body composed of the Board of Governors (one per member). The Executive Directors of the Bank, limited to 12 in number, "exercise all the powers delegated to them by the Board". The Directors have some powers, the Governors cannot take away, such as the power to elect a President.*

[53] *Article 12.4 provides that the CDM "shall be subject to the authority and guidance of the COP/MOP and be supervised by an executive board of the clean development mechanism." It may be tempting to read in "overall authority and guidance" but this is not what the text says.*

Composition

The composition of a body refers to its size and the capacity in which its members should serve. The Executive Board could be of limited or open-ended membership. It could be a board "of Parties" comprising all or a mixture of government representatives, or made up of independent experts, or by representatives of existing institutions such as the GEF, or a mixture of these.[54] A limited membership body would allow for efficient functioning of the CDM by saving valuable COP/MOP time. Intersessional meetings of the Executive Board would also allow the activities of the CDM to be supervised at all times. An open-ended Executive Board could not supervise the CDM efficiently on a day-to-day basis. This is true whether the CDM emerges as a clearinghouse mechanism or something akin to a portfolio manager and CER supplier.

But the UNFCCC has not successfully established any bodies of limited membership on either a temporary or permanent basis. Parties have resisted efforts to establish Technical Advisory Panels or an Implementation Committee to deal with non-compliance along the lines of those established under the Montreal Protocol.[55] The most recent example of Parties' reluctance to delegate authority to smaller bodies took place during the June meeting of the Ad Hoc Group on Article 13. The US insisted that the Committee comprise government delegates drawn equally from Annex I and non-Annex I Parties. The Group of 77 insisted it reflect the traditional UN geographical representation, which gives developing countries four out of five regions.

Negotiations to define the composition of the CDM are likely to be problematic. Parties may look to the executive boards of financial institutions, funds administered by various UN bodies or those operating pursuant to a convention for guidance. The Montreal Protocol and the governance structure of the GEF are well known to many negotiators. But there are many other choices that illustrate the diversity of options. Table 2 summarises the salient institutional features of a number of such boards, including their voting procedures and administrative support. Parties may wish to study these institutions, and perhaps even invite some of them to share their experiences, before deciding the institutional framework of the Executive Board. In addition, or alternatively, Parties may find it helpful to request the Secretariat to prepare a paper outlining the way in which the executive boards of other financial institutions operate.

Voting

All the executive boards listed in Table 2 aim for consensus decisions. But where this is not possible, decisions may be taken by majority vote. What counts as a "majority" differs. In some case, this is a simple majority. But in many others, including the Montreal Protocol, GEF, and World Bank, voting is weighted to reflect the balance between donors and recipients. In institutions such as the International Tropical Timber Council, voting is also weighted to balance geographical representation with the need to ensure the voice of countries that are particularly important, either as consumers or producers, is reflected.[56]

UNFCCC Parties have failed to agree on majority voting procedures for the plenary body, the COP/MOP.[57] This factor will hinder the consideration of voting procedures for a limited membership body like the Executive Board. The Executive Board's day-to-day functioning would be considerably hampered without voting rules underpinning its work. Executive Board members could block decisions at the board level knowing these would then have to be dealt with in the

---

[54] *During Kyoto, the text on the CDM had at one stage specified that the EB be "an executive board of Parties." As this would have excluded GEF representative from being a full member of the EB, a number of developed country delegations requested deletion of the phase "of Parties" to allow for such a possibility.*

[55] *The June meetings of the Ad Hoc Group on Article 13 floundered precisely on the question of composition of the committee that would look at questions of implementation.*

[56] *Similar considerations apply to the International Civil Aviation Authority.*

[57] *Rule 42 dealing with voting majorities remains bracketed. Article 12.5 of the Protocol applies the COP's rules of procedure to the COP/MOP mutatis mutandis unless agreed otherwise by the COP/MOP by consensus.*

FUND	REVENUE SOURCE	SUPREME BODY	EXECUTIVE BODY AND FUNCTIONS	BODY REPRESENTATION	VOTING	SUPPORT
Global Environment Facility (GEF)	Public – new, additional & adequate	Assembly (3 years)	Council – developing, adopting, evaluating operational policies and programmes for GEF-financed activities	32 members (16 DCs: 6 Africa & Asia, 4 Latin America, 14 ICs, 2 EITs) – meets twice per year or as necessary	Consensus or double – majority of participatory countries and 60% donor support	Secretariat (World Bank) & STAP (UNEP)
Montreal Protocol	Public – new, additional & adequate	MOP	Executive Committee of the Multi-lateral Fund – developing, adopting implementation of operational policies, guidelines, including disbursement of funds	14 members (7 DC, 7 ICs)	Consensus whenever possible. If no agreement, 2/3 majority of the Parties present and voting, representing a majority of Parties operating under Art. 5.1 and a majority of Parties not so operating present and voting.	Independent Secretariat (Montreal)
UN Population Fund (UNFPA)	Public	Policy supervision by ECOSOC	Executive Board	36 members, equitable geographical representation (8 Africa, 7 Asia & Pacific, 5 LAC, 4 EITs, 12 WEOG)	ECOSOC rules on voting apply	UNDP
Int'l Tropical Timber Council (ITTC)	Public	Council (annual)	No Executive Body. Council exercises all powers & functions to carry out provision of ITTA (includes funding for projects)	One representative per member	Council votes 2000:1000 producers & 1000 consumers. Within these two categories votes distributed to reflect geographical representation, importance of country as exporter & size of forests (for producers). For consumers, each country has 10 initial votes with rest weighted to reflect net imports of tropical timber	Independent Secretariat (Japan)
Int'l Civil Aviation Organisation (ICAO)	Public	Assembly (3 years)	Council – continuous direction of ICAO's work including negotiation & adoption of new standards & practices	33 members – selected under 3 headings: states of chief importance in air transport, those making largest contribution to provision of air navigation facilities & those designated to ensure all areas are represented	Consensus otherwise simple majority vote of the members of the Council.	Independent Secretariat & permanent specialist committees
Int'l Sea-Bed Authority (UNCLOS & 1994 Agreement)	Public, but is intended to access private sector	Assembly	Council – administration of activities in sea-bed area & exploitation of natural resources	36 members: 4 largest consumers or importers of minerals, 4 largest investors, 4 major exporters, 6 DCs with special interests, 18 geographic representation	Consensus, or failing that voting with a majority within each of 4 chambers of countries in Council.	Secretariat (Jamaica), Legal Technical Commission, Finance Committee
CITES	Contributions of Parties to a Trust Fund est. by UNEP – in accordance with the UN scale of contr.	COP	Standing Committee – management, oversees action taken by the Parties, decides on issues re restriction on Parties	Representatives or Alternate Representatives of 7 regional members from at least 4 regions (15 to 30 Members from Africa, Asia, CSC, EU, NA, Oceania and Others.	Consensus unless a vote is requested by the Chair or Representatives or Alternates of seven regional members or alternate regional members from two regions – simple majority of the regional members or alternate regional members voting.	Secretariat
World Bank	Financial markets (bond selling) and shareholders capital retained earnings. IDA depends on contr. of the wealthier governments.	Board of Governors consisting of a Governor appointed by each Member State	Executive Directors – matters of policy and approval of all the loans made by the Bank.	12 Executive Directors (they do not need to be Governors), 5 appointed by each of the 5 Members having the largest n. of shares and 7 appointed by all Governors rather than the 5 above. They are appointed or elected every 2 years.	Consensus or quorum shall be a majority of the Directors exercising not less than one half of the total voting power. Developing countries have half of the votes.	Officers and Staff
'Int'l Fund Convention' for Compensation for Oil Pollution Damage	Private sector – contributions from crude & fuel oil cargo receivers based on tonnage received	Assembly (annual)	Executive Committee – approves settlement of claims against Fund, advises Director on Fund administration, and prepares annual report on Fund activities. Meets several times a year	One third of seven Assembly members but not < 7 or > 15. Equitable geographic representation but including States exposed to risk of oil pollution & Parties with larger oil tanker fleets	Each member has one vote. Decision by 2/3 or 3/4 majority depending on type of decision	Independent Secretariat headed by Director

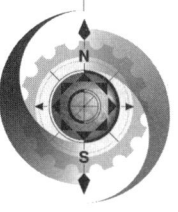

ISSUES & OPTIONS

The Clean Development Mechanism

[58] *The author would like to thank Tania Wasserstein for her research assistance in preparing this table.*

plenary body, the COP/MOP, where decisions are also made by consensus. This would render any delegation of authority by the COP/MOP to the Executive Board unworkable.

The wider of issue of voting procedures for the COP and the COP/MOP should be resolved, at least in relation to the operation of the CDM.

Operational entitites, auditing and verification bodies

Certification of emission reductions must be undertaken by "operational entities" designated by the COP/MOP. Before looking at bodies suitable for designation, it is important to consider who will undertake the auditing and verification functions.

Article 12.7 specifies that auditing and verification must be "independent," i.e. cannot be undertaken by those directly involved in development, finance or implementation of the project. The key question is who will undertake the auditing and verification functions most effectively and efficiently. Each of these tasks could be undertaken by the private sector, or by national or international bodies.

Auditing bodies

Auditing could be undertaken by the private sector through firms offering consultancy services in this area.[59] It could also include accounting firms or similar organisations. Non-profit organisations with relevant expertise are another possibility. Examples of *national institutions* include public auditing offices. The various standardisation organisations accredited by the International Standards Organisation (ISO) represent a hybrid example of private/public national bodies.

At the *international level*, the Climate Change Secretariat is the most obvious candidate. It is independent, has expert knowledge of national circumstances and inventories, could apply standards consistently and may be able to extend its capacity to cover these new functions

at modest cost. It could apply a standard fee for each project. Keeping the CDM's transaction costs as low as possible is important.

A possible first step in this process is for UNFCCC Parties to gather more information about costs and benefits by organising a "beauty parade" of interested organisations. Such a step could help the COP to better understand the advantages, disadvantages and costs of different options before elaborating modalities and procedures referred to in Article 12.7.

Verification bodies

Verification involves assessing whether the emissions reductions claimed in project documentation have, in fact, occurred. It involves on-site inspection and/or other tools for "reality" checking. Verification of all CDM projects would be prohibitively expensive and time-consuming. Random checks of a certain fraction of projects may prove a cost-effective alternative.

Verification and auditing involve different types of expertise. Verification can only be done effectively by experts with technical knowledge of the CDM projects. A CDM energy sector project may require someone with an appropriate engineering background, while a sinks project would require someone with a sound scientific understanding of carbon sequestration.

To generate confidence, verification must be undertaken by a respected and trusted institution whose impartiality is beyond question, one that can report easily to the COP/MOP and the Executive Board. The Climate Change Secretariat is held in high esteem by Parties, has expertise in relevant areas and could undertake verification of CDM projects. It could enhance its verification capacity by establishing teams of experts to undertake random verification of projects, akin to the In-Depth Review Teams coordinated by the Secretariat to examine Annex I Parties' national commitments.[60]

Some Parties may resist the international scrutiny inherent in an independent verification process. They may seek to limit or weaken

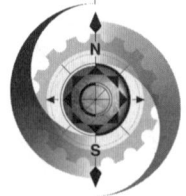

---

[59] *One prominent example is Société Générale de Surveillance (SGS).*

[60] *See H. Ott, Operationalizing Joint Implementation.*

verification procedures. Alternatively, they may promote a more decentralised verification process that stresses the role of national institutions. It is difficult to see how the impartiality and integrity underpinning verification could be maintained if it were carried out by a network of national institutions. Parties participating in the CDM may have to accept international scrutiny as the price worth paying for the financial and technological resources flows generated by CDM projects. Poor verification may destroy the value of CERs, as markets will lose confidence and ultimately weaken the CDM.

Certification bodies

Certification of emission reductions produced by projects must be undertaken by "operational entities" designated by the COP/MOP. These could also be national or international bodies or the private sector (or a mixture of these). It is important to recognise that the Kyoto Protocol does not require "operational entities" to be "independent," but that the certification is not done by the COP/MOP or the Executive Board.

Operational entities could be organisations involved in the development, financing and implementation of CDM projects. The current implementing agencies of the GEF, (UNEP, UNDP and the World Bank) could, for example, be certifiers of emission reductions, as could international financial institutions or private investment funds or national bodies that had been designated by the COP/MOP.

Certification bodies would be involved in an essentially managerial task that involves verifying that project activities conform with all the standards[61] and processes[62] specified by the COP/MOP. If they do, CERs can be issued for Annex I Parties to use in achieving compliance with their Article 3 commitments.

Prior independent auditing and verification procedure would ensure operational entities could only issue CERs for projects that had satisfied the independent auditors and met

verification standards. This would provide a powerful check on "operational entities" to minimise bureaucracy, incompetence and inflated claims for CERs. If an operational entity continually failed to satisfy the auditors and/or if verification revealed gaps between project documentation and reality, the COP/MOP could suspend the right of that entity to certify projects. And if problems persist, the COP/MOP could ultimately reconsider its designated status.

Article 12 does not provide any guidance for how operational entities should be selected for designation. In the initial phase, the COP/MOP should be encouraged to designate more than one "operational entity" to encourage competition between entities, reducing costs and improving efficiencies.

The COP/MOP may want to ensure, for example, that Parties have a choice of operational entities at the national, regional, and international level for their certification needs. International organisations may have to prove they have a certain level of national or regional presence and the human and technical resources to cope with the certification process. Organisations such as UNDP, with country offices, and a strong mandate in capacity building, technical assistance, and sustainable development, could be at an advantage, as could organisations like the International Energy Agency.

National institutions could be also be designated as operational entities provided these could demonstrate relevant expertise and resources. Numerous treaties dealing with trade in waste, chemicals, and pharmaceuticals rely on national institutions to undertake permitting or certification. The 1973 Convention on International Trade in Endangered Species of Wild Fauna and Flora (CITES), is a good example. CITES establishes a global system of trade controls based on permits and certificates covering the export, import, and re-export of flora and fauna listed in CITES appendices. Permits and certificates are issued by national institutions, minimising supra-national regulation, which

---

[61] *i.e., the tests for deciding environemtantl benefits and additionality, etc.*

[62] *i.e., the independent auditing and verification procedures.*

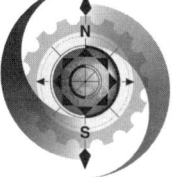

may influence Parties traditionally sceptical of international bodies.

CITES, and the other treaties, are an example of a "mutual recognition" model.[63] These rely essentially on a workable measure of compatibility between national systems, and mutual respect for national authorities. In the CDM context, this compatibility would have to be based on international regulation by the COP/MOP in order to standardise CERs and to prevent Parties from generating endless amounts of CERs based on subjective baselines and additionality assumptions.[64] The mutual recognition model also requires the support of "epistemic" co-operation between specialists across national boundaries.

National certification processes have other advantages over international operational entities. They are more likely to enhance human development and capacity building efforts in developing countries than international agencies. They might also generate greater public awareness and private sector involvement in developing countries than a more remote, international agency could. Finally, the global market for CERs will spawn a new service industry. To maximise economic gains from the CDM, developing countries need to develop expertise in these new areas of economic activities. Otherwise, they risk becoming dependent on foreign consultants and agencies.

Participation of public and/or private bodies

Article 12 sanctions participation in the CDM by public and private entities subject to the "whatever guidance" is provided by the Executive Board. The Executive Board has to deal with the following issues:

- whether to allow public institutions funded by ODA from Annex I Parties to participate in the CDM

- how to exercise its institutional authority over public and private institutions that are outside the Convention/Protocol

- how to resolve disputes arising between the COP/MOP, itself and public and private institutions.

Publicly funded bodies

The direct participation of public bodies funded by ODA contributions from Annex I Parties in CDM projects raises the controversial issue of financial additionality discussed above. To avoid the CDM getting "bogged down" in highly political but practically irresolvable debates surrounding additionality, it is suggested Parties agree that public funds from Annex I Parties will not be used to generate CERs. Public entities could participate in the CDM but should not use the ODA funded elements of their operational budgets for claiming CERs for donor countries. If the GEF began to leverage private funds for CDM projects, it could become involved in the generation of CERs, but this involves competing with the World Bank initiative for the Prototype Carbon Investment Fund.

The participation of public entities in the CDM should focus on supporting activities linked to the development and certification of CDM projects. Capacity building and training projects are an obvious example. GEF public funds could, for example, support capacity building efforts, particularly of the work of its implementing agencies like UNDP, to help develop endogenous capacity relevant to the CDM.[65] This could include setting up national certification institutions or CDM focal points.

ISSUES&OPTIONS
The Clean
Development
Mechanism

[63] The "mutual recognition" typologies are drawn from P. Sands, Lessons learned in global environmental governance. WRI, 1990. Sands poses this as a contructive alternative to supranational regulation. p.22.

[64] In CITES, a permit has no value unless it corresponds to a physical specimen.

[65] By COP-3, only three developing countries had AIJ projects. Although many more have designated focal points and are developing AIJ projects, the majority have no direct experience of setting up and reporting on an AIJ projects and are not practically familiar with the complex methodological and technical issues relating to the calculation of environmental benefits or baselines.

Exercising institutional authority over entities

The CDM will involve a partnership of actors of diverse legal character: national and international and public and private, not-for-profits and otherwise. The guidance issued by the Executive Board will have to generate legal and regulatory certainty among these entities as to their roles and ensure its guidance is being respected and is otherwise effective.

Parties have a fair amount of experience of "contracting out" certain tasks to other international bodies. The GEF's operation of the Convention's financial mechanism is the best example. The relationship with the Intergovernmental Panel on Climate Change (IPCC) is another. By contrast, the COP has not had any formal relationship with private entities and those that have participated in the Convention process have done so as non-governmental organisations.[66]

The COP/MOP will have to decide who will enter into any contracts or memorandum of understanding with such entities[67] as well as specifying the following issues:

◆ tasks each entity must undertake and the time-frame

◆ frequency of guidance

◆ reporting requirements, e.g. annual/quarterly reports, oral presentations at COP/ MOP, subsidiary body or Executive Board sessions

◆ institutional arrangements, e.g. a joint working group of officers, "observer" status for officers of the entity at the Executive Board level, an inter-entity coordination committee etc.

◆ frequency and basis of performance reviews of each entity

◆ incentive/sanction structure suitable for each entity type· to ensure adherence to guidelines.

Dispute resolution

The COP/MOP may have to establish mechanisms for dispute settlement between the COP/MOP (and Executive Board) and public and private institutions participating in the CDM. The legal framework for dispute settlement created by Article 14 of the UNFCCC is not well suited to creating legal certainty, even for Parties.[68] It is not applicable to entities that may be contracted or designated by the COP/MOP.

One approach might be to allow non-Parties access to trigger the non-compliance procedure to be established pursuant to the provisions of Article 18 of the Protocol. Another would be to specify that all entities engaged have to accept to be bound by a common arbitration procedure at an appropriate body.

CONCLUSIONS

Annex I Parties face ratification challenges and many are keen to mobilise the Kyoto momentum to secure early operation of the CDM. Other countries are more cautious and want time to reflect on the implications of what was agreed before launching a major new economic instrument such as the CDM. The main purpose of this article was to analyse in more detail the analytic work needed to implement the provisions of Article 12 of the Protocol. The pace at which it is done will depend on Parties. ■

---

[66] *The role of the business community and other NGOs has been on the Subsidiary Body's agenda since 1995 when COP-1 requested examination of the possibilities in response of a New Zealand proposal to establish a business consultative mechanism. Parties have failed to adopt any far-reaching conclusions.*

[67] *It could be the COP/MOP or, through delegation, the Executive Board.*

[68] *Article 19 applies this,* mutatis mutandis, *to the Protocol.*

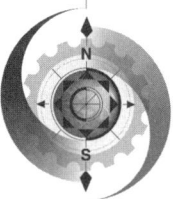

Next Steps

Chapter 6

EQUITY, SUSTAINABILITY AND SOLIDARITY CONCERNS

Benjamin Dessus
Programme Ecodev, Centre National
    de la Recherche Scientifique (CNRS)
Meudon, France

Summary: As the Clean Development Mechanism (CDM) moves from an idea to reality, it is important that it not exacerbate current inequities between industrialised and developing countries, and among developing countries themselves. Given the different priorities and concerns of the Annex I and non-Annex I countries, ecological criteria alone are not sufficient to qualify projects as pertinent for the mechanism. Indeed, in order to honour the spirit of the Rio Conference, the principles of equity, sustainability, and solidarity must be incorporated into the way the CDM operates.

Article 12 of the Kyoto Protocol defines a Clean Development Mechanism (CDM), the purpose of which shall be "to assist Parties not included in Annex I in achieving sustainable development and in contributing to the ultimate objective of the Convention, and to assist Parties included in Annex I in achieving compliance with their quantified emission limitation and reduction commitments (QERLCs) under Article 3."

The wording of this article is the outcome of a debate which took place in Kyoto around several contrasting and/or complementary ideas:

◆ the bilateral mechanism of Activities Implemented Jointly (AIJ) between an Annex I country and a non-Annex I country (now in its pilot phase)

◆ a stock-exchange mechanism matching projects for reducing greenhouse gas emissions in non-Annex I countries and investors in Annex I countries, allowing the latter to get credit for reductions made in the host country

◆ a fund to accelerate technological transfer, the "leapfrogging" of climate friendly technologies to non-Annex I countries (Brazilian proposal)

◆ a fund to help particularly vulnerable countries adapt to the effects of climate change.

Initially designed to channel private funds, the mechanism does not exclude public fund participation.

Through these debates, the main concerns and priorities of the various Parties were revealed:

◆ **for the developing countries:** development, technological transfer between industrialised and developing countries, assistance in adapting to climate change

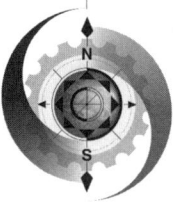

ISSUES&OPTIONS
The Clean
Development
Mechanism

◆ **for the industrialised countries:** reducing greenhouse gas emissions at the lowest possible marginal costs, introducing flexibility through a mechanism of greenhouse gas exchange between industrialised and developing countries, starting to integrate non-Annex I countries in the common effort of greenhouse gas emission limitation, mobilising private funding to finance the required investments in developing countries.

The project selection criteria, as well as the mode of operation and management of the CDM, should be defined in the light of these concerns and priorities.

PROJECT SELECTION CRITERIA AND OPERATION MODE

Article 12 specifies that non-Annex I countries are to benefit from project activities resulting in certified emission reductions (CERs). It also specifies that these projects must bring about both "real, measurable, and long-term benefits related to the mitigation of climate change" and "reductions in emissions that are additional to any that would occur in the absence of the certified project activity."

These two points explicitly refer to the ecological additionality, as does the framework of Joint Implementation. However, given the concerns of both the developing and industrialised countries, in particular that of development and sustainability, the ecological additionality criteria is not enough to define a project as pertinent for the mechanism.

Projects benefiting from recognised ecological additionalities can present widely different characteristics in terms of development for the host country. Take the example of an afforestation project in a country with intense competition for the use of agricultural soils. Its development advantages are not the same as those of a technology transfer project or a capacity building project. In fact, those projects could lead, in the long term, to widespread adoption of development paths that are more ecologically sensitive.

It is thus important to clarify the criteria or the type of projects and programmes that best match both the development requirements of the host countries and the ecological additionality requirements.

Durability

The durability aspect is referred to in the phrase, "measurable and long-term benefits related to the mitigation of climate change." Durability should be a major criterion for the selection of projects for two complementary reasons. First, the emission credit generated in the Annex I country that funds the project is directly related to the lifetime of this project. At its end, the country that temporarily benefited from the credit linked to this project is required to satisfy the new quantitative commitments in force at that time. This might mean new domestic measures, or the purchase of the right to emit in an Annex I country, or the financing of a new project in a non-Annex I country.

Second, at the end of the project's lifetime, the emissions of the host country are likely to be increased correspondingly and contribute once again to the greenhouse gas emission increase of the non-Annex I countries, if the latter do not renew the initial investment. Thus, durability is central for global reasons – the long-term efficacy of the mitigation actions – but also for the national concerns of Annex I and developing countries.

However, it does not seem productive to adhere to a rigid notion of durability. For one thing, because development criteria can lead to priorities counter to the criterion of "maximum project lifetime," as suggested by the afforestation project mentioned above. But also, the dynamics of technical progress must be taken into account. In today's rapidly changing world, a project with a very long lifetime may inhibit the development of new technologies.

The sustainability of climate change mitigation measures relies on learning more about the synergies between development and the global environment. Thus, capacity building, project

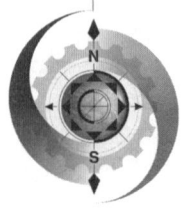

replicability, technology pre-dissemination and transfer must be fully applied under the CDM approach.

Conceivably, the number of CDM projects could be significant in terms of meeting Annex I country commitments. However, their impact will be minor compared with the projected growth of non-Annex I country emissions. In a 1997 report on Activities Implemented Jointly,[1] Pierre Cornut gave a rough estimate of the annual potential for reduction of 27 Metric Tons of Carbon (MtC) in 2010 due to North-South Activities Implemented Jointly. This compares with emissions growth of some 1200 or 1500 MtC in developing countries between 1990 to 2010, according to World Energy Council scenarios (1700 in 1990 and 4000 in 2020).

In terms of climate protection, then, three levels of action are needed:

◆ In the non-Annex I countries, promote the institutional, technical and financial conditions of clean development.

◆ In the Annex I countries, collect temporary credits for emission reduction.

◆ In the international community as a whole, actively use CDM projects as a way of

> **Conceivably, the number of CDM projects could be significant in terms of meeting Annex I country commitments. However, their impact will be minor compared with the projected growth of non-Annex I country emissions.**

learning about how development and environment interconnect.

Ecological benefit and incremental costs

Eligible projects should result in "reductions in emissions that are additional to any that would occur in the absence of the certified project activity." This criterion, common to both the CDM and Joint Implementation, implies both ecological additionality and additional costs. The ecological additionality is expressed as the difference of emissions (for example, annual emissions) between the project to be implemented in the host country and a baseline project or "reference scenario" in the same country. The same sort of reckoning can be applied to figure the incremental cost of the project. The choice of a baseline has a major influence both on the assessment of both the added ecological benefits and incremental costs.

The difficulties associated with selecting this reference scenario have been extensively debated within the Global Environment Facility (GEF), the Fonds Français pour l'Environnement Mondial (FFEM) and during the AIJ pilot phase. The experience accumulated through these institutions should, at least for the energy sector, provide minimum guidelines for action.

ECONOMIC CRITERIA AND FINANCIAL IMPLICATIONS

The above considerations show that neither the scope of direct greenhouse gas emission reductions nor the marginal cost of reductions for each project is sufficient to rate projects. The dynamic and long-term impacts on clean development of the projects that would most likely be financed under such a scheme would probably remain negligible, and finally, hardly beneficial, both for the host and the investing countries.

Cost/benefit analysis thus should only be used as one selection criterion when comparing projects of the same nature (such as two heavy industrial establishment projects). It should not preclude use of a multi-criteria analysis integrating the criteria of development, capacity building, technological transfer, and future benefits generated by the dissemination of clean technologies. The economic and financial

---

[1] *"L'application conjointe dans le cadre des négociations climat"* - Pierre Cornut, 1er octobre 1997. See also Box 1, page 88.

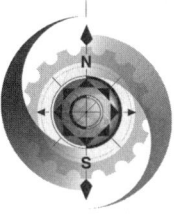

ISSUES&OPTIONS

The Clean
Development
Mechanism

assessment of these possible benefits raises some important methodological problems. It implies projections that are difficult to integrate in a market-type approach and by specific project.

Take the case of heavy infrastructure investments (transport, energy networks, urban development, buildings), for example. The rationality of initial choices in these domains will have considerable consequences on greenhouse gas emissions for very long periods. Since the CDM targets countries that are entering the phase of heavy infrastructural development, these central concerns must be taken into account, even though it may be difficult to measure and assess the global benefits of projects in this area.

However, it is possible, in some cases, to approximate the benefits through retrospective comparisons with projects of the same type. We can estimate potential emission savings over long time periods by looking at industrialised country experience over the past 50 years. The investment choices for transport infrastructure, urban zoning, housing thermal standards and service sector construction have very long-term effects on energy expenses and thus on greenhouse gas emissions. The relative magnitude of these consequences are widely known. For instance, we know that urban development decisions in cities (American vs. European) can affect mobility needs, and thus energy use, at a ratio of 1 to 6. Transport infrastructure decisions (rail vs. road) and housing construction standards can affect energy needs in a ratio of 1 to 4. Thus, the difficulties of measuring the ecological benefits of a project or programme should not be considered as a real obstacle to CDM support.

EQUITY ISSUES

This article addresses three categories of equity problems raised by the CDM: equity between the industrialised and non-Annex I countries; access equity among non-Annex I countries to the benefits of the CDM; and equity with regard to the climate change adaptation efforts. These issues are discussed below.

> **Three categories of equity problems are raised by the CDM: equity between industrialised and non-Annex I countries; equity of access among non-Annex I countries to the benefits of CDM; and equity with regard to the climate change adaptation efforts.**

developing countries of "cream skimming." This is why the problem of the CDM cannot be treated independently from the commitments of various countries in the medium- and long-term. In particular, how does the CDM relate to the equitable and simple rules of convergence for emission management targets for all the countries of the world? This question demands consideration of both the initial situations (per capita wealth and emissions) and the development requirements (population growth and economic growth) of the various countries. While the quantitative commitments made by the Annex I countries at Kyoto appear quite disparate (from an eight per cent reduction for Europe to an eight per cent increase for Australia), they are, in fact, much more convergent if they are analysed in terms of development goals. Graph 1 illustrates this point. When current rates of emission and targets are plotted against productivity (GDP per capita), the data reveals that the efforts of

Equity between the industrialised and the non-Annex I countries

The new financial investments flowing from Annex I to developing countries as a result of the CDM may indeed improve the balance between countries in the North and South. But its implementation has to be considered in a larger framework of problems inherent to the Climate Change Convention and of past responsibilities, climate change impacts and future responsibilities. In particular, the CDM must take into consideration the fear expressed by all the

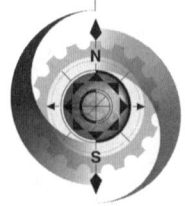

ISSUES&OPTIONS

The Clean
Development
Mechanism

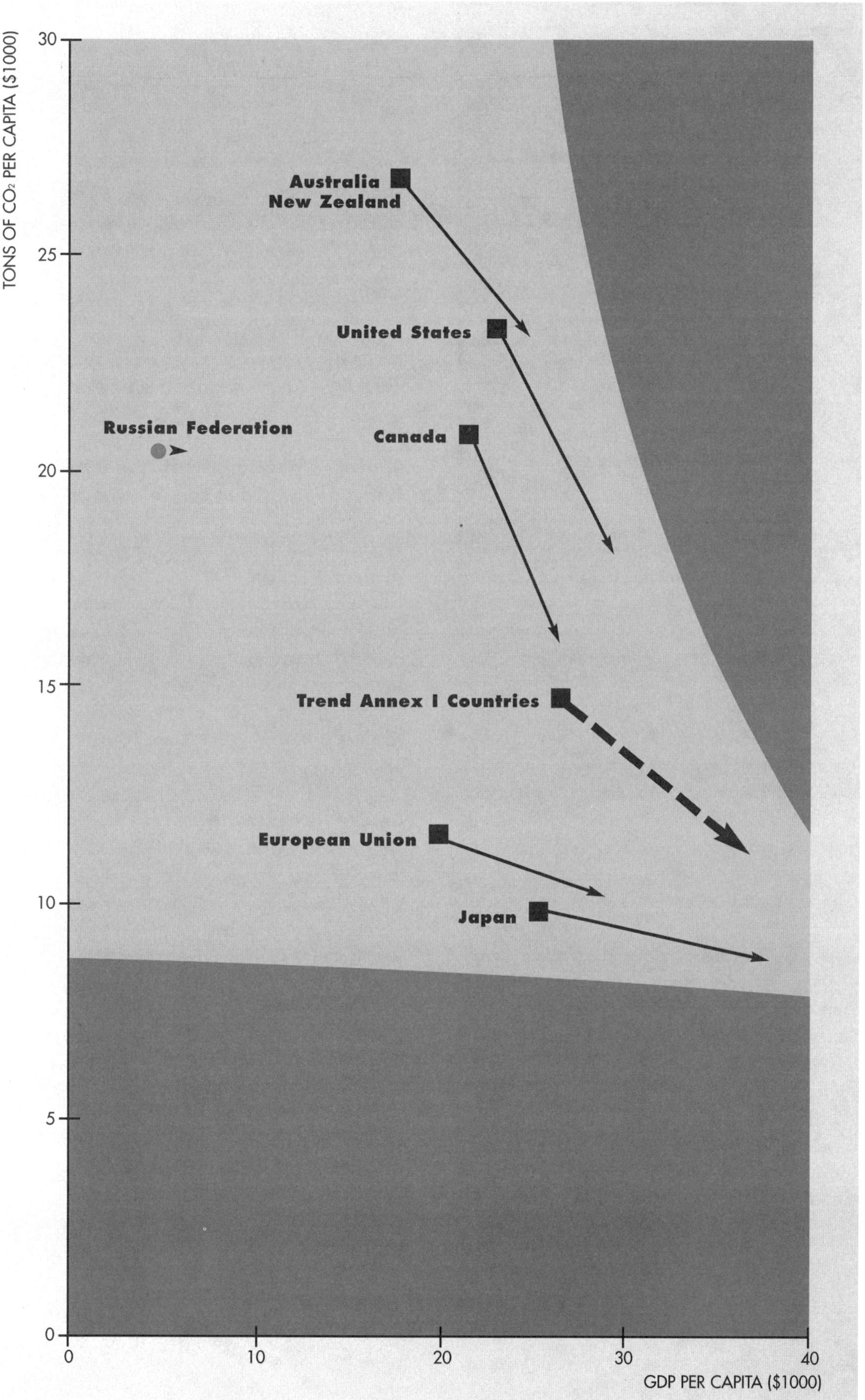

TONS OF CO$_2$ PER CAPITA ($1000)

30

25

Australia
New Zealand

United States

Russian Federation

Canada

20

15

Trend Annex I Countries

European Union

10

Japan

5

0

0   10   20   30   40

GDP PER CAPITA ($1000)

Graph 1. Kyoto Commitments

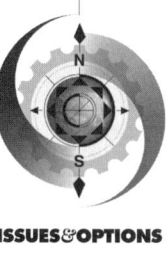

ISSUES&OPTIONS

The Clean
Development
Mechanism

Table 1. EU reduction proposals for 2010

COUNTRY	EU REDUCTION PROPOSAL FOR 2010
Denmark	- 25 %
Sweden	+ 5 %
Finland	0 %
Luxembourg	- 30 %
France	0 %
Germany	- 25 %
Austria	- 25 %
The Netherlands	10 %
Belgium	- 10 %
United Kingdom	- 10 %
Italy	- 7 %
Ireland	+ 15 %
Spain	+ 17 %
Greece	+ 30 %
Portugal	+ 40 %
Europe	- 10 %

the various parties are, in a real sense, converging, a fact that is not immediately obvious.

The same applies to the internal sharing of efforts among the European Union (EU) countries before Kyoto. Graph 2 also shows (with a few exceptions) a convergence that strongly corrects the impression of divergence produced by simply listing the commitments (Table 1) of each country.

The EU example also provides another lesson: It demonstrates that a common environmental objective can be accomplished, even while allowing for considerable differentiation among countries. In this case, it requires taking into account their current situations, in terms of both development and emissions, as well as their respective development needs. Such a perspective clarifies why Portugal, whose initial stage of development and per capita emissions are the lowest in the European Union, is allowed to significantly increase its emissions and in effect

to "catch up" with the other member countries. Here again, the apparent differentiation in fact reveals a solidarity of effort among the European Union countries around a given common target.

These examples deserve consideration in as much as they permit, in the long run, a redefinition of differentiated quantitative objectives for all countries (including non-Annex I countries) that in turn target a common objective. The preceding examples demonstrate that convergence criteria that seems essential in a long-term international negotiation is perfectly compatible with widely differentiated quantitative objectives.

Equity of access among the non-Annex I countries to CDM benefits

Within the group of non-Annex I countries, there may be considerable imbalance between emerging countries and less-developed ones in gaining access to the CDM. The largest greenhouse gas savings potentials are located in the larger and more advanced developing countries. The CDM, if not carefully crafted, could exacerbate this imbalance in financial flows.

Equity in access to climate change adaptations

Countries that need to adapt to climate change are not necessarily those countries that stand to gain from the emission reduction CDM projects. The "natural" orientation of financial flows towards countries with a higher potential for emission credits thus raises problems of equity with respect to countries that contribute very little to emissions, but which are the most vulnerable to climate change, for instance the small island states. Addressing this issue implies at least a partial redistribution of the benefits generated through the CDM.

SHARING THE INCOME

The CDM acknowledges and seeks to leverage the marginal cost difference in reducing greenhouse gas emissions between Annex I and non-

Annex I countries. It is designed to help the Annex I countries comply with their commitments through the flexibility generated

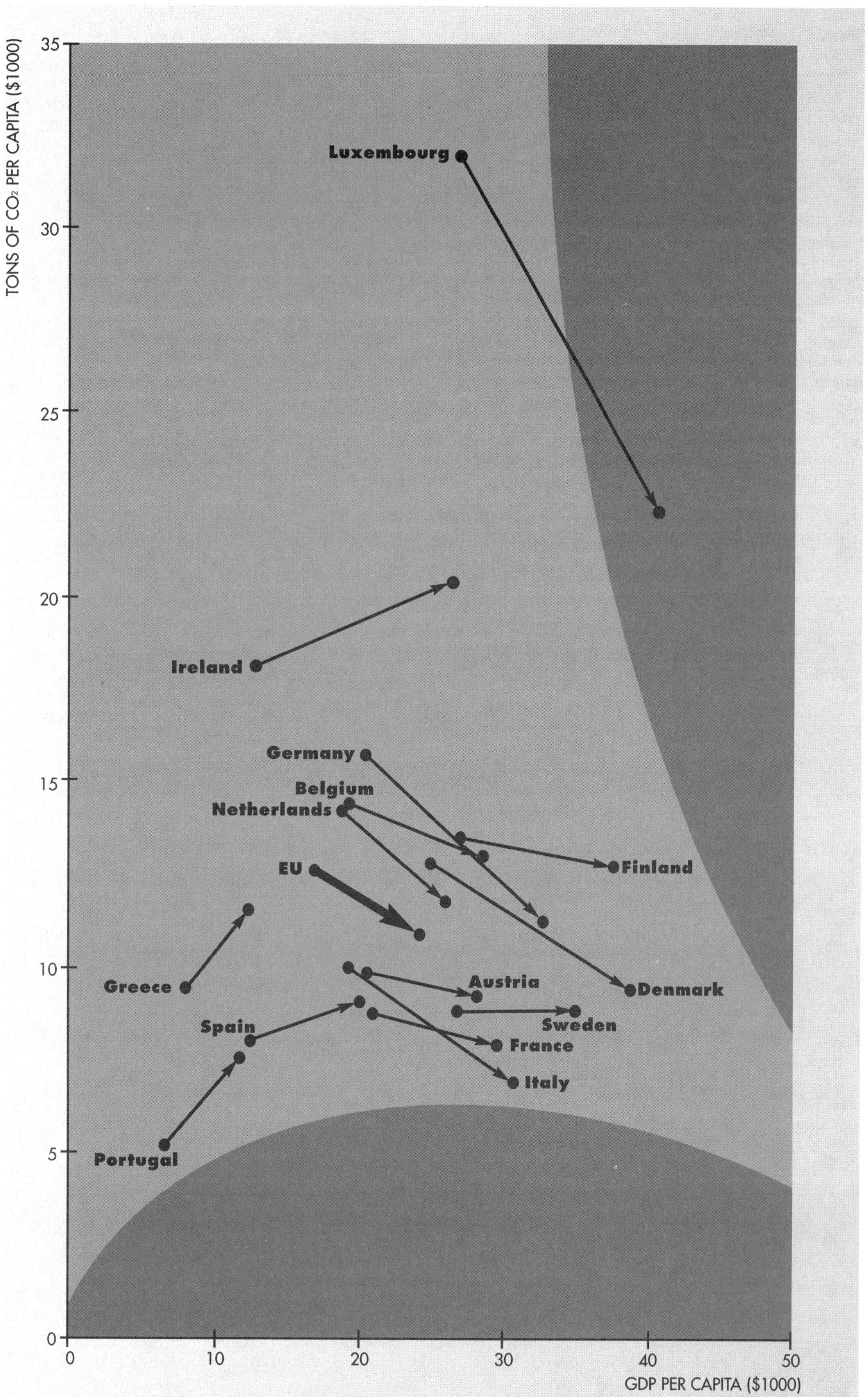

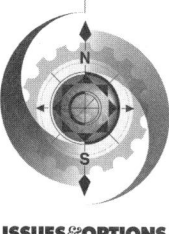

TONS OF CO$_2$ PER CAPITA ($1000)

35

30

25

20

Luxembourg

15

Ireland

Germany

Belgium

Netherlands

EU

10

Greece

Spain

Austria

Portugal

Sweden

France

Italy

Finland

Denmark

5

0

0   10   20   30   40   50

GDP PER CAPITA ($1000)

Graph 2. European Proposal of Commitment Sharing at the European Council, March 1997

ISSUES&OPTIONS

The Clean
Development
Mechanism

Box 1. Calculating future emissions reductions

In calculating the emissions potential for North-South Activities Implemented Jointly (AIJ) projects in 2010, Pierre Cornut[1] considered a medium reduction objective for Annex I countries of 10 per cent below 1990 emissions levels in 2010 (two times the Kyoto QELRCs). He supposed that a limitation would be placed on North-South Joint Implementation, so that domestic measures in Annex I countries would have to reach at least a - 9 per cent of 1990 levels (i.e. Annex I countries commit to reduce at least nine per cent below 1990 at home, and 10 per cent including North-South Joint Implementation). The annual 2010 potential for North-South Joint Implementation would then be equal to 1 per cent of Annex I countries' 1990 emissions. However, since Eastern European countries are not supposed to "buy" Joint Implementation reductions from developing countries, Cornut considered only the other Annex I countries' 1990 emissions, which were 2700 MtC. The annual potential for North-South Joint Implementation in 2010 would then be one per cent of 2700 MtC, or 27 MtC. This potential could reach 60 MtC per year if, for example, the limitation put on North-South Joint Implementation was two per cent of 1990 levels. (This would mean that domestic measures in Annex I countries would constitute an eight per cent reduction below 1990 instead of nine per cent.) This compares with an emissions growth in developing countries of some 1200 or 1500 MtC between 1990 to 2010, according to World Energy Council scenarios.

by the access to emission reduction potentials at costs lower than would be possible domestically. The difference between these marginal costs constitutes a revenue – the product of the quantity of carbon avoided multiplied by the cost differential. The distribution of this revenue between the investing countries and enterprises and the host countries should reflect as closely as possible a balance between the various principles and criteria analysed above: development and sustainability criteria and equity.

From the point of view of emission credits, it seems that the baseline for the calculation of avoided emissions should not be the local baseline (the project that would have been implemented in the host country in the absence of the CDM) but that which the investor would have carried out in his own country to respect its commitments if he had not invested in the host country. We could thus legitimately consider the domestic project "avoided" by the investor as the reference project for the calculation of the emission credit. Adopting this formula presents the advantage of limiting the quantity of emission credits

accessible and thus avoiding the risk of speculation based on "cream skimming." Without this precaution, one could easily imagine that some multinational enterprises could find financial benefits in relocating their activities to unduly profit from part of the cream skimming revenue. Moreover, it opens the way and gives some guidelines to a possible credit sharing between the host country and the funding country.

Principles of management and organisation

In the light of these various considerations, we can define a few principles concerning the management and organisation of the CDM. These principles would permit all partners to access its benefits in terms of emission reduction, development, and adaptability for the countries most vulnerable to climate change.

Give preference to categories of projects that couple development advantages and reasonably measurable ecological benefits. Initially projects in the energy area – those that promote energy efficiency as well as produce energy – seem to offer the most promise. Within this category, weight should be given to the development of infrastructure, whether urban, residential, or industrial, that heavily impacts energy consumption. On the other hand, given the current state of knowledge, projects linked to carbon storage in biomass should be considered with caution. Although it is possible to estimate the amount of carbon stored, projects in this category tend to produce few benefits in terms of technological transfer or sustainable development for the host country. Afforestation projects are a case in point. While they may yield long-term benefits in terms of climate change, they do not result in short-term benefits for the host country. The result may be that afforestation projects in some areas simply exacerbate deforestation in other areas due to agricultural needs. This could be particularly true for Africa. An exception could be made in the short and medium term for agricultural intensification operations, in particular in Africa, inasmuch as they are win-win-win projects: for development, for carbon storage and for forests.

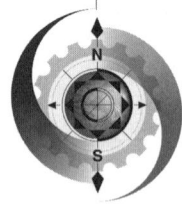

Ensure transparency of the system by avoiding as much as possible direct bilateral transactions that could lead to what the economists call "hot air" (CO_2 reductions that are not real). In this field, establishing a "clearing house" system and a certification independent from private actors and countries could be an important step.

Limit the use of the various flexibility mechanisms (tradable permits, Joint Implementation, CDM) to ensure a sufficient level of domestic effort to induce technological and behavioural

> The CDM should be crafted to closely link the mechanism to the concerns of development, equity, solidarity, and global environment protection that lay the foundation for the Climate Convention in the spirit of the Rio Conference.

evolution in the Annex I countries.

Impose a levy on all CDM transactions in order to fund for the adaptation of the most vulnerable countries to climate change.

We will insist, in conclusion, that the CDM should be crafted without neglecting any of its principal aspects and closely linking the mechanism to the concerns of development, equity, solidarity, and global environment protection that lay the foundation for the Climate Convention in the spirit of the Rio Conference. ∎

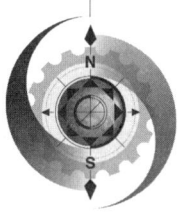

ISSUES&OPTIONS

The Clean
Development
Mechanism

Chapter 7

OUTSTANDING ISSUES

Domenico Siniscalco, Alessandra Goria, Josef Janssen
Fondazione ENI Enrico Mattei
Milan, Italy

Summary: The Clean Development Mechanism (CDM) arrangements as currently defined in the Kyoto Protocol leave room for many options. This paper will examine status and available options regarding four outstanding issues: institutional, administrative, and financial arrangements; criteria for certification of emission reductions; criteria for operational modalities, including eligibility criteria for projects; and sharing of CDM credits and the market structure.

GENERAL ASPECTS

Economic and environmental rationale

The Kyoto Protocol provides for four "flexibility" mechanisms to help Annex I Parties achieve their emission reduction commitments, while contributing to the mitigation of global climate change:

◆ Bubbles, in Article 4
◆ Joint Implementation, in Article 6 and referred to in Article 3.10 and 3.11
◆ Clean Development Mechanism (CDM), in Article 12 and referred to in Article 3.12
◆ Emission trading, in Article 17, and referred to in Article 3.10 and 3.11

The economic rationale of Joint Implementation, the CDM, and emissions trading is to exploit the differentials in marginal costs of climate change mitigation between countries. Joint Implementation refers to "emission reduction units" resulting from projects between Annex I Parties. The CDM refers to "certified emission reduction" resulting from projects between Annex I and non-Annex I Parties. Emissions trading refers to the transfers of "any part of an assigned amount" of emission reduction units between Annex I Parties and is not necessarily project-based. Bubbles refers to a group of countries wanting to jointly comply with the Kyoto commitments, with trading confined to countries inside the bubble, such as the European Union).

The CDM is the only instrument that allows for joint emission reductions between industrialised and developing countries, essentially allowing for Joint Implementation between Annex I and non-Annex I Parties. CDM projects would basically be international efforts, with Annex I Parties investing in emission reduction projects and non-Annex I countries hosting them. For investing countries, the main return on investments through CDM projects would be the crediting of certified emission reductions to meet their commitments.

From an economic point of view, CDM projects would attract investors if reducing emissions under the CDM were less costly (or more efficient) than any other available option under Joint Implementation, emissions trading or domestic actions. Therefore, all four would be competing investment options

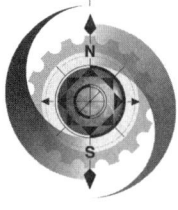

ISSUES&OPTIONS
The Clean
Development
Mechanism

for emissions reduction: a mix of them would generally be the optimal investment portfolio for individual Annex I Parties.

For the host countries, projects under the CDM would bring direct and secondary benefits related to climate change mitigation, preparing as well the respective countries to face possible future emissions limitation or reduction commitments.

> **CDM, Joint Implementation, emissions trading and domestic actions would be competing investment options for emissions reduction; a mix of them would generally be the optimal investment portfolio for individual Annex I Parties.**

Under this perspective, the CDM could play a very important role not only in assisting Annex I Parties to comply with their emission reductions or limitations commitments, but even in assisting developing countries to achieve sustainable development and in contributing to the ultimate objective of the United Nations Framework Convention on Climate Change (UNFCCC). This would occur by accelerating the transfer and diffusion of clean or more efficient technology to the less developed countries, by enhancing human capital and generating secondary economic benefits, and by providing more efficient solutions for the mitigation of global climate change. However, the effectiveness of the CDM in pursuing these objectives depends upon many crucial aspects that need to be further explored.

Definition of the CDM in the Kyoto Protocol

Article 12 in the Kyoto Protocol defines the rules for the CDM, as also referred to in Article 3.12, as follows:

- Annex I Parties may use the certified emission reductions accruing from project activities to contribute to compliance with part of their quantified emission limitation and reduction commitments (QERLCs) under Article 3, as determined by the Conference of the Parties serving as the meeting of the Parties to the Protocol (COP/MOP).

- Non-Annex I Parties will benefit from project activities resulting in certified emission reductions.

- The CDM shall be subject to the authority and guidance of the COP/MOP and shall be supervised by an Executive Board.

- The COP/MOP will designate operational entities for the certification of emission reductions.

- The COP/MOP shall ensure that a share of proceeds from certified project activities is used to cover administrative expenses as well as to assist developing countries Parties that are particularly vulnerable to the adverse effects of climate change to meet the costs of adaptation.

- Participation under the CDM may involve private or public entities, and is to be subject to the guidance of the Executive Board.

- Certified reductions achieved from 2000 onwards can be used to achieve the first commitment period (2008-2010) targets.

CDM OUTSTANDING ISSUES

These rules as currently defined leave room for many options. This paper will examine four outstanding issues, grouped as follows:

1) institutional, administrative and financial arrangements

2) criteria for certification of emission reductions
3) criteria for operational modalities, including in particular eligibility criteria for projects
4) sharing of CDM credits and the market structure.

Institutional, administrative, and financial arrangements

The institutional setting and the procedural structure of the CDM should be attractive for the private sector, in such a way as to create valid investment options and to channel private investments towards globally efficient mitigation projects.

This implies that CDM institutional arrangements should aim to minimise set-up and administrative costs and provide economic incentives to fund and implement projects to both investing and host parties. The outstanding institutional, administrative and financial arrangements requiring action are:

◆ further defining the relative functions of the governing bodies (COP/MOP and the Executive Board) and the operational entities.

◆ agreeing on what share of proceeds from certified project activities will be used to cover administrative expenses as well as to assist most vulnerable developing countries to meet adaptation costs, and on how this share of proceeds will be administered.

◆ agreeing on how the CDM would channel private investments. Should it be a project-related bilateral mechanism, a fund-based multilateral procedure, or a combination of multilateral and bilateral means, involving multiple institutions and the market?

Functions of the governing bodies and operational entities

Article 12 of the Protocol states that the Executive Board shall be in charge of supervising the CDM and provide guidance on participation under the CDM, which may involve private or public entities (paragraphs 4 and 9). It will carry out these functions based on authority and guidance coming from the COP/MOP (paragraph 4) and using CDM modalities and procedures to be elaborated by COP/MOP (paragraph 7). In addition, COP/MOP will determine how Annex I Parties may use the certified emission reductions accruing from CDM project activities to contribute to compliance with part of their quantified emission limitation and reduction commitments (paragraph 3). It will also designate the operational entities in charge of certifying emission reductions resulting from each project activity (paragraph 5).

These provisions leave room for various options regarding the procedural and institutional arrangements of these bodies, all aspects of which shall be addressed at the next Conference of the Parties (COP-4). Generally, these arrangements should guarantee for the effectiveness and efficiency of CDM investment projects.

A possible institutional arrangement would be to designate an impartial central secretariat body to support the Executive Board in its supervision of the CDM. Certification and verification should occur within a competitive market structure, supervised by the Board.

One of the main issues will be whether to create new bodies, or whether to build upon already existing expertise. The latter solution, minimising set-up and operational costs, may be more economically viable and attractive, although it may not appeal to those non-Annex I countries that are not yet sufficiently involved in the existing mechanisms.

The Global Environment Facility (GEF) and its Implementing Agencies have considerable relevant experience, particularly in the financing of emission reduction activities in developing countries and in the assessment of financial and environmental additionality. Therefore, the GEF could conceivably be involved in this process and be institutionally linked to the CDM Executive Board.

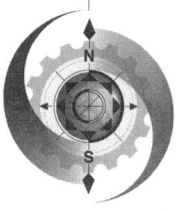

ISSUES&OPTIONS
The Clean Development Mechanism

The designation of the Executive Board in particular should depend on a clear specification of its functions and on whether existing bodies already have the relevant experience. Non-Annex I countries may be willing to create a new, more independent "COP-based" body, where they could play a more significant role. Or they may at least advocate higher decentralization of an already existing body.

Operational entities need to be able to insure an objective verification and certification of emissions reduction. A single certifying institution would probably not be able to deal with the volume of CDM activities, and would not be economically attractive, since it might lead to an inefficient and bureaucratic monopolistic structure. Conceivably, these functions could be carried out by auditors or accountants, operating under the authority and guidance of a central body. Their "objectivity" in the verification and certification of emission reduction should be carefully evaluated, since the profitability of overestimating emission reductions for both investing and host Parties under the CDM could encourage morally hazardous actions.

Share of proceeds

Article 12.8 of the Kyoto Protocol provides that "the COP/MOP should ensure that a share of the proceeds from certified project activities is used to cover administrative expenses as well as to assist developing countries Parties that are particularly vulnerable to the adverse effects of climate change to meet the costs of adaptation."

Basically this share of proceeds may be interpreted as a CDM investment tax. Obviously, this tax would increase the costs of investing through the CDM, favouring other investment options such as Joint Implementation, emissions trading, or domestic actions in Annex I Parties. At present, the exact meaning of "proceeds" needs to be clarified: what is the tax base and what is the quantitative definition of the share (or the tax rate)?

Furthermore, it is not clear what share will be devoted to administrative expenses versus assistance to developing countries. Nor is it clear who will decide on the allocation and based on what criteria, in particular which "particularly vulnerable" Parties would benefit from this distributional mechanism.

The management and allocation rules of the cumulative amount of these proceeds will certainly help determine the overall attractiveness of the CDM for both investing and host Parties and private entities.

A multilateral mechanism could probably provide for an efficient and equitable management and allocation of the total shares of proceeds. It represents an economically attractive option, since it would face low transaction costs and diversify risk. It would also be an effective mechanism for equal redistribution of the resources generated through the CDM. Equity issues in the reallocation of a share of the proceeds from the CDM to cover adaptation costs will arise not only between Annex I and non-Annex I Parties, but in particular among non-Annex I Parties.

A multilateral structure to manage the cumulative share of proceeds would avoid any strong influence that bilateral political and economic interests may have on the allocation criteria: non-Annex I Parties still struggling to fulfil their basic needs and most vulnerable to the effects of climate change may benefit from such structure. However, this multilateral system to manage and allocate the shares of proceeds should be complementary to any institutional structure under which CDM projects will occur and CDM resources will be generated. (The CDM structure, whether a multilateral mechanism, a bilateral mechanism, or a mix of both is discussed in the following section.)

Clearly, in order for CDM projects to be attractive for investors, the net marginal benefits of CDM projects, after subtracting administrative expenses and adaptation costs, must be higher than under other competing investment options. This implies that the CDM offers efficient channels for international investments that should be competitive with respect to the other flexibility instruments and any domestic options for climate change mitigation.

Nature of the CDM funding mechanism

Also undefined are the institutional, administrative, and procedural settings that would pro-

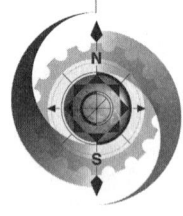

vide sufficient incentives for private investments under the CDM. The CDM could be designed as a multilateral, fund-based, mechanism, or as a bilateral, project-based, mechanism, or as a mechanism which involves both the multilateral and the bilateral structure.

In a bilateral option for international investments, the Parties could negotiate a framework agreement setting the criteria and rules for project realisation and crediting of emissions reduction. Projects could be negotiated freely between private or public entities of both investing and recipient countries.

In a multilateral option mechanism, investing Annex I Parties would make contributions to an independent fund. Non-Annex I Parties could offer projects competing for the CDM fund's sources, and each investor would receive a credit proportional to its share of the project portfolio.

On one hand, a multilateral mechanism may imply the following disadvantages:

◆ Investors would not be able to select projects according to their own preferences (regional, geo-political, technological and sectoral).

◆ Low project identification may imply less incentive for transfer of technology and human capital, and generally may lead to lower positive externalities.

◆ Investing parties would have fewer opportunities for trade promotion, not being able to exploit bilateral options.

◆ The management of a multilateral mechanism by an international bureaucracy may lead to inefficiencies because of low competition.

On the other hand, multilateral arrangements would lower transaction costs and allow for better risk-diversification. To overcome some of the inefficiencies of a public multilateral

A CDM structure which allows for both multilateral and bilateral options seems to be the optimal solution more likely to foster investments, promote innovation, and at the same time guarantee that structures are competitive, enhancing efficiency.

fund, it would be possible to create national or international funds managed by private entities, such as investment banks. Conceivably, such mutual carbon investment funds would be structured according to specific sectoral and regional criteria, as well as risk-return based criteria, leading to a multiplicity of distinct investment portfolios.

From an economic perspective, channelling private or public finance for CDM activity directly from investors to recipients, rather than through a public multilateral institution, could lead to a more efficient solution. However, it could also be advantageous for some CDM activity to take place through joint-risk sharing mechanisms, in order to provide incentives for a broader and more diverse participation of investors. The World Bank has recently launched an initiative in this direction by creating a "Carbon Investment Fund," in which several Parties and multinationals have already agreed to invest. The performance of the 'Carbon Investment Fund" will represent a useful experience to take into account in defining the structure of the CDM funding mechanism.

Based on our previous considerations, a CDM structure that allows for both multilateral and bilateral options seems to be the optimal solution. In fact, this approach, involving multiple institutions and markets, is more likely to foster investments, promote innovation, and at the same time guarantee that structures are competitive, enhancing efficiency.

Criteria for certification of emission reductions

A rigorous certification of emission reduction, which ensures real emission reductions, is essential to the effectiveness of the CDM.

However, the CDM, while enhancing private investments between industrialised and developing

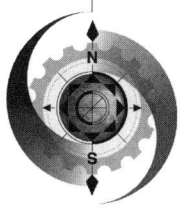

ISSUES&OPTIONS

The Clean
Development
Mechanism

countries, may also create a potential loophole. This could arise in two ways. First, in many non-Annex I Parties, there is a current lack of expertise and capacity to manage and monitor emissions accurately; thus, emission reductions could be overestimated. Second, certified emission reductions acquired under the CDM are outside the Annex I cap – a potential loophole that could be widened by the opportunity of pre-commitment period crediting.

In order to avoid loopholes and the risk that emission reductions will not reach the committed levels, pre-commitment crediting should not be allowed until transparent guidelines on emission reduction certification are approved.

Therefore, appropriate guidelines for a rigorous certification are needed in order to demonstrate real emission reductions. To avoid loop-holes, pre-commitment crediting should not be allowed until the guidelines on certification are approved. Guidelines will not be finalised before the first session of COP/MOP.

Guidelines shall be based on Article 12.5 of the Kyoto Protocol, which states that operational entities shall certify emission reductions on the basis of:

- ◆ voluntary participation approved by each Party involved

- ◆ real, measurable, and long-term benefits related to the mitigation of climate change

- ◆ reductions in emissions that are additional to any that would occur in the absence of the certified project activity.

These criteria need to be further elaborated. Identifying real, measurable and long-term benefits of CDM projects related to the mitigation of climate change requires specific competence and expertise.

Capacity for monitoring and verification, and its accuracy, should be enhanced in the developing world, where CDM projects will be undertaken. Appropriate capacity building will, in fact, be required to monitor the project performance against a "baseline," and

independent verification should be carried out.

The criterion of additionality is particularly difficult to address: "additional" reductions are certified with respect to the "baseline," which needs to be defined, taking into account environmental and economic factors. The definition of the "baseline" and of "additional" emission reductions will require a detailed analysis of the project potential against the "business as usual" trend, taking into account energy and other sectors' projections in the developing world.

The GEF and its Implementing Agencies may provide some useful expertise in the design of these criteria. In particular GEF's methodology for estimating "agreed full incremental costs" of its activities may be useful. Other institutions with relevant expertise include the International Energy Agency (IEA), the Food and Agriculture Organisation of the UN (FAO) and the UN Industrial Development Organisation (UNIDO). Private companies in the field of energy contracting face the problem of baseline determination of energy projects in the context of their usual business.

In general, project-by-project determination of additionality will lead to higher transaction costs and hence will reduce the efficiency gains of CDM projects. Efficiency could be improved by using standards or benchmarks for the determination of additionality. These standards should take into account the project type and the local current and expected market conditions and institutional settings. Such differentiated standards could be elaborated by private companies and supervised by the CDM Executive Board.

Criteria for operational modalities

Operational modalities shall be elaborated at the first session of the COP/MOP 1, according to Article 12.7 of the Kyoto Protocol. Guidelines on the operational modalities of the

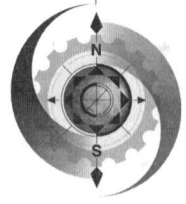

CDM need to be addressed in particular with respect to:

◆ restrictions of CDM transactions, i.e. which "part" of Annex I Parties' commitments can be met under the CDM

◆ pre-commitment crediting of emission reductions under the CDM

◆ the eligibility criteria for projects under the CDM.

Article 12.3 (b) states that "under the CDM, Annex I Parties may use the certified emission reductions accruing from project activities to contribute to compliance with part of their quantified emission limitation and reduction commitments under Article 3, as determined by the COP/MOP". What "part" means needs to be specified, with obvious consequences on the relative attractiveness of the CDM versus other flexibility instruments and domestic measures of mitigation, as well as on the overall efficiency of global mitigation actions.

Article 12.10 states that certified reductions achieved from 2000 onwards "can" be used to achieve the first commitment period (2008-2010) targets. This possibilistic statement leaves Parties with some uncertainty. As already discussed, in order to avoid loopholes and the risk of real emission reductions below the certified levels, pre-commitment crediting should not be allowed until transparent guidelines on emission reduction certification are approved.

The eligibility criteria for CDM projects are not clearly specified. Some eligibility factors are reflected in the criteria for certification of emission reductions from project activities in Article 12.5, including requirements for additionality and long-term mitigation benefit. Specific sectors, regions or categories of projects are not identified. In particular, it is not clear if sink projects will be eligible for CDM projects, because only emission reductions are explicitly mentioned.

The operational modalities of CDM should take into account the economic and strategic interdependence of the CDM with the other flexibility instruments. Guidelines on both the operational modalities and the criteria for auditing and verification should be consistent with the guidelines developed for emissions trading and Joint Implementation between Annex I Parties. Furthermore, they should enhance the incentive for developing countries to increase their involvement in emission limitations and should be consistent with sustainable development policies.

Sharing of CDM credits and the market structure

CDM projects will lead to additional emission reductions that will be credited towards the investors, in compliance with part of their quantified emission limitation and reduction commitments under Article 3. The equitable sharing of the CDM credits between the investor from an Annex I Party and the host in the non-Annex I Party needs to be considered carefully. Since non-Annex I Parties do not have any reduction or limitation commitment they will not be interested in sharing these technically quantified and certified emission reductions in order to comply with any specific commitment. However, non-Annex I Parties will have a vital interest in sharing the monetary value of the certified emission reductions.

From an economic perspective, the concrete sharing schemes for this monetary value will be influenced by the structure of the CDM projects market. Conceivable market structures on the demand and/or supply side vary from monopolistic to more competitive markets.

Generally, monopolistic structures on the demand side will give the Annex I Parties the greatest share of the efficiency gains of CDM projects. Monopolistic structures on the supply side, analogous for instance to the OPEC cartel, will lead to efficiency gains for the non-Annex I Parties. In a bilateral monopoly, the CDM project's price will depend on the relative bargaining power of both Parties.

Competitive markets will tend to generate a more fair and equitable distribution of efficiency gains, depending on the price elasticity of

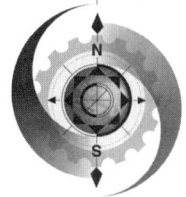

ISSUES&OPTIONS
The Clean
Development
Mechanism

supply and demand in the markets of CDM projects. The market structure will be determined by technological and institutional restrictions, by the availability and diffusion of information and knowledge, and by strategic considerations as they occur with the OPEC cartel. Important institutional restrictions which may hamper the evolution of competitive markets for CDM projects include monopolistic and bureaucratic certification processes.

Capacity building can improve the availability and diffusion of information and knowledge about the potential of the CDM and give it a boost in competitive markets and transparency. The financing of case studies on the CDM as part of National Strategies in non-Annex I Parties would, for instance, contribute to capacity building and to a better understanding of the CDM potential.

Overall, the design of principles, guidelines and rules for the CDM should promote competitive market structures. ∎

REFERENCES

Heller T., "Additionality, Transactional Barriers and the Political Economy of Climate Change," in *Working Paper 10.98*, FEEM, 1998.

Janssen J., "Strategies for Risk Management of Joint Implementation Investments," in *Greenhouse Gas Mitigation: Technologies for Activities Implemented Jointly*, Riemer P., Smith A. and K. Thambimuthu Eds., 1998, p. 357-365.

Michaelowa A. and Dutschke M., "Interest Groups and Efficient Design of the Clean Development Mechanism under the Kyoto Protocol," paper presented at the Second International Conference of the European Society for Ecological Economics, Geneva, 4-8 March, 1998.

Mohr E., "Sustainable Development and International Distribution: Theory and Application to Rainforests," in *Review of International Economics*, 4.1996, p. 152-171.

Chapter 8

DEFINING AND OPERATIONALIZING THE CDM

Rajendra K. Pachauri
Tata Energy Research Institute (TERI)
New Delhi, India

Summary: A close textual analysis of what Article 12 says and does not say, including nuances and implications, can be a first step in moving towards a definition of the Clean Development Mechanism (CDM). Paragraph by paragraph, this paper suggests possible interpretations, clarifications, and options, and then explores issues involved in getting the CDM into operation.

INTRODUCTION

Article 12 of the Kyoto Protocol begins with the clause "A Clean Development Mechanism is hereby defined." From that statement, we might expect to read the Article and end up understanding how the extent and impacts of climate change can be mitigated globally. As currently drafted, however, it raises more questions than it provides clear solutions. The word "defined" in the English language carries the connotation of precision. Something cannot be treated as defined if its shape and contours defy precise delineation. In fact, it would perhaps take several rounds of negotiations and considerable intellectual effort to clarify what the CDM truly is or can be.

Toward that end, this chapter first discusses Article 12 paragraph by paragraph, and then looks at some key issues that arise in the context of possibilities for putting the CDM into operation.

TEXTUAL ANALYSIS AND DISCUSSION

Paragraph 2 of Article 12 states first that the purpose of the CDM "shall be to assist Parties not included in Annex I in achieving sustainable development and..." The implications of this clearly stated purpose of the CDM could indeed be powerful. Even before we discuss activities that would be admissible under the CDM, this statement of purpose provides a rationale for identifying ineligible activities. Any measure that goes against the overall objectives of development in a non-Annex I country should not qualify for consideration under the CDM. In other words, non-Annex I Parties should essentially examine proposed CDM activities against the background of their own perceptions of sustainable development. The Protocol, once ratified, would be like any other agreement sanctioned by the United Nations: by its very nature, it would address a global problem, but in a manner that supports and upholds national sovereignty. If, for instance, a particular non-Annex I country decided that a proposed activity is not consistent with its sustainable development objectives, this should truly be the last word on the subject.

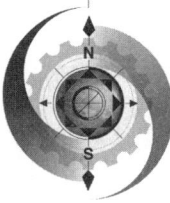

ISSUES&OPTIONS

The Clean Development Mechanism

Paragraph 2 goes on to mention the ultimate objective of the Convention and the CDM's second purpose: "to assist Parties included in Annex I in achieving compliance with their quantified emissions limitation and reduction commitments under Article 3." This clearly implies that activities to be implemented in non-Annex I countries, while supporting their own national objectives of sustainable development, would also assist the Annex I countries in reducing the latter's emissions. The developing countries – that is, the non-Annex I Parties – need to keep this reality truly in focus, because emission reduction should not become the overriding purpose, subordinating the purpose of achieving sustainable development in the non-Annex I Parties.

Understanding these nuances and possible implications is critical in terms of the different objectives of the two groups of countries, but also with respect to the cost of CDM activities and associated financial transactions. If the purpose is to achieve sustainable development, then financial transfers cannot be limited to only those narrow components of an activity or project that help in reducing emissions, ignoring other aspects of sustainable development that would be vitally important to the developing countries. In fact, a prerequisite for developing countries should be substantially to improve their understanding of sustainable development and their preparation of projects that vest them with maximum, lasting benefits.

Paragraph 3 of the Article states in part (a) that "Parties not included in Annex I will benefit from project activities resulting in certified emissions reductions." How these non-Annex I Parties would actually benefit is not indicated. Of course, there would be a variety of other benefits beyond those of a global nature and those bringing emission reduction credits to Annex I Parties. These might include employment generation, introduction of new technologies, reduction in local pollution, and the conservation of natural resources in the host countries. Clearly, in future negotiations, the developing countries will have to find some way of specifying the types of benefits that would accrue to them from CDM mitigation projects.

Part (b) of paragraph 3 is clear and certainly establishes the major driving force behind the inclusion of the CDM in the Kyoto Protocol.

The genesis of the CDM goes back to the Brazilian proposal for a Clean Development Fund submitted almost six months before Kyoto. However, the CDM differs substantially from the proposed fund. The Brazilian proposal intended to impose financial penalties on those Annex I Parties that do not meet their commitments, and using the revenues for promoting activities in developing countries related to climate change. If the CDM were funded in this way, then obviously it would not become operational before the commitment period 2008-2012. But the proponents of the CDM at Kyoto were seeking to advance this timetable, perhaps to establish the "meaningful participation" by key developing countries that has been referred to frequently before, during and after Kyoto.

Paragraph 4 specifies that the CDM will be under the authority and the guidance of the Parties to the Kyoto Protocol and supervised by an Executive Board of the CDM. This raises the important issue of the governance of the CDM. Several models could be considered:

◆ At one extreme would be an Executive Board consisting only of Annex I Parties. Since they are committed to emissions limitations, they could be considered legitimately entitled to being in the driver's seat.

◆ The other extreme would be a Board consisting of only non-Annex I Parties. The argument is that, since projects in their countries must meet their sustainable development objectives, it is these Parties that should oversee the functioning of the CDM.

◆ Between these extremes would be some kind of joint or mixed composition, such as has been evolved for the Global Environment Facility (GEF).

◆ One set of proposals would entrust the GEF with responsibility for implementing the CDM. The GEF has developed expertise on climate change and emissions reduction projects, and has a governing structure which is now largely acceptable to both developed and developing countries. A disadvantage of such an arrangement relates to GEF financing. If

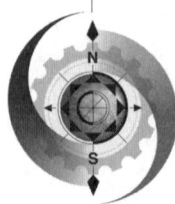

ISSUES&OPTIONS

The Clean
Development
Mechanism

CDM-related activities reach a certain large scale of operation, there might be a dwindling of support for GEF projects. However, this danger exists irrespective of the governance structure of the CDM.

The governance structure is bound to be a contentious subject on which it would be difficult to reach quick agreement. Hence, this is an issue that needs to be taken in hand for discussion, debate and negotiations very early.

Paragraph 5 deals with "voluntary participation," on the one hand, and with "real, measurable, and long-term benefits related to the mitigation of climate change," on the other. These are mentioned in the context of certification of emissions reduction. How and by whom such certification will take place is a subject that would also require some detailed consideration. Ideally, the authority to certify emissions should be given to independent non-government institutions around the world and helping them, where necessary, to acquire adequate expertise. The acquisition of such expertise could take two to three years in some cases, but several institutions are already quite competent to handle the task. An even geographical spread of such institutions or organisations would help ensure objectivity and involvement of every region in CDM-related activities.

The term "real, measurable, and long term benefits" used in paragraph 5(b) raises an interesting question of what would constitute long-term benefits and what would be excluded. For instance, would training of energy auditors or helping to form energy service companies qualify as action that would create long-term benefit? Comparing this issue to the purpose stated in paragraph 2, one can see a clear correspondence and synergy in such capacity-building measures and long-term benefits.

Paragraph 5 (c) specifies that, to qualify under the CDM, emission reductions would have to be "additional to any that would occur in the absence of certified project activity." This presupposes that baselines and benchmarks would be firmly established so that this additionality could be identified.

> If a particular developing country decided that a proposed activity is not consistent with its sustainable development objectives, this should truly be the last word on the subject.

Paragraph 6 specifies that the CDM shall "assist in arranging funding of certified project activities as necessary." Some agreement will have to be reached on the source of such funding. Perhaps it should be specified that funding for such purposes should be additional to existing bilateral development assistance. This would address the concern of developing countries that climate change-related financing should not be at the cost of existing bilateral or multilateral development assistance.

It will also have to be established whether the CDM organisation will maintain a shelf of projects that would be eligible for funding. This would imply that project activities will have to be certified in advance of funding being arranged; but whether that is possible in reality needs to be considered. At least in the initial period, it appears that certification of specific projects and funding possibilities will have to move hand-in-hand. In other words, if a particular project is being developed and certified, simultaneous discussions with potential donors should be arranged to elicit their support and ensure that funding is available by the time the project is certified, fully appraised and ready for implementation.

Paragraph 7 discusses the need for the very first session of the Parties to this Protocol to "elaborate modalities and procedures with the objective of ensuring transparency, efficiency and accountability through independent auditing and verification of project activities." Obviously, these desirable characteristics can only be realised if the entire action – certifying projects, auditing them, and verifying the nature of the activities involved – is de-bureaucratised to the extent possible. This can happen only if a number of institutions around the world are identified to carry out these independent tasks. In order to ensure objective evaluation, verification, and certification, an institution located in country A should not have anything to do with the projects in the same country, but may be asked to carry out its functions in countries B or C. In this way, not only is objectivity

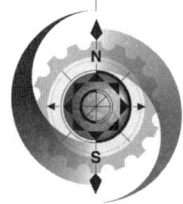

maintained in the entire process, but it fully appears to be so.

Indeed, it would be necessary in some cases to provide some support and help in capacity-building of some of the institutions that could be commissioned for this purpose, particularly for some developing country institutions. However, a number of developed country institutions would also require such capacity-building, because they may not be aware of ground realities in several parts of the world. Nor would they necessarily understand issues of sustainable development consistent with the overall objectives of the Protocol. These issues would have to be discussed in the first meeting of the Parties to the Protocol. The intellectual groundwork for implementation needs to occur before the first meeting actually takes place.

> **Providing for credits in the period 2000-2008 offers specific incentives to ensure the harnessing of initiatives and enterprise for the development of technologies which could make CDM a successful venture.**

Paragraph 8 specifies that the Parties to the Protocol "shall ensure that a share of the proceeds from certified project activities is used to cover administrative expenses as well as to assist developing country Parties that are particularly vulnerable to the adverse effects of climate change to meet the costs of adaptation." Clearly, the reference here is to the small island states, but since the wording of the Protocol does not specify this group of countries, it can be assumed that such assistance could apply to other states which face the likelihood of serious impacts of climate change in the future.

It would be necessary to lay down some formula or specify a percentage of the transactions that are to take place through this provision such that adequate revenues are generated not only for meeting administrative costs, but also for providing adequate assistance to the most vulnerable developing country Parties. However, this is another issue that would have to be decided and some scenarios of the level of activity that can be projected would be necessary as also would it be necessary to lay down some level of assistance that would be required to the Parties that have to be helped in meeting the adverse effects of climate change and to carry out adaptation measures. It would also be essential to clearly specify the kind of organisational structure that would be required for managing the administrative activities of the CDM, so that a clear estimate of administrative expenses can be arrived at.

For the sake of efficiency, the administrative and secretariat expenses should be kept to the barest minimum. Only then can a certain level of confidence be developed in the functioning of the CDM organisation. If administrative expenses turn out to be very high in the initial stages, it would become very difficult to change this situation in subsequent periods.

Considerable clarity is also required in defining, elaborating, and describing the kinds of adaptation activities and protection measures that would have to be undertaken by the vulnerable developing country Parties. Some degree of prioritisation would also be useful. This is essential so that funds are used efficiently, but also because considerable data and experience would be advisable before undertaking any large-scale efforts to protect against adverse effects of climate change. Science in this regard is still far less than perfect, and there are uncertainties about how to assess possible impacts as well as how to counter them.

Paragraph 9 lays down the possibility of participation in the CDM by "private and or public entities, subject to whatever guidance may be provided by the Executive Board" of the CDM. This is an important provision, because if activities under the CDM are to build up rapidly, participation should be open to as many organisations and types of organisations as possible. The Executive Board would be well advised to provide open and unfettered involvement of all kinds of organisations as long as the procedures laid down for certification and verification are followed faithfully. Full harnessing and utilisation of market forces

serves the CDM purpose of mitigating climate change, given that necessary regulatory actions would be put in place by the CDM.

Paragraph 10 provides that "certified emission reductions obtained during the period from the year 2000 up to the beginning of the first commitment period can be used to assist in achieving compliance in the first commitment period." This important provision would provide a certain level of practical benefit to the Parties that are going to be implementing greenhouse gas reduction measures. It would not be wise to postpone credits until the beginning of the period when commitments become binding. A great deal of uncertainty and some level of experimentation would be required before countries can arrive at definite and measurable benefits arising out of mitigation measures.

This provision is also important because it would lead to the development of technologies, which necessarily involves a certain time lag. Hence, if technology can be employed and evolved in the period before 2008, then by the time the first commitment period begins, some countries may even be able to increase their commitments and reduce greenhouse gas emissions beyond the levels specified in the Protocol. One reason that projects in the pilot phase of Activities Implemented Jointly (AIJ) prior to Kyoto did not quite take off to the extent expected is that there were no possibilities for credits accruing to countries undertaking these measures. Hence, providing for credits in the period 2000-2008 offers specific incentives to ensure the harnessing of initiatives and enterprise for the development of technologies which could make the CDM a successful venture.

KEY ISSUES FOR PUTTING CDM INTO OPERATION

Several questions arise about the measures needed for making the CDM operational in a manner that fulfils the various provisions of Article 12.

Project eligibility

What types of projects would be admissible under CDM criteria and certification processes? Since the first stated overall objective of the CDM is to help non-Annex I countries achieve sustainable development, this becomes the key criterion for deciding which projects would be eligible for CDM operations. Sustainable development has to be determined by each country in keeping with its own objectives, constraints, and natural resource endowments. Thus, the criteria for defining sustainable development cannot be global in nature. Undoubtedly, there are general principles for determining what sustainable development is, with global applications; but their interpretation within a specific national context necessarily has to be driven by national concerns and objectives.

However, given that several types of projects would have relevance to most countries of the world, it would be possible to specify the types of activities that would be eligible for the CDM. One example is projects in the energy sector, such as the use of renewable energy technologies, the promotion of energy efficiency, and the move from fuels that are highly intensive in greenhouse gas emissions to those that are less intensive. Also, given the fact that the Kyoto Protocol has included sinks in all estimates of net greenhouse gas emissions, the inclusion of forests and creation of carbon sinks through afforestation also becomes an eligible set of activities under the CDM.

The identification of activities that contribute most effectively to national sustainable development objectives would, of course, need careful preparation and analysis by specific countries and organisations situated therein. For instance, a large country with little green cover would likely benefit from enhancement of sinks and forest cover. Another country with remote, spread-out habitations might benefit from a project involving decentralised generation of energy using local resources and renewable forms. Still another country with substantial coal resources and significant levels of poverty could implement a project using clean coal

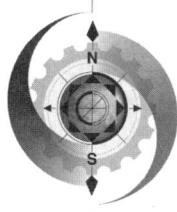

technologies for power generation; the premise is that every unit of electricity generated would perhaps help through lighting for literacy programmes, education in general, provision of drinking water, and other developmental benefits. While trying to mitigate climate change, we should not lose sight of the fact that there are two billion people in this world who have no access to electricity. One cannot talk about sustainable development without addressing this very basic need. Finally, a country that has energy-intensive industry or even small-scale industries using energy in not very efficient ways can benefit by implementing energy efficiency projects. Clearly, in identifying sustainable development projects, countries themselves must have a paramount role in determining what would be of benefit to them.

> **In looking at actions to mitigate climate change, we should not lose sight of the fact that there are two billion people in this world who have no access to electricity. One cannot talk about sustainable development without addressing this very basic need.**

Range of projects, and phasing

There is some question as to whether sufficient capacity exists to assess, certify, and monitor a diverse range of activities worldwide. Purely from the operational point of view, therefore, it may be useful to think in terms of prioritising and phasing projects. While retaining flexibility to suit national objectives and concerns, it might be useful to think in terms of a three- or four-year period when certain types of projects would be preferred over those that could be perhaps taken up in the second phase, let us say starting in the year 2004 or so. However, it can be argued that a more inclusive first phase of CDM operation might be advisable. Very valuable experience, data, and institutional responses could emanate from carrying out activities that are comprehensive and complete in every respect. Undoubtedly it would help to draw in as many non-Annex I countries as possible, to ensure that the CDM is not exclusive in any sense and that a whole range of project types can be implemented even in the initial phase. This certainly is an issue that needs considerable discussion and debate.

In political terms, the Executive Board may decide on an initial mix of projects as a broad guideline in the first phase extending, for instance, from the year 2000 to 2005. An example of the type of mix to be specified could be 25 per cent of project expenditures in the renewable energy sector, 25 per cent related to energy efficiency, 25 per cent covering sinks, and perhaps a 25 per cent share which is flexible and undefined, thereby promoting the generation of good ideas, experience and expertise. Needless to say, considerable analytical work would have to be done by the Secretariat to help in arriving at prioritisation and phasing of activities proposed.

Avoiding loopholes

Another area that raises a number of relevant questions is the enormous set of loopholes inherent in the implementation of CDM activities. A great deal of scepticism and even suspicion has arisen among non-Annex I countries about Joint Implementation projects and projects in the AIJ pilot phase. They are concerned that these projects can become a soft option for at least some of the Annex I countries. These countries may find it far more attractive to perform no emission reduction activities within their own territories and instead achieve their targets purely by the soft options of Joint Implementation and emissions trading. For this reason, it may be necessary to lay down some limits on the extent to which extra-territorial credits can be claimed by any Annex I country.

There is also a genuine fear that, given the current situation in Russia as well as some of the other former Soviet Union states, some Annex I Parties may trade and seek credit for the 400 million tonnes of carbon available as so-called "hot air" in some of these countries. Since their 1990 levels of emission were registered, reductions have already taken place on account of economic and other factors.

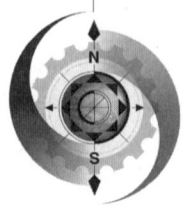

Clearly, some limits will have to be placed on trading of this hot air, which would be counter to the basic objectives of the Convention and the Protocol. Such a restriction can be pursued at this stage because the rules and procedures for emissions trading are yet to be worked out.

Additionality

A related question arises out of paragraph 5 (c) which refers to reductions and emissions that are additional to any that would occur in the absence of certified project activity. Perhaps the most effective and simplest approach to this issue would be to ensure that, at least in the initial phase of CDM operations, such reductions are not to be allowed, simply because between the period 2000 and 2008 any CDM activities that result in limitation or reduction of emissions would actually be providing credit only in the period 2008 to 2012. Hence, the evaluation of activities pointed at in paragraph 5 (c) would only complicate the whole issue of verification, monitoring, and evaluation. It would, therefore, be desirable to postpone any evaluation against this particular provision of the Protocol. Other general issues related to the functioning of the CDM are discussed below.

Verification

The first relates to verification of emission reductions and development benefits over time. As far as emission reductions are concerned, the Executive Board of the CDM would have to work in coordination with, if not under the direct control of, the Climate Change Secretariat. This issue would need to be decided as early as possible and certainly no later than the Fourth Conference of Parties (COP) to the United Nations Framework Convention on Climate Change. Verification will have to be carried out not by a large bureaucratic organisation which functions in a centralised manner, but through the empowerment of specific organisations around the world who would be given authority to carry verifications under a specified system, much in the manner that auditors are certified and empowered to carry out audit operations in a corporate organisation.

Emission reductions would perhaps be far easier to verify than development benefits. But, given the fact that the major objective of the CDM as stated at the outset is to assist non-Annex I Parties in meeting sustainable development objectives, development benefits will have to be verified and evaluated also. For this purpose, a very broad set of criteria defining these development benefits would need to be specified. These development benefits resulting from projects would certainly include income benefits, employment benefits, and benefits to the local environment in physical and possibly economic terms. Another valuable set of benefits would derive from the increased local capacity to sustain and build on the project activities.

CDM operating processes and structure

Finally, the operating processes and structure of CDM need to be considered. As mentioned earlier, the composition of the Executive Board needs to be settled as early as possible. In order to ensure consistency of actions carried out under the CDM and those carried out under the Kyoto Protocol in general, it may be desirable to locate the Executive Board in the Climate Change Secretariat. This does not mean that the Secretariat should have unfettered control over the Executive Board, but it should have essential and adequate representation on the Executive Board. The Secretariat would service the Executive Board and provide the Board Secretary from among its staff.

The Executive Board should function in a decentralised manner and avoid the establishment of a large bureaucracy. It is also important to keep the administrative costs as low as possible. It would be useful to arrive at a percentage based on some estimation of revenues to be generated and the total cost of administering the CDM. These scenarios need to be generated by the Secretariat of the Convention and placed

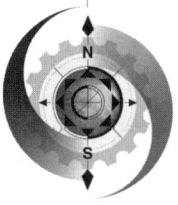

ISSUES&OPTIONS
The Clean
Development
Mechanism

before the Subsidiary Body for Scientific and Technological Advice (SBSTA) and perhaps the next COP, so that an initial percentage can be fixed. This figure, of course, can be reviewed from time to time by the Parties to the Protocol as well as by the SBSTA or another group that the COP will designate.

Initially, it would be desirable to see that the projects implemented under the CDM are handled in a co-ordinated manner. For this purpose, the approach and the processes followed by the Global Environment Facility (GEF) appear the most attractive for ensuring consistency between what has been learned in implementing climate change-related projects and what needs to be done under the CDM. The GEF, of course, has its designated agencies, namely the World Bank, the United Nations Development Programme, and the United Nations Environment Programme, for carrying out projects it funds, but it does have a largely unified approach and decision-making structure. Perhaps a similar approach could be considered in this case also.

In this paper, a large number of questions have been raised but not answered in any definitive way. Only through the identification of the right questions that emanate from the wording of the Kyoto Protocol can solutions be found through a process of discussion, negotiation, and consensus building.

The CDM is indeed one of the most important provisions of the Kyoto Protocol. While it has enormous potential, it also has certain inherent dangers that could create confrontation and a great deal of contentious bickering over a period of time. It is, therefore, necessary to proceed on a cautious basis, so that in the months and years ahead the CDM is seen as a means for helping not only the Annex I countries to achieve their targets and limitation goals, but also non-Annex I Parties to meet the overall objective of sustainable development. Promoting this objective can build confidence in the CDM, making it in the ultimate analysis an acceptable mechanism around the world in keeping with the intentions underlying the introduction of Article 12 in the Kyoto Protocol. ■

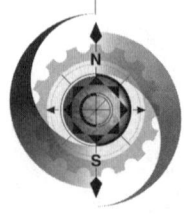

ISSUES&OPTIONS

The Clean
Development
Mechanism

ISSUES&OPTIONS
The Clean Development Mechanism

Special Issues

Chapter 9

WHAT PROSPECTS
FOR AFRICA?

**Youba Sokona, Stephen Humphreys
and Jean-Philippe Thomas**
Energy Programme, ENDA Tiers monde
Dakar, Senegal

Summary: The details of the Clean Development Mechanism (CDM) have not yet been decided. The vast majority of work underway at present is taking place in the countries that have the resources and information to move quickly, and represents their interests. However, since the CDM is explicitly designed to overcome the controversies of Joint Implementation and Activities Initiated Jointly (AIJ), the crucial aspect in its make-up must be its ability to balance the interests of the various Parties. The CDM is not merely a mechanism for ensuring cost-efficient emissions reductions and involving the private sector, but also for promoting sustainable development in developing countries. The key factor in determining the CDM must therefore be equity. The factors that have led to the exclusion of African countries – signatories to the United Nations Framework Convention on Climate Change (UNFCCC) – from the AIJ pilot phase must be explicitly countered in the formation of the CDM. To ensure equity the CDM must (a) function on a multilateral basis, (b) assure that *avoided future emissions* have priority status as "emission reductions," and (c) operate according to an explicit set of criteria that prioritise sustainable development as well as emissions mitigation. These criteria must be embedded in the notions of certification and baselines as well as in the constitution of the Executive Board and operational entities.

INTRODUCTION

In Africa, climate change was originally seen strictly as an environmental issue. The diversity and complexity of specific local environmental problems, unparalleled anywhere else in the world, obscured the global and developmental aspects of the situation. In fact, however, the issue of climate change unites the problems of development and the environment – particularly in the African context. The process that began in Rio in 1992 gave Africans an unprecedented opportunity to revisit the development paradigm, first in terms of the central notion of "sustainability," second in terms of the mechanisms put in place to support this idea (particularly in the Climate Change Convention), and lastly in terms of the international will and support to achieve these objectives.

The focal areas for cooperation identified in the United Nations Framework Convention on Climate Change (UNFCCC), such as the provisions for technology transfer, financial assistance, and capacity building, have generated much interest. Capacity building – the creation and maintenance of strong institutions and of efficient structural linkage between these institutions – is perhaps the most essential element recognised by the Convention, for without it long-term policy and strategy is difficult if not impossible. The creation and maintenance of an organisational and administrative infrastructure to cope with global environmental issues, which is largely absent or nascent in Africa, is vital not only to the overarching development objective but also to the success of the climate change initiative, globally as much as locally.

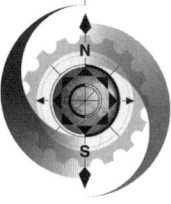

ISSUES&OPTIONS
The Clean
Development
Mechanism

Unfortunately, progress in these focal areas has been slow. Partly, this is because precedents are being set, and international cooperation on this scale is unfamiliar to the majority of actors. In addition, the differing interests of the various actors make agreement difficult. One mechanism designed to foster North-South cooperation, Actions Implemented Jointly (AIJ), more or less passed Africa by – only one out of 75 AIJ pilot projects currently reported to the UNFCCC secretariat is being implemented in Africa. Remarkably, an entire continent in the developing world has been effectively excluded from a process intended to strengthen the relationship between North and South on the basis of mutual interest.

THE CLEAN DEVELOPMENT MECHANISM

The Clean Development Mechanism (CDM) is the result of the desire of the various Parties to the Convention to produce a flexible mechanism that would allow for concerted action while preserving national sovereignty. The CDM is intended to provide enough flexibility to ensure that the differing objectives of the industrialised and developing worlds can be met simultaneously, thereby underpinning the global cooperation necessary to successful implementation of the UNFCCC.

The CDM may be seen as an overarching accord for organising, structuring, and financing initiatives that involve North-South collaboration with the objective of treating the global problem of climate change with mutual benefit to participating countries. Article 12 of the Kyoto Protocol, which establishes the mechanism, also introduces the notion of "certification" as a means of evaluating collaborative programmes. It specifies that an "Executive Board" will be set up to oversee the process of certification. To date, the criteria for both certification and the constitution of the Executive Board remain to be defined, as does the operation of the mechanism as a whole.

Emission reductions versus sustainable development?

The critical issues of disagreement and discussion at Kyoto stemmed from the differing emphases in the interpretation of the UNFCCC by industrialised and developing countries in terms of their respective concerns and priorities. An apparent contradiction emerged between the demands for the reduction of greenhouse gas emissions at the lowest possible cost and the participation of developing countries in this effort, on the one hand, and equity in terms of development and access to technologies and funding, on the other. The goals of emission reduction in the North and sustainable development in the South often appear to be in conflict. However, they are not mutually exclusive: the UNFCCC was specifically designed to encourage concerted global action, and it recognises the differing priorities of different countries and regions of the world. The differing sets of priorities, as they arose at Kyoto, are roughly as follows:

INDUSTRIALIZED COUNTRIES	DEVELOPING COUNTRIES
Emissions reduction	Sustainable development
Emissions trading and credits	Equity
DC participation	Common but differentiated responsibilities
Joint Implementation	Technology transfer
Sinks	Financial assistance
Compliance and verification	Special circumstances
CDM?	CDM?

CDM's role in balancing differing priorities - the equity issue

The principle of common but differentiated responsibilities between Northern and Southern countries is a primary concern of the

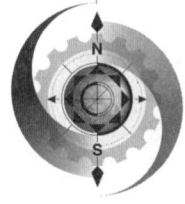

CDM. Questions then arise about the provisions for financial assistance and technology transfer contained in the UNFCCC: is the CDM the mechanism through which these commitments are finally to be implemented?

The essential issue in implementing the CDM will therefore be balancing the differing sets of priorities above. It is important in this context to note the wording of the Protocol, Article 12, paragraph 2:

> "The purpose of the Clean Development Mechanism shall be to assist Parties not included in Annex I in achieving sustainable development and in contributing to the ultimate objective of the Convention, and to assist Parties included in Annex I in achieving compliance with their quantified emission limitation and reduction commitments under Article 3."

The Protocol offers differentiated purposes for Annex I and non-Annex Parties and therefore proposes two criteria by which the success of the CDM must be measured. The demands for sustainable development have equal status with those of emission limitation and reduction. Therefore, we submit that the key issue is *equity*[1]. The benefits of the CDM for Annex I countries are evident: the fulfilment of their obligations at the lowest possible cost. For non-Annex I countries, with the goal of sustainable development to the fore, there must be *equity in terms of the benefits* of the CDM, and *equity of access* to the CDM. There must be *equity between* non-Annex I countries and Annex I countries first of all, and also *equity amongst* non-Annex I countries, all of whom have ratified the Convention and will be signatories to the Protocol in the near future.

To date, the debate around the CDM has large-

A CDM that exists merely to issue certificates on the validity of the emission reductions of given projects, and that allows market forces to determine the content, extent, and location of those projects will result in the same disequilibrium that we have seen in the AIJ pilot phase.

ly focused on the economics of emission reduction, the complexities of emission trading, and the market mechanisms to allow this. Although these issues are clearly of fundamental importance, they prioritise the concerns of Annex I countries over those of non-Annex I countries and tend to neglect the original intent behind the CDM. A CDM that exists merely to issue certificates on the validity of the emission reductions of given projects, and that allows market forces to determine the content, extent, and location of those projects, will result in the same disequilibrium that we have seen in the AIJ pilot phase. Since the inherent imbalance of market forces underpins the entire notion of cost-effectiveness in this context, to rely on them would be to recreate this imbalance on a global scale and thereby ignore the criterion of sustainable development in non-Annex I signatory countries.

Non-Annex I countries are marked by a wide variety of radically dissimilar conditions on the economic, political, social, and technological levels. Some of the countries, those termed "Least Developed Countries" (LDCs), have no significant basic infrastructure as well as negligible greenhouse gas emissions. The situation of "Economies in Transition," primarily in Eastern Europe, and the "Newly Industrialised Countries," primarily in Asia, is considerably closer to that of the industrialised countries in terms of both infrastructure and emissions. Others lie between these two extremes. LDCs, and those countries closest to them, such as many in Africa, are not in a position to reduce emissions and will therefore be excluded from the process unless equal attention is given to the possibility of avoiding future emissions through CDM projects in these countries. Avoidance of future emissions matches both the demands of sustainable development and the overall objectives of the Convention. If the focus remains on mitigating

---

[1] *The importance of equity, particularly in regard to guaranteeing international cooperation, has been well expressed by Jepma and Munasinghe in their book* Climate Change Policy, *Cambridge University Press 1998, pp. 64-65.*

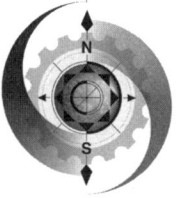

present emissions, many of the developing countries of the world will be excluded from the mechanism *a priori*.

A problem with the dual purpose of the Protocol is that while emissions reduction is relatively measurable, sustainable development is barely measurable, if at all. The objectives of Annex I countries tend to gain priority by default simply because they can be validated. Indicators for measuring development have been notoriously difficult; nevertheless, a number have been developed, notably the UN Development Programme Human Development Index (HDI). If the benefits of a given project in terms of its impact on emissions are to be measured in terms of additionality, perhaps additionality in terms of sustainable development – which could be measured using the HDI – should also be introduced. The CDM has to align these differing objectives by adopting projects and programmes that lead to certifiable emission reductions with measurable impacts on development.

> A problem with the dual purpose of the Protocol is that while emissions reduction is relatively measurable, sustainable development is barely measurable, if at all.

The implication of the private sector is an area requiring much debate. In most Annex I countries, the participation of the private sector is an inevitable consequence of the commitments of the states. Greenhouse gas emissions are largely produced by private bodies in the industrial countries, and states will pressure the private sector, through legislation or regulation, to cut their emissions. Furthermore, the technologies and financial resources that can address the problem are mostly in the hands of the private sector. These technologies and resources will, of course, also be sought after in developing countries, and many of the programmes and projects that the CDM will certify or oversee will be financed or initiated by Northern private bodies for implementation in Southern countries. The treatment of this issue in the CDM is therefore a central question.

THE AFRICAN CONTEXT

As is well documented, current emissions of greenhouse gasses in Africa are practically negligible in global terms due to the low level of industrialisation. The entire continent is estimated to be responsible for less than seven per cent of global emissions, and only about four per cent of CO_2 emissions. As a result, the options for mitigation in Africa are very limited. In fact, the entire debate over emission reduction largely escapes the needs of this continent.

Africa is currently recovering from the economic and political ravages of the 1980s and early 1990s. These years witnessed a steep decline in Official Development Aid (ODA), as well as the shock and debatable consequences of structural adjustment programmes. Foreign direct investment (FDI) in Africa, which according to current economic thinking ought to alleviate this decline, increased from US\$0.9 billion in 1990 to over US\$5 billion in 1996. This remains a rate of increase far below that of the rest of the developing world, and vastly insufficient to the developmental needs of the continent.

Africa's exclusion from the AIJ pilot phase

Now that AIJ has been tested and effectively rejected in developing countries, its failure can be examined to ensure that the CDM does not make the same mistakes. As noted above, African countries were virtually excluded from the AIJ pilot phase. The main reasons for this can be listed as follows:

◆ The AIJ emphasis on emission reductions: Africa is not in a position to benefit substantially.

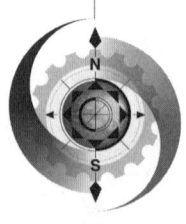

- AIJ relied largely on market forces: Africa's comparatively weak markets are not attractive to investors unless there is a longer-term incentive.

- The relative absence of the necessary administrative and technical infrastructures on the continent.

- The lack of a strategic vision on the continent concerning the potential benefits of AIJ.

Emphasis on emission reductions. For African countries, the crucial criterion for fulfilling their UNFCCC obligations, and therefore for certification, is that expressed in Paragraph 5(b) of Article 12: "real, measurable and long-term benefits related to the mitigation of climate change." As noted above, it is necessary to think in terms of avoided future emissions in Africa rather than emission reductions. With the emphasis on Northern reduction commitments in the UNFCCC, however, emission reduction has become the default option in climate change-related projects. Projects that reduce existing rather than *future* reductions are easier to grasp and quantify. In effect, this means that countries that cannot contribute to emission reductions will not be targeted for such projects. It is crucial that the Certified Emissions Reduction Units (CERUs) mentioned in the Kyoto Protocol include avoided future emissions.

> **Genuine sustainable development can be assured by placing the climate change issue in the context of African development policy, by dealing with it as a primarily regional (global) rather than national issue, and by directing the resources it offers towards building basic infrastructures.**

Market forces. Rather than relying on market forces that are presently weak, the process of encouraging sustainable development must involve stimulating the existing nascent markets and reinforcing the infrastructure (in terms of energy supply, transport and communications) to ensure the smoother operation and growth of the market. Private sector investment is crucial to both the African market and the CDM. The CDM will stimulate the flow of FDI if the necessary

incentives and procedures are put in place to allow it to operate as such a channel. Furthermore, the certification process of the CDM can assure investor confidence in the viability of projects undertaken. A well structured CDM can ensure that "win-win" scenarios are prioritised. However, in the short to medium term, private investments cannot substitute for ODA.

Infrastructural deficiencies. The development of strong and well conceived basic infrastructures, both technical and organisational, will have the greatest impact on the reduction of future emissions of the continent. Genuine sustainable development can be assured by placing the climate change issue in the context of African development policy, by dealing with it as a primarily regional (global) rather than national issue, and by directing the resources it offers towards building basic infrastructures. This is why the CDM is important for Africa: it can, as articulated, make a decisive contribution to sustainable development for the future.

Need for strategic vision. Despite widespread publicity, a certain amount of ignorance persists about the possibilities of the CDM in Africa, which renders a common position difficult. Informational resources are far weaker in Africa than elsewhere (Internet access, for instance, is approximately 1 in 5000 as opposed to 1 in 6 in the North). While progress has been made in informing and preparing African decision-makers – at the African Experts Workshop held in Dakar, May 1998, for example – construction of an effective CDM will require the informed participation of involved stakeholders. This is key to the cooperative spirit underpinning the Convention.

In the African context, a wide vision of the possibilities of mitigation must be taken. Strong interventions on behalf of the sustainable development of the continent will have the

immediate effect of lowering the baseline of future emissions scenarios. Conceiving of the situation in these terms will allow for the fulfilment of the dual objectives of the CDM, as well as stimulating private sector investment constructively. Questions then arise about the establishment of baselines and the measurement of developmental impact.

TWO MECHANISMS FOR NORTH-SOUTH COOPERATION: THE GEF AND THE CDM

While both the Global Environmental Facility (GEF) and the CDM are intended to promote North-South cooperation, they must be regarded separately. The GEF is a "mechanism for international co-operation for the purpose of providing new and additional, grant and concessional funding to finance programmes and projects that will achieve global environmental benefits" in the area of climate change among others. It has since "emerged as both a facilitator and a funding mechanism for integrating global environmental concerns into the developmental process." The First Conference of Parties (COP-1) designated its current priority area of activity: enabling activities focused on capacity building (Operational Strategy, GEF, 1996).

The GEF therefore exists to support projects that will allow developing countries to fulfil their obligations, often of a technical nature, according to the UNFCCC; to finance programmes and projects for adaptation to the effects of climate change; and also reduce the market barriers to the introduction of new technologies through high-risk projects. These roles must be maintained by the GEF, and must not become blurred by the essentially different objectives of mutual benefit behind the CDM. The GEF is supported by voluntary contributions and will never have the stability to take on major infrastructural development programmes (e.g. in transport, housing, or energy supply).

An important role that could be fulfilled by the GEF, however, is the carrying out of background studies and prospectives for developmental projects that could then be implemented through the CDM. By creating an enabling environment in developing countries, the GEF will also reduce the transaction costs of programmes that can later be funded through the CDM.

The CDM, on the other hand, is as yet undefined, and could operate on a quite different basis. It could provide several functions that, as we see from the above, are not yet covered, or insufficiently covered, by the GEF and AIJ. Most important among these will be its ability to support projects and programmes that promote greater North-South equity, and greater equity among developing nations. If it is well constructed, the CDM will be able to focus on sustainable development in developing countries through an emphasis on avoided future emissions, while also contributing to the emission reduction commitments of Annex I countries. Unlike AIJ, the CDM can operate on a *multilateral* basis. Another key difference, particularly for Africa, is the CDM's potential to focus on large, regionally based technical and organisational infrastructure projects that are outside the reach of GEF. These are the projects that will have the greatest impact on the future emissions of the continent.

The operations of the CDM must be separated from those of the GEF, in order to ensure financial autonomy. In addition, in order to avoid disparities, proposed AIJ and Joint Implementation programmes should be required to pass through the CDM certification process.

Three apparent roles can be pinpointed for the CDM at this stage:

As a certification body for transfer of emission credits. This is the most basic role, which will require a series of guidelines allowing the Executive Board to evaluate the developmental benefits of a given project in a host country alongside the emission credits of the same project in an industrialised country. Here the CDM can serve as a regulatory body to ensure transparency and standardisation of application and crediting.

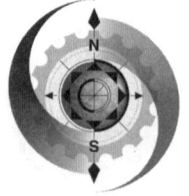

ISSUES&OPTIONS

The Clean
Development
Mechanism

As a project clearing house. The CDM can be imagined as a meeting point for those with projects and programmes to implement and those with the means to implement them. Projects could be submitted from either Northern or Southern private or public actors and matched through the CDM. Here a larger role could be envisaged in identifying and implementing the most appropriate programmes for the various different actors according to flexible criteria of overall objectives.

As a project coordinating body and funding agency (broker). In an expansion of the previous role, funds would be actively sought and accumulated through the CDM and projects and programmes actively elicited. The CDM would apply defined criteria to the acceptance of projects and the allocation of funds. Guidelines would be put in place to ensure an even geographical distribution of activities and finances, and to ensure that defined objectives are met in terms of both emission reduction and sustainable development and in accordance with an overall perspective of regional and global stakes.

In the first of these three roles, the CDM is little

more than an adjunct to AIJ: there is a standardisation of results, but essentially no safeguards of equity. The latter two roles would allow the CDM to function as multilateral body, which would give it considerably more flexibility than Joint Implementation and AIJ currently have, and allow it to focus also on sustainable development. However, without clear criteria for operation and a clear overview of the common motivation behind different programmes and projects, as is the case in the second role, it is difficult to see how the maximal potential for development would be realised.

Ideally the CDM should operate in the third role. A body that applies standards and criteria to the choice and efficiency of projects could assure equity. Such a body could ensure that equal weight is given to the aims of emission reductions and sustainable development; that avoided future emissions remain a priority in Africa and the developing world; that there is coherence among different projects in the same regions; and that funding is available for projects initiated in developing countries. Large-scale and regional infrastructure development projects could also be adopted by a coordinating and funding CDM.

DESIGNING THE CDM

In order to balance the interests of Annex I and non-Annex I countries and promote equity, the CDM needs to incorporate a number of key elements. These include regionalised quotas; carefully designed baselines; independence and transparency in the Executive Board and operational entities; careful selection of appropriate programmes and projects; and built-in incentives to ensure developing country participation. These elements are discussed in greater detail below.

Region-based quotas

In the interests of equity of access to the UNFCCC mechanisms, programmes and projects must be fairly distributed amongst regions. As indicated above, funding that passes

through the CDM will tend to be driven towards mitigation-based programmes in non-African countries unless a mechanism is specifically introduced to ensure that this is not the case. This bias can be avoided through a quota-based system (for instance, by specifying that a third of the projects are to be implemented on the African continent and/or within LDCs). African (and other developing) countries will then be able to commit themselves to the new mechanism in the full assurance that they will have the support they need to achieve infrastructural development. The same applies to the "share of the proceeds from certified project activities that is to be used to assist developing country Parties that are particularly vulnerable to the adverse effects of climate change to meet the costs of adaptation" (Article 12, paragraph 8). Adaptation financing

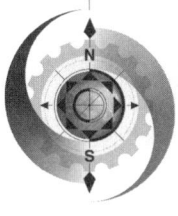

ISSUES&OPTIONS
The Clean
Development
Mechanism

should also be distributed regionally on a quota basis. These considerations may be included in the guidelines for the operation of the CDM at the COP/MOP or Executive Board stage.

Criteria for baselines

One of the essential elements of the CDM will be the definition of baselines, according to which the additionality of projects is to be measured and certification subsequently applied. Baselines may be configured according to a country or an individual project: in the former case they will show the greenhouse gas emissions of a host country according to a developmental path, which itself must be defined according to a given scenario.

How these scenarios are to be adopted is a thorny question. Are they to be based on the 1990 emission levels or on the projected levels of (say) 2010, which would be more informative but less accurate? Following the implementation of a project, is the original baseline to be maintained or is the (presumably lower) post-project baseline to be adopted? In an African country, for example, where emissions are currently low, are we to assume development according to current growth of Gross Domestic Product (GDP) and population, using available resources and technologies? A "business as usual" scenario would not necessarily imply large emissions growth. On the other hand, there are fears of the establishment of "inflated" baselines that would be in the interests of both the investing and host Parties, but not of the environment.[2] A predictive baseline model using economic and demographic growth (such as the Stockholm Environment Institute's PoleStar model) would undoubtedly be most accurate, but may be time-consuming and expensive. Furthermore, in many African countries much of the economic data necessary for such a prediction is simply unavailable. The demand for such criteria could easily operate as a block on CDM initiatives in African and other developing countries. Accurate measurement of national baselines should be seen rather as a long-term goal, to be achieved in parallel with the capacity building efforts to construct accurate national inventories.

The CDM will require a standard for baselines in order to fix the value of CERUs. In the meantime, following Michealowa (1998), we suggest that a combination of national and project-specific baselines be used. Thus, the baseline for constructing a new fuel-efficient power plant where there was none previously, should take into account the likelihood of the construction of a less efficient plant, but also the national demand for electricity and how it is to be met. The criteria for fixing baselines will need to be reviewed in any case after a first stage of projects have been implemented.

The Executive Board and the operational entities

The Executive Board will be the responsible body for drawing up guidelines for the operation of the CDM based on the directives of the COP/MOP, and for establishing the contractual conditions for the operational bodies. The neutrality and transparency of the Executive Board will be crucial in aligning the differing interests of the Parties concerned. The Board need not be large but should include a representation of more than fifty per cent of non-Annex I Parties to ensure that a veto is possible. The Board should also include environmental and non-governmental bodies. Operational bodies will be the implementing agencies of the mechanism and therefore they must be independent organs in the host countries. The guidelines governing their behaviour, particularly with regard to issuing certification and baseline delineation, must be explicit and applicable. With the establishment of explicit guidelines, there will be no need for excessive bureaucratisation or large administration costs.

Criteria for certification

Article 12 of the Kyoto Protocol refers to "certified emission reductions" (paragraph 3) and "certified project activities" (paragraph 6), but certification is not defined. CERs are the bread and butter of the CDM. Once a system of calculating CERs has been established, they will provide the essential incentive for private sector involvement. They will also form the

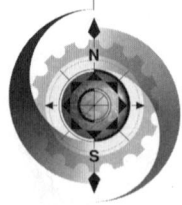

---

[2] *See Axel Michaelowa*, "Joint Implementation - The Baseline Issue," Global Environmental Change, *1998. Also see Axel Michaelowa and Michael Dutschke,* Interest groups and efficient design of the Clean Development Mechanism under the Kyoto Protocol, *HWWA Discussion Paper No. 58, Hamburg, March 1998.*

basis for emission credits for Annex I countries. It is not clear, however, how this framework is to benefit sustainable development or act as an incentive to developing countries. One suggestion allocates a share of the CERs resulting from a project to the host country, but the details are difficult to envisage, since a market for CERs does not yet exist, and the host countries do not have reduction commitments. Furthermore, the conversion of the mechanism into a simple form of paying off developing countries for their low emission potential (also referred to as cream-skimming) is precisely what the CDM was created in order to avoid.

We suggest, therefore, that *certified project activities*, as indicated in the protocol, can serve as a means of incorporating sustainability indicators into the certification process. A certified project activity would indicate the verifiable CERs of a project and also a number of other key indicators: technologies introduced; economic and social impact (jobs created, reduction of imports, revenue increases); environmental impacts (such as other pollutants, biodiversity, and water resources) coherence with national developmental objectives; and impact on HDI, among others. A project would only be certified if it reached a certain level, determined in advance, according to these parameters.

Once again, this raises the question of measurability and verifiability. To a certain extent, this may be resolved by relying on the procedures of the Subsidiary Body of Scientific and Technological Advice (SBSTA) and other bodies already involved in the measurement of data of this kind (such as UNDP and the World Bank). However, certification of a project could also incorporate the reliability and accuracy of the data presented. Such a broad notion of certification will ensure the optimal functioning of the CDM as it is intended: a mechanism for achieving a global objective through the concerted efforts and participation of a number of actors for their mutual benefit.

Guidelines for choosing programmes and projects

The success of the CDM, as well as the fulfilment of its potential to achieve the aims outlined above, will depend on the kind and breadth of programmes and projects that it supports. A number of basic elements can be identified as critical to this process.

First among these should be an emphasis on the basic energy-related infrastructure on the continent. Programmes that focus on energy use, energy provision and energy management should be prioritised as having the most immediate impact both on future emissions and on providing essential infrastructure for all the elements of development. Such programmes can be evaluated quickly and precisely – both in terms of emissions avoided and in terms of their concrete impact on development. Moreover, they are not difficult, in relative terms, to plan and execute, and can benefit from the experience of countries and regions worldwide. Support of the energy-related infrastructure will help to define a lifestyle for the future on the continent.

The next important element to be considered in CDM programmes is regional or sub-regional cooperation. Programmes are generally carried out on the national level, and may lead to a debilitating competition among individual nations rather than the cooperation that can bring huge benefits in terms of infrastructure. A regional emphasis will provide enormous opportunities in such areas as the transport sector, electricity provision, and even housing. Furthermore, projects that support the region will finally work towards the opening and development of African markets. The absence of reliable market conditions has also contributed to the paucity of AIJ projects on the continent. The CDM offers an opportunity to help create more reliable markets, and this can be achieved through a focus on infrastructural development on a regional basis. The idea of a "North-South-South triangle" is applicable here also: projects that have been successfully applied in one developing country could then be brought to another, via the first.

Examples of areas that would benefit enormously from such projects abound. A number of railway-lines, dating from colonial times, traverse sections of the continent, but have regressed in the thirty-plus years since independence. Their restitution and extension would provide an invaluable infrastructural resource in the region. Likewise, a major housing construction programme could take

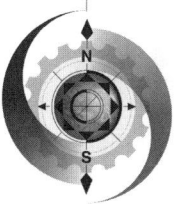

advantage of energy efficiencies and thus avoid future emissions. Such projects have been implemented on a small scale in certain countries, and the potential benefits of wide-spread dissemination in those countries, as well as on the continent at large, are enormous. Africa also possesses tremendous potential for natural gas and hydroelectric and solar power, the immense resources of which remain virtually untapped. Agricultural techniques are also in need of a major shift, from the traditional extensive systems (and the associated land-degradation) to intensive or mechanised systems, in order to increase labour efficiency and productive capacity. A large number of existing and potential large-scale interregional projects (such as regional power sharing – the delayed Manantali dam is an example) remain stalled for financial reasons.

Building incentives into the calculation of incremental costs

The question of equity in terms of the benefits of mutual projects can best be addressed at its root: the costs and distribution of benefits of projects. One of the central notions behind North-South AIJ was the low cost (in terms of labour, resources and overheads) of implementing projects in developing countries compared to industrialised countries. The CDM addresses a similar problem but from a different angle. The difference in the marginal cost (in dollars

per ton of greenhouse gas emissions avoided) of a similar project in the two areas frequently reaches a factor of 10 or more. These gains will be wholly available to the financing (Annex I) rather than the host (non-Annex I) country, unless a safeguard is put in place to ensure a more equal distribution. Indeed, the main advantage of a mechanism such as the CDM for Annex I countries is to achieve precisely this margin of cost-effectiveness in fulfilling their commitments. Clearly, a margin of cost-effectiveness must remain as an incentive to Annex I countries, but it is vital that a similar incentive be offered to developing countries to ensure their participation as equal partners.

In the pilot AIJ projects to date, the incremental cost per ton of greenhouse gases avoided or reduced in a collaborative project is calculated with reference to the host country, and the huge difference in cost is recovered by the financing country. An equitable distribution of the gains of such a project would require that the incremental cost in the financing country is also taken into account: this would give an intermediary cost baseline between the incremental cost of a ton of greenhouse gas emissions avoided in the Annex I country and in the non-Annex I country. The CDM could act as a regulatory body to ensure this equity, which would allow non-Annex I countries to benefit from collaborative programmes as much as Annex I countries.

CONCLUSION: WHAT PROSPECTS FOR AFRICA?

Having outlined the potential opportunities for Africa presented by the climate change negotiations in general and the CDM in particular, we can answer the question posed in the title, "What Prospects for Africa?" The CDM can, if properly designed, make a decisive contribution to sustainable development on that continent.

The primary potential benefit of a well-constructed CDM for Africa will be the possibility of implementing large-scale infrastructural development projects and programmes. Second, the CDM could act as a driving force for regional cooperation in Africa. To achieve sustainable development and avoid potential

future greenhouse gas emissions, Africa's top priority is the development of regionally based technical and organisational infrastructures. Whereas the other mechanisms put forward to address climate change (GEF and AIJ) have not been adequate to address this priority, the CDM has the potential to do so. The stated objective of sustainable development for host countries must be prioritised if this is to happen, and equity must be a primary consideration in the construction of the CDM. Guidelines and the criteria for certification and the establishment of baselines must be set forth so as to reflect the differing interests of the Parties involved and align their objectives. ■

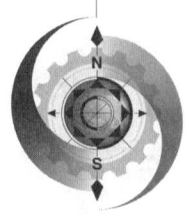

ISSUES&OPTIONS
The Clean Development Mechanism

Chapter 10

PRACTICAL APPROACHES IN THE ENERGY SECTOR

Robert Hamwey and Francisco Szekely
International Academy of the Environment
Geneva, Switzerland

Summary: As a framework for cooperative implementation of greenhouse gas emission reduction projects between industrialised and developing countries, the Clean Development Mechanism (CDM) aims to protect the climate system while also supporting wider sustainable development goals. Ongoing development of the CDM is guided by requirements for it defined in Article 12 of the recently negotiated Kyoto Protocol. Specifically, CDM projects must demonstrate additionality of emissions reductions and promote sustainable development. Furthermore, financing and crediting for projects must be equitably managed. With particular focus given to projects in the energy sector, we examine some of the main issues and problems facing the international community as it strives to build a CDM and discuss practical options that can be used to address them in a sustainable and equitable manner. Options presented include: a simplified and transparent framework to define and use project baselines; a surplus credit system providing emission reduction credits to countries hosting projects; a proposal that sustainable development screens be established to filter prospective projects; and a hybrid model of financing that facilitates both bilateral and multilateral approaches to project selection and investment.

INTRODUCTION

The Kyoto Protocol recently opened new opportunities for Joint Implementation activities by parties to the United Nations Framework Convention on Climate Change (UNFCCC).[1] Under the auspices of the Clean Development Mechanism (CDM), the Protocol permits Annex I Parties (mainly industrialised countries that may act as sponsors) and non-Annex I parties (developing countries that may act as hosts) to jointly conduct greenhouse gas emission reduction projects. Aiming to supervise projects meeting criteria for eligibility and certification to be agreed upon multilaterally, the CDM represents a framework for jointly implemented projects between industrialised and developing countries. It thus serves as a governance mechanism; its projects are essentially CDM-governed Joint Implementation projects, or simply CDM projects.

Negotiators will develop CDM rules and procedures at future UNFCCC sessions. In the meantime, a variety of stakeholders seek to ensure that the CDM is built to respond to their needs. Many want it to become an efficient and equitable mechanism that can successfully address and arbitrate long-standing concerns associated with Joint Implementation, such as additionality,

[1] *See the following JI review articles: Reinhard Loske and Sebastian Oberthür, "Joint Implementation under the Climate Change Convention," in* International Environmental Affairs, Vol. 6, No. 1 *(1994); Jyoti Parikh, "Joint Implementation and North-South Cooperation for Climate Change," in* International Environmental Affairs, Vol. 7, No. 1 *(1995); Anne Arquit Niederberger and Marie-Thérèse Niggli, "Un nouvel instrument de politique environnementale: la «joint implementation»," in* La vie économique – Revue de politique économique, *(Bern: OFIAMPT, 1997); and L. D. Danny Harvey and Elizabeth Bush, "Joint Implementation: An Effective Strategy for Global Warming," in* Environment Vol. 39, No. 8 (1997).

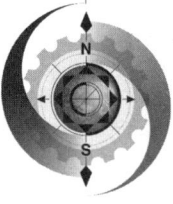

benefit sharing, and sustainability.[2] Can such a CDM be developed? Enthusiasts are optimistic that it can be. The result would be a CDM that fosters broad international cooperation in sustainable development and does more for the world than simply reducing global emissions.

Little can be said of what the CDM is today. It remains a mere framework to be elaborated in future negotiations of the parties. However, a great deal can be said of what it should become, and in this paper we will examine major unresolved issues surrounding the CDM and explore options to address them.

REQUIREMENTS FOR THE CDM

The CDM should be a mechanism that objectively and equitably fulfils the purposes and functions ascribed to it in Article 12 of the Kyoto Protocol.[3] Below, we review key requirements for the CDM outlined in Article 12 and discuss issues that must be managed by CDM modalities, procedures, and criteria for project eligibility and certification.

The nature of CDM projects

With numerous greenhouse gases and a wide range of associated economic activities, various types of emission offset projects can be conceived. We limit our discussion here to the principal class of offset projects: carbon offset projects. These projects either reduce carbon dioxide (CO_2) emissions from facilities that burn fossil fuel to generate electricity, heat, and/or other forms of power, or they sequester atmospheric CO_2 through enhanced forest sinks.[4]

Although carbon offset projects of both types make up over 70 Joint Implementation projects currently underway in the pilot phase of Activities Implemented Jointly (AIJ), the Protocol's Article 12 indicates that the CDM

only authorises projects resulting in "certified emissions reductions."[5,6] The Article makes no mention of projects resulting in an enhancement of sinks, i.e. afforestation or reforestation projects. Was this restrictive wording drafted intentionally? Some argue it was not and that carbon sequestration projects remain valid as CDM activity.[7] However, others insist the restriction was intentional to ensure the CDM promotes clean "development" benefiting from the transfer and use of clean technologies; otherwise, they say, the CDM would favour a transfer of trees that might further limit development options by locking host countries into long-term commitments to maintain limiting land use patterns.[8] Supporting this claim, AIJ experience shows that, on average, the costs for sink projects in the forestry sector (US $18/tC) are significantly less than those for emission reductions in the energy sector (US $136/tC) on an equivalent carbon offset basis (i.e., per tonne of carbon sequestered or reduced).[9] Because of this cost differential, CDM sponsors would likely prefer to secure CDM offsets through sink projects over technology projects if sink projects were CDM-eligible. In view of these considerations, it is uncertain if negotiators will agree that CDM

---

[2] See Note 1

[3] See United Nations, "Kyoto Protocol to the United Nations Framework Convention on Climate Change," document FCCC/CP/1997/L.7/Add.1, (Geneva: UN, 1997).

[4] CO_2 emissions from fossil fuel consumption contribute to roughly half of the global warming potential. See Intergovernmental Panel on Climate Change, Second Assessment Report of the IPCC (Cambridge: Cambridge University Press, 1995).

[5] "Activities Implemented Jointly Under the Pilot Phase: Update on Activities Implemented Jointly," document FCCC/SBSTA/1998/INF.3, (Geneva: UN, 1998).

[6] No similar limitation is placed on Joint Implementation between Annex I parties.

[7] Refer to discussions in Session 8 of the SBSTA, Bonn, June, (1998).

[8] Philippe Cullet and Annie Patricia Kameri-Mbote, "Activities Implemented Jointly in the Forestry Sector: Conceptual and Operational Fallacies", in The Georgetown International Environmental Law Review, X, 1, (1997).

[9] Michael Ridley, Lowering the cost of emission reduction: Joint implementation in the Framework Convention on Climate Change, (Dordrecht: Kluwer, 1998).

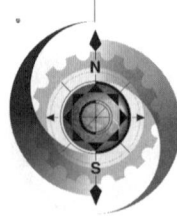

projects may include offset projects involving carbon sequestration. Only future negotiations can answer this question.

Keeping in mind the long-term nature of the Climate Change Convention, a phased approach to CDM implementation may represent an attractive option to UNFCCC parties. In a first phase, CDM projects may be limited to a class or classes of offset projects that are most attractive to potential host countries and for which certification can be most readily effected. Emission reduction projects involving a specified greenhouse gas such as CO_2, and taking place within a specified sector such as the energy sector, could be selected for the first phase of CDM implementation. In later phases – as CDM experience is accumulated and methodologies needed to certify other project types are developed – other classes of projects, including sequestration projects, might qualify for the CDM.

> In a first phase, CDM projects may be limited to a class or classes of offset projects that are most attractive to potential host countries and for which certification can be most readily effected.

Measurably additional emission reductions

The underlying rationale for the CDM is the encouragement of *bona fide* emissions reductions where marginal mitigation costs are lowest in order to promote a highly efficient international allocation of capital to mitigate climate change. As required by Article 12, this can be achieved for CDM projects that result in:

◆ real, measurable, and long-term climate change mitigation benefits

◆ emission reductions that are additional to any that would occur in the absence of project activity – a condition known as 'additionality'.

In order to ensure these conditions are met by projects, there is a need to both measure a project's emissions (technically feasible through monitoring) and compare these against the emissions baseline that would have

occurred in the project's absence (difficult to estimate accurately). Modalities and procedures for baseline definition thus remain critical to determinations of the additionality and advancement of the CDM.

An equitable mechanism for cooperative implementation

According to Article 12, the purpose of the CDM is to assist developing countries in achieving sustainable development and in contributing to the Convention's ultimate objective, and to assist Annex I parties in achieving compliance with their emission reduction commitments. CDM projects must thus:

◆ provide a level of credit flow to industrialised countries sponsoring project activity

◆ meet agreed upon criteria for sustainable development

◆ provide a level of *"enabling"* financing to developing countries hosting project activity.

The CDM must define modalities and procedures that can ensure project selection and implementation will satisfy each of these above objectives. Accomplishing this, CDM modalities should aim to produce win-win transactions, wherein each partner makes appropriate contributions to a project while receiving an attractive sharing of project benefits.

Credit sharing

Industrialised countries, and a wide range of public and private actors based within them, support the CDM because it provides them with a flexible option to effect new legally binding emission reductions at marginal costs lower than those available domestically. Their investment in projects is made when credit for reductions directly attributable to their investments can be accrued and used to meet domestic

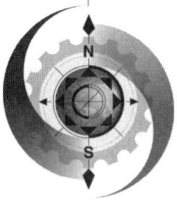

commitments. They therefore require that the CDM provide credits to compensate the additional financing they will provide to projects. On the other hand, some developing countries have argued that as participants hosting CDM projects – and indeed making them possible – that a portion of credits yielded by a project be apportioned to them. They could either sell such credits in global markets, or possibly use them against their own future emission reduction commitments. The CDM will thus have the difficult task of developing appropriate modalities to ensure equitable credit sharing occurs without significantly diminishing the magnitude of credit incentives that motivate potential project sponsors to finance CDM projects.

Supplementarity

As a related equity concern, developing countries have long sought to place limits on industrialised countries' ability use the CDM to meet national commitments by requiring supplemental domestic actions. It is specifically mentioned in Article 12 that Annex I sponsors of CDM projects may use CDM credits to contribute to compliance with only *"part of"* their quantified emission limitation and reduction commitments (QELRCs) under the Protocol. The CDM might thus seek to ensure that supplementarity (at an agreed level) is demonstrated before CDM credits can be used by industrialised countries to meet their QELRCs.

Sustainable development

The CDM should develop criteria for project eligibility that ensure projects promote sustainable development. At the host country level, a range of non-climate related environmental criteria as well as economic and social criteria should be met by CDM projects. Too many criteria may obstruct project development and overly restrict a host country's choice in serving its national priorities; too few criteria may permit highly profitable yet unsustainable projects to go forward. The CDM must carefully

> **CDM modalities should aim to produce win-win transactions, wherein each partner makes appropriate contributions to a project while receiving an attractive sharing of project benefits.**

balance its aim to ensure sustainable development with the need to build open and robust CDM markets.

Project financing

Developing countries have accepted the CDM because they see it as a significant means to promptly acquire modern technologies needed to support enhanced development paths. Two options are available to govern how financing will be transacted for CDM projects. Project financing could take place through pooled investments to be globally managed and allocated by an oversight committee (multilateral approach), or it could occur through direct sponsor-host transactions at the project level (bilateral approach). Although promoting equity and spreading risk, the former option might result in a slow and overly bureaucratic apparatus, unattractive to many potential project sponsors and hosts. However, the latter option, although fostering competition, may result in investments flowing only to those host countries with strong capacities to identify and market projects while neglecting more attractive, yet unidentified, projects in countries lacking such capacities.

The successful development of a vigorous and efficient CDM market will likely depend on whether a multilateral or bilateral approach to project financing is adopted by the CDM. Article 12 specifically states that the CDM *"shall assist in arranging funding"* of project activities *"as necessary."* AIJ experience indicates that in many instances such assistance is not necessary. For various political and economic reasons, however, some developing countries were unsuccessful in attracting sponsors for viable projects within the AIJ pilot phase. Thus for CDM project financing, a hybrid model employing a mix both bilateral and multilateral approaches may be needed. It could allow free-market bilateral deals to proceed unimpeded while at the same time providing a multilateral mechanism to assist those host countries unable to independently attract sponsors to valid CDM projects.

Key issues to address

We have outlined above some of the main issues related to the development of the CDM: baselines and additionality, credit sharing, supplementarity, sustainable development, and project financing. In the remainder of this chapter, we will discuss innovative options that may represent attractive approaches to addressing these issues. Emphasis is placed throughout on identifying options that are universal, objective, equitable, and easy to both apply and evaluate. We focus on defining issues and describing options as they relate to future CDM projects to reduce CO_2 emissions in the energy sector, and more specifically, for power generation activity (Figure 1). Energy sector projects are expected to represent a major class of CDM projects, and as mentioned above, a potential class of project to be implemented early if CDM activity assumes a gas- and sector-specific phased implementation.

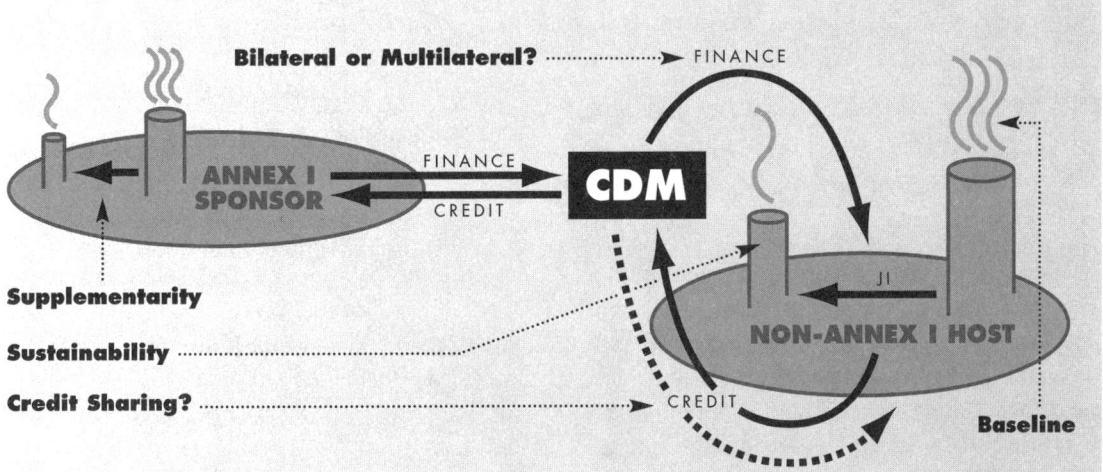

Figure 1. CDM governed Joint Implementation Projects in the Energy Sector transform a 'baseline' facility into a CDM facility of equal utility but lowered emissions. Issues to be resolved include baselines, credit sharing, supplementarity, sustainability, and the mode of project financing – bilateral or multilateral.

BASELINES AND ADDITIONALITY

The most prominent project criterion set forth by the CDM is the requirement that CDM activities must pass an additionality test, in other words, that they must bring about *"real, measurable, and long-term benefits related to the mitigation of climate change resulting in emission reductions that are additional to any that would occur in the absence of certified project activity."* The CDM must provide a consistent, systematic, and objective framework whereby these project assessments can be made.

For CDM projects in the energy sector involving the replacement of an existing facility by one with higher efficiency, or the retrofitting of an existing facility, additionality is readily demonstrated by comparing CO_2 emissions of two real facilities.[10] Additionality is more difficult to demonstrate for CDM projects that involve replacing a purportedly planned facility that does not exist. In the latter case, additionality could be assessed on a project-by-project basis by validating that a real CDM project's CO_2 emissions are less than those arising from a virtual baseline project that would have been implemented in the absence of CDM project activity. Here, difficulty in assessing additionality centres on estimating

[10] *Edward Parson and Karen Fisher-Vanden,* Joint Implementation and its Alternatives: Choosing Systems to Distribute Global Emissions Abatement and Finance, *Belfer Center for Science and International Affairs, John F. Kennedy School of Government (Cambridge: Harvard University, 1997).*

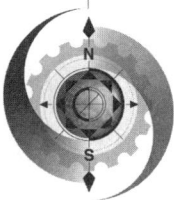

baselines – since baseline projects are counter-factual, baselines cannot be objectively determined.[11]

Observable baselines

For CDM projects in the energy sector, use of an *observable baseline framework* outlined below can remove the uncertainties associated with baselines.[12] Unlike current approaches to defining baselines, observable baselines are calculated from *"observable"* data – a country's existing energy and emissions data – and not from the particularities of a hypothetical baseline project.

Current approaches to the baseline problem infer what a business-as-usual project's greenhouse gas emissions might be on a project by project basis. In contrast, the observable baseline framework assumes that, at any given time, the baseline emissions for any project is simply an extension of nationally averaged current emissions to energy production in the host country.[13] In the energy sector, the CDM project baseline is simply the host country's *national emission factor* Ω: the sector average of CO_2 emissions with respect to energy generated in the year t_o just prior to year t_o+1 of a CDM project's certification:

$$\Omega(t_0) = \textit{national emission factor in year } t_o = \left(\frac{\textit{total annual emissions of } CO_2}{\textit{total annual energy generated}} \right)_{\text{energy sector}}$$

$$= \textit{observable baseline for use in year } t_o + 1$$

where total annual CO_2 emissions and energy generated derive only from fossil fuel combustion, and not from nuclear or renewable, facilities.[14] This restriction is made to ensure a level playing field for various countries with different access potentials to nuclear and renewable energy sources. Additionally, to ensure that technical progress is reflected in the observable baseline, only the top tier of highest efficiency ranking facilities are included in the calculation (Figure 2). The observable baseline thus calculated, remains fixed over the CDM project's lifetime.

Within this framework, baseline emissions of a project are uniquely determined based on real projects that a country has already implemented, rather than any uncertain or subjective assumption

of projects that might be implemented in the future. For both a sponsoring industrialised country D, and hosting developing country d, respective values of national emission factors Ω (i.e., Ω_D and Ω_d) can be calculated from emissions data on existing power generation facilities accounted for in national inventories.[15,16] Furthermore, for any given CDM project to be implemented in host country d – a "real" project with known technical and operational characteristics – its ratio of CO_2 emissions to energy generated or project emission factor, ω_{CDM}, is readily approximated in advance. It can be used to estimate future emission offsets of the project. Once the project is in place, ω_{CDM} can be calculated using actual data for any year t of its operation:

$$\omega_{CDM}(t) = \textit{project emission factor in year } t = \left(\frac{\textit{total annual project emissions of } CO_2}{\textit{total annual project energy generated}} \right)$$

[11] *Joel Swisher, "Joint Implementation under the UN Framework Convention on Climate Change: Technical and Institutional Challenges," in* Mitigation and Adaptation Strategies for Global Change, 2, (1997).

[12] *Robert Hamwey, "A Sustainable Framework for Joint Implementation" in* International Environmental Affairs, Vol. 10, No. 2, (1998).

[13] *A floor for facility power generation capacities to be included in the average is needed, since data for smaller facilities (such as those in buildings, small factories, and remote communities) are not easily available and difficult to estimate. In many settings, 1 MW could provide a suitable floor.*

[14] *Alternatively, an N year running average of annual emissions to annual energy production could be used to flush out annual emission anomalies resulting from year-to-year fluctuations in weather, economic activity, and corresponding changes in load patterns and fuel mixes.*

[15] *To ensure that all numerical calculations are comparable, emissions are expressed in kilograms of carbon, energies in MWh, and emission factors in kg of carbon per MWh. Furthermore, to simplify details of the calculations, we use a zero project lead-time assumption; i.e., it is assumed that a CDM project certified in year t becomes operational in the same year.*

[16] *Under current UNFCCC reporting requirements, however, national greenhouse gas inventories only report data on total emissions of greenhouse gases from stationary energy generation sources, and not data on total energy generated. The latter data are also needed to calculate national emission factors.*

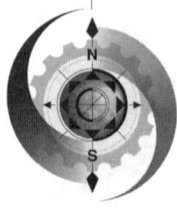

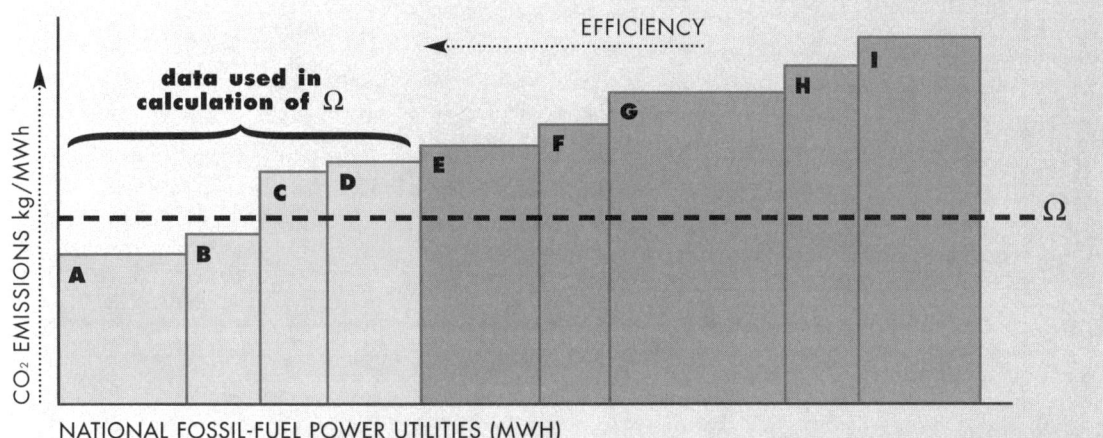

Figure 2. Calculations of the national emission factor or national baseline, W, include only the top 'production weighted' tier (or other agreed subset) of efficiency ranked facilities. In the figure, the calculation for W is made based on data from facilities A – D and not from the lower efficiency facilities E – I. Restricting data for the calculation in this way ensures that technical progress is incorporated into evolving values of Ω. In any given year, new facilities from the previous year's CDM projects would be incorporated into Ω, whereas any newly established highly emissive non-CDM facilities would not. The restriction thus blocks any perverse incentive a host country might have to inflate its national baseline by establishing new highly emissive facilities in parallel with low emission facilities established through CDM engagements.

Emission reductions attributable to the project over its lifetime are:

$$\Delta = \sum_{t_0+1}^{\tau+t_0+1} e_{CDM}(t)\left(\Omega_d(t_o) - \omega_{CDM}(t)\right)$$

where $e_{CDM}(t)$ is the energy generated by the CDM project in year t, the project start date is in year t_o+1, and t is the project's lifetime.

Assuming a 100 MW facility runs at X % capacity in each year of its Y year lifetime, emissions avoided, Δ, are readily estimated to be:

$$\Delta = \left(\Omega_d - \omega_{CDM}\right)\frac{kg}{MWh} \times \underbrace{100\,MW \times X\%}_{e_{CDM}} \times Y\,yrs \times \left(\frac{8760\,h}{yrs}\right)$$

With Δ thus determined, certification, implementation, and monitoring could proceed.[17] Other CDM projects also certified in the same year would use the same previous year's national emission factor as a baseline. At year end, all certified projects, as well as all non-CDM-related activity occurring during the year, would be culled together and used to adjust the sectoral inventory for the subsequent year. This would give a new (likely lower) value of Ω_d for use as the following year's observable baseline.

Observable baselines are dynamic in the sense that they change from year to year reflecting changes in a country's energy sector infrastructure over time. Projects implemented in the future will use the future observable baseline existing at the time they seek CDM certification. It is important to note, however, that once a project is certified the baseline against which emissions over its lifetime are measured is fixed to the observable baseline existing at its certification date. Baseline certainty is thus secured by hosts and sponsors over the entire

---

[17] *The CDM would necessarily need to objectively monitor w and X on a yearly basis in order to calculate D.*

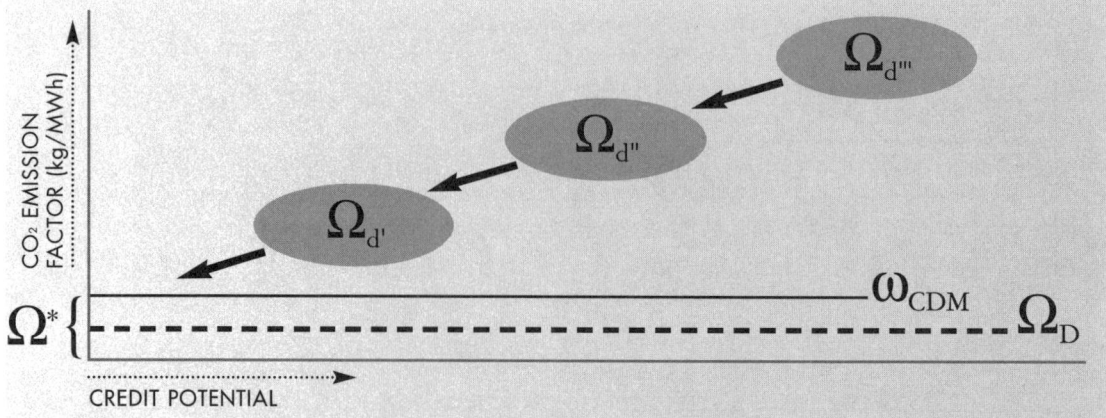

Figure 3. For a sponsor country D with a national emission factor Ω_D, a CDM project with emission factor ω_{CDM} would yield a varying quantity of emission reduction credits depending on the host country d where the project is implemented. It is assumed that CDM projects will involve state-of-the-art technologies widely used in country D, thus the value of wCDM is in the neighbourhood of WD. The figure shows three host countries d', d", and d''' with increasing national emission factors. The CDM project shown is most attractive in country d''' and least attractive d'. Market forces to lower national emission factors in d', d", and d''', whose magnitude and direction are indicated by the vectors, would result in convergence over time of W in countries d', d", and d''' towards Ω^*, the average value of Ω in sponsoring countries.

lifetime of the project permitting investment decisions to be made.[18]

Observable baselines and sustainable development

Observable baselines dynamically evolve in a way that ensures many sustainable development objectives are met by CDM activity. Sustainable development criteria inherently met by the framework include:

True mitigation in a host country d: For the project to qualify as a CDM project and generate offset credits, it must provide an improvement to a host country's national emission factor (i.e., its observable baseline). Meeting this criterion in year t requires $\omega_{CDM}(t) < \Omega_d(t)$. Because the national emission factor is used as the baseline, viable CDM projects automatically represent improvements on existing emission performance in the host country.

Dynamically directing CDM investments to countries where energy efficiency is lowest: The framework would drive global energy efficiency by making CDM most attractive in countries where overall sector efficiencies are lowest (Figure 3). It would thus direct investment flows to developing countries where emission reductions are most needed (those with the highest sectoral average emissions).[19] This process would then repeat itself as the years pass until such point that national emission factors for all countries converge to a common level where marginal mitigation costs in host countries would be in equilibrium with marginal mitigation and/or emission costs (e.g., the cost of emissions permits or taxes) in sponsor countries.

Promoting action to reduce emissions earlier rather than later and encouraging prompt technology transfer: Because evolving CDM activity in a host country acts to lower its national emission factor over time, the greatest emission reduction credits are accrued in the initial years of the CDM regime before rounds of additional CDM activity significantly lower host country baselines. Thus, an early participation mechanism is automatically present in this framework. Prompt global technology transfer would thereby be encouraged.

---

[18] *Elsewhere in the literature, the term 'dynamic' baseline is often used to describe a baseline that, for a given project, is adjusted, and thus changes, periodically during the project lifetime. Project hosts and sponsors have no certainty on what baseline will be used for a given project in future periods of the project's lifetime making investment decisions difficult.*

[19] *Assuming all other factors – political, economic, etc. – are equal. In general this would not be the case because project financing includes a range of non-CDM offset elements which also strongly influence investment attractiveness.*

Ease and transparency of implementation:
Averaged emissions are readily and accurately calculated based on the most recent national baseline inventory reported to the UNFCCC. Once a new project is realised, average sector emissions are appropriately adjusted in an evolving manner as each year's projects are subsequently included in revised baseline inventories for the following year.

Lowered transaction costs: High transaction costs associated with CDM projects are a serious threat to the emergence of a CDM market. Costs associated with assessments of additionality for potential projects are a major component of these costs. Since the observable baseline framework readily provides a unique baseline for all projects of any size, feasibility evaluations of potential projects can proceed rapidly and at minimal cost. Overall transaction costs of a resulting CDM project would thereby be reduced.

Assuring that projects are cost-effective: By adding an additional eligibility criterion to CDM projects measured against observable baselines, projects can be guaranteed to be cost-effective. Specifically, if during any year $t = t_0+1$ a project, between a developed country D and a developing country d, is eligible as CDM if and only if: $\omega_{CDM}(t) < \Omega_D(t)$. The project must then not only represent a performance improvement in the host country, but it must also be a project that, if implemented in the sponsor country, would also represent an improvement to the sponsor's national performance. Such a project could provide emission reductions in the sponsor or host country, and sponsors would seek to implement it where it would be most cost-effective. If the project is proposed as CDM, it would by default be more cost-effective

to implement in the host country than in the sponsor country, and cost-effectiveness of the CDM project could thus be assured.

The observable baseline framework outlined above is conceptually simple: managing a CDM transaction in the energy sector using emission factors of the host country, sponsor country, and the proposed CDM project. By virtue of this simplicity, the framework has many attractive features at the project level of a CDM transaction and at the global level of the CDM regime.

At the project level, the observable baseline is simply the host country emission factor, a quantity calculated from the country's aggregate energy and emissions data. Requiring only these two data as input, each of which can be accurately determined, observable baseline calculations are easily performed and results easily reproduced. In contrast to other approaches, since calculations do not make reference to future events, baseline uncertainties are reduced. If relevant data were to be included in national reporting requirements under the UNFCCC, the framework could provide a credible and transparent approach to baseline determinations that could be applied universally in any project setting.

At the global level, because additionality is assessed relative to the host country's national emissions performance, and project eligibility conditions can be placed on sponsor country's national emissions performance, the framework forces CDM activity to generate global environmental benefits, prompt action and technology transfer, lowered transaction costs, and cost-effectiveness. These features respond to many of the sustainable development and international equity objectives sought by the international community as it develops a workable CDM that is acceptable to all stakeholders.

CREDIT SHARING AND SUPPLEMENTARITY

Despite advances made in Kyoto, Convention negotiators must still elaborate how CDM transactions shall be equitably governed. Specifically, parties require that the CDM

should provide an equitable distribution of benefits to project partners and should not become a means by which industrialised countries shift their responsibility for domestic

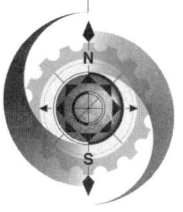

reductions to developing countries.[20]

Most generally, Joint Implementation is characterised by a symmetry between parties – two countries voluntarily work together to meet the commitments of one or both through joint mitigation projects. This symmetry is broken for Joint Implementation transactions between industrialised and developing countries due to their differentiated responsibilities and commitments under the Convention. While these require that CDM financing be assumed by industrialised countries, they need not require, as is often assumed, that emission reduction credits flow exclusively to industrialised countries since developing countries have no current commitments.

Developing countries will likely have to assume emission reduction commitments as their economies grow; thus credits acquired for CDM participation today could provide them with significant and deserved future benefit. Indeed, CDM credit flows should be an economic imperative for developing countries since most low-cost mitigation domestic options will be exploited in initial years of CDM activity, leaving only high-cost options available when they confront future commitments. These costly options will be no different from those industrialised countries seek to avoid tackling today through Joint Implementation and CDM.

The Intergovernmental Panel on Climate Change underlines that "equity concerns both *process* issues and *outcomes* in terms of the distribution of costs and benefits internationally."[21] Therefore, in the context of the CDM, not only should the process be equitable – which developing countries have contested since industrialised countries may overly exploit CDM to avoid domestic actions – but further its outcomes should be equitable, with a fair sharing of project benefits.

> **A project sustainability screening procedure can ensure that projects, which are otherwise eligible for the CDM, will generate environmental, social, and economic benefits.**

Integrating equity into CDM projects remains a primary task of the CDM, which aims to assist developing countries in contributing to the Convention's ultimate objective – the stabilisation of greenhouse gas concentrations through emission reductions. For industrialised countries, the Protocol defines a CDM that generates CDM credits and authorises their use in meeting commitments. Strikingly, no mention is made of credit acquisition and future use by developing countries. If indeed the CDM is meant to assist developing countries in contributing to climate change mitigation, it should include provisions to credit their efforts. CDM credits would provide a powerful incentive for their enhanced participation in near-term mitigation activity. Furthermore, although the Protocol states that sponsor countries may utilise CDM credits to contribute to meeting 'part of' their QELRCs, the Protocol fails to quantify this "supplementarity" constraint.

A surplus matched crediting system

New thinking is needed for the CDM to successfully address credit sharing and supplementarity issues.[22] We propose a surplus matched crediting system for the CDM to address these issues. For a CDM project resulting in a CO_2 equivalent emission reduction of X tons, and a surplus credit parameter $\alpha < 1$, the system would allocate a total credit of $X + \alpha X$ tons. X tons would then be distributed to the industrialised sponsor country and the artificial surplus of αX tons to the developing host country. Both could redeem acquired CDM credits against commitments only when matched by equivalent domestic reductions. With provisions that such credits can not be sold or transferred, they would have value only to the recipient country when domestic actions are pursued. Alternatively, provisions for

---

[20] *Many review articles on JI describe these and other barriers to JI's acceptance. See for example references cited in note 1.*

[21] *Intergovernmental Panel on Climate Change,* Second Assessment Report of the IPCC, *Cambridge University Press, (1995).*

[22] *Robert Hamwey and Christine Batruch, "Reducing Global Emissions Equitably", submitted,* Environment, *(1998).*

trading credits could be made – for example; any recipient country could trade credits only when it is engaged in a commitment period.

Such a crediting system could promote equitable credit sharing since both sponsors and hosts receive an apportionment of credits with a greater share flowing to sponsors to compensate their financing of the project. Exactly how much credit would flow to project hosts? This depends on the value of a employed in the system – a value to be set by the CDM. Additionally, by requiring that CDM credits be matched 1:1 by domestic reductions, the system could ensure supplementarity at a level of at least 50 per cent for all countries. Matching requirements other than 1:1 could be used to strengthen or relax this constraint.

The most attractive feature of a surplus matched crediting system is that it provides increased incentive for prompt emission reductions, while maintaining current incentives perceived by project sponsors. Credit acquisition could induce a wider range of potential project hosts to participate in

> **CDM projects must address local and regional environmental concerns that now play an increasing role in energy sector decision-making.**

early CDM activity. The system is not unlike marketing mechanisms that generate increased proceeds in commercial applications – double bonus mileage for air travel, double coupons in supermarkets – by inducing increased consumption of a good by consumers.

If econometric models indicate surplus crediting can generate sufficiently enhanced CDM participation, global CDM emission reductions could be considerably greater than those achieved using single crediting approaches. As an example, suppose $\alpha = 1/2$ is employed in a surplus matched crediting system leading to an increase in the level of global CDM activity from X1 tons of emission reductions under a single crediting system to a level X2 (see Figure 4). Then, provided X2 is at least twice the value of X1, long-term global mitigation levels would be enhanced. Thus, although some may argue that surplus credits could artificially lower reductions required by parties, they could likely result in a level global of CDM activity that more than compensates for lowered reduction requirements perceived at the party level.

SUSTAINABLE DEVELOPMENT

The CDM aims not only to mitigate climate change but also to promote *"clean development."* In other words, to promote a type of development that is compatible with environmental, social, and economic systems in a sustainable fashion over time. Many developing countries have been cautious about fully supporting Joint Implementation in the past, and the CDM today, because it is not clear to them that projects within these schemes will necessarily promote sustainable development in host countries. Accordingly, developing country willingness to enter vigorously into CDM partnerships as hosts will not materialise unless

their concerns over project sustainability are satisfactorily addressed.[23] In particular, they must be assured that the CDM provides them with prompt tangible benefits supporting sustainable development.

An operational framework could be developed to ensure that all CDM projects could achieve this goal. But should sustainable development criteria be used in selecting potential CDM projects? Some host governments might consider judgements of project sustainability to be within their domain as they assess prospective projects against national priorities. External

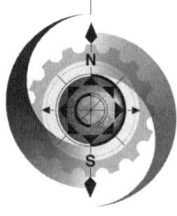

ISSUES&OPTIONS
The Clean
Development
Mechanism

---

[20] *For a discussion of these concerns, see Jyoti Parikh, "Joint Implementation and North-South Cooperation for Climate Change," in* International Environmental Affairs, *Vol. 7, No. 1 (1996), and R. Shakespeare Maya, "Joint Implementation: Cautions and Options for the South," in* The Feasibility of Joint Implementation, *ed. Catrinius Jepma, (Dordrecht: Kluwer, 1995).*

evaluations of project sustainability by a central CDM body – perhaps its executive board – may be perceived by these host governments as an interference with national decision-making. However, long-term (25-50 year) project sustainability may not figure highly among national priorities in some countries with overriding short-term economic objectives. Thus, some form of central sustainability screening will likely be required under the CDM, despite likely objections from certain quarters.

The CDM should establish specific sustainable development criteria to be met by prospective projects to ensure that only those projects that promote sustainable development are accepted for the CDM. A project sustainability screening procedure can ensure that projects, which are otherwise eligible for the CDM, will generate environmental, social, and economic benefits. It employs a combined series of three sequential sustainability screens to evaluate candidate CDM projects:

Assessing the environmental impacts of projects

Environmental sustainability will be achieved by projects that generate net environmental benefits that can be sustained over time. Any prospective project that reduces greenhouse gas emissions but also generates undesirable environmental side effects would be excluded from the CDM.

Assessing the social aspects of projects

Social sustainability will be achieved when a CDM project enhances the welfare of the local population, and at the national level, improves living standards through the services it provides and enhances commercial activity through project-related activities.

Assessing economic benefits and costs associated with projects

Economic sustainability will be achieved by projects that are commercially and economically

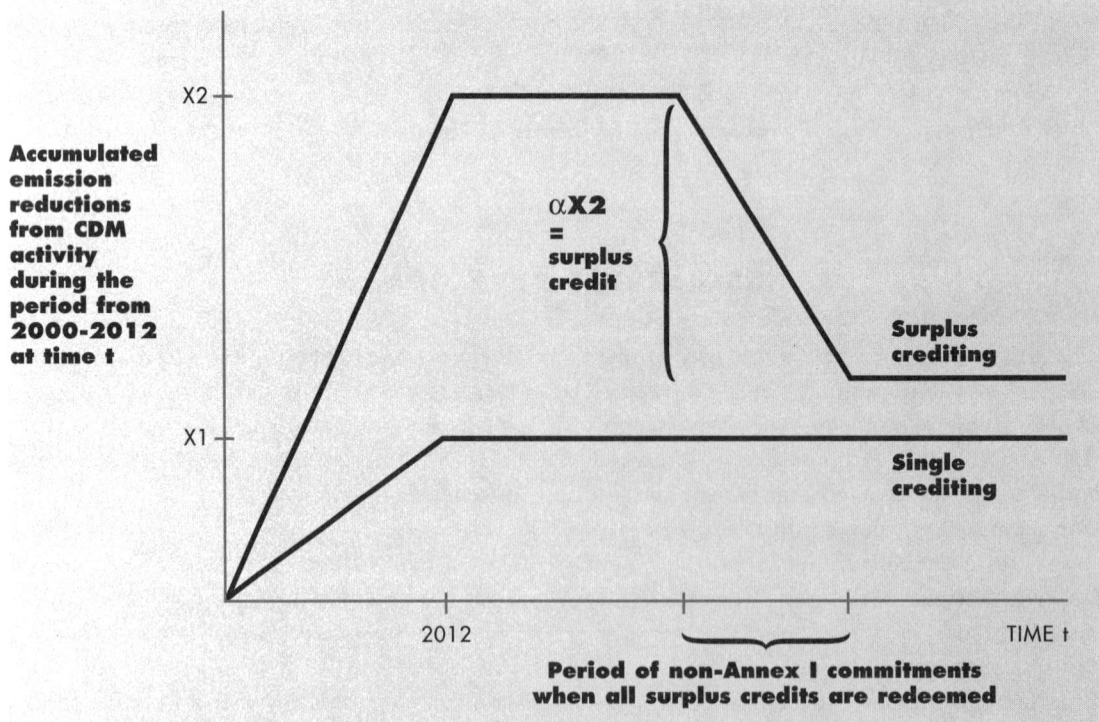

Figure 4. The figure shows net CDM-related emissions reductions from 2000 – 2012 on an accumulated basis (post 2012 reductions are not shown). With single crediting some level X1 is achieved by 2012 and all of this is permanent. With surplus crediting, the additional incentive of credits to non-Annex I hosts leads to a greater CDM activity level X2 by 2012. But αX2 of these latter reductions are not permanent since they are redeemed as matching credits at a future date. Nevertheless, long-term permanent reductions with surplus crediting will be greater than those with single crediting if X2–αX2 is greater than X1 as shown. Furthermore, the X2 reduction over the short-term (before redemption of surplus credits) is always greater than X1.

viable – providing larger net economic benefits than costs to the host country.

Only those projects satisfying all criteria comprising the three screens would achieve sustainability status for CDM. Most national governments seeking to host CDM projects will add an additional national screen, reflecting national priorities, to select the most appropriate projects from a portfolio of eligible CDM projects:

National Priorities

In the last few years, mainly after the Rio Summit, most developing countries have undertaken the task of identifying their national sustainable development priorities. Accordingly, most governments have national economic development plans and strategies that explicitly include sustainable development priorities and targets to be achieved over the short and long term. CDM projects should support and directly contribute to meeting such priorities and targets.

Screening criteria would comprise both positive screens to qualify projects, and negative screens to disqualify projects. Projects passing through a positive screening criterion meet or exceed agreed minimum standards. Projects blocked by a negative screening criterion would be in conflict with principles of sustainable development. The three sustainable development screens, and the national screen, are shown in Figure 5. Potential screening functions they might provide are briefly outlined below as they relate to energy sector power generation projects.

Environmental screening

An important component of environmental screening is an assessment of environmental impacts. CDM projects must address local and regional environmental concerns that now play an increasing role in energy sector decision-making. In evaluating a CDM project, such improvements may be measured relative to an existing business-

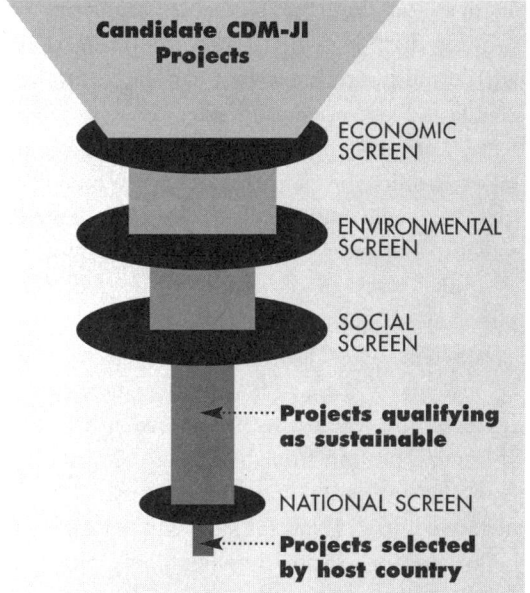

Figure 5. Sustainable development criteria for CDM projects can be applied as a series of three distinct sustainability screens to be used in the project evaluation process. Only projects passing through all three screens would qualify as CDM and be 'certifiable'. A national screen could be applied at the host country level to identify, according to national priorities, the most attractive project(s) among these.

as-usual project or a plausible baseline project. Positive environmental screens could help ensure that non-climate related environmental improvement in the local ecosystem results from a project.[24] For example, a gas-fired facility 'replacing' a coal-fired, wood burning, or hydropower facility could result in improved local air quality, reduced deforestation and desertification pressures, or enhanced downstream water quality respectively.

Negative environmental screens could disqualify potential CDM projects that would place an increased burden on stressed local environmental resources. Most types of energy sector technologies can negatively impact the local environment in some way. When environmental impact assessments (EIAs) indicate that such impacts would critically stress the local environment, or run counter to aims of a multilateral environmental agreement, a project should be disqualified as CDM.[25] For example, coal-fired

---

[24] *To estimate environmental improvements yielded by a CDM project a reference "non-CDM" project must be assumed. Recall, however, that to estimate and measure credits for emissions reductions a more objective procedure is required, for example, using the observable baselines described earlier in this chapter.*

[25] *Impacts from projects should be screened against MEAs such as the Conventions on desertification, biodiversity, wetlands, transboundary air pollution, etc.*

ISSUES&OPTIONS
The Clean
Development
Mechanism

facilities can emit considerable quantities of sulphur dioxide which, through interactions with atmospheric moisture, can create highly acidic and corrosive acid rain on a regional scale. For sites in which regional forests and lakes would be significantly affected by increased acid rain such facilities must be screened out from CDM options. As another example, forest and woodland degradation, sometimes leading to desertification, can result from biomass-fired facilities when forests cannot be sustainably managed. For sites where forest resources are already stressed, disqualification of biomass projects from CDM may be required. Negative environmental screens must identify negative impacts, and for sites where they may be significant, disqualify threatening projects from CDM. In questionable cases, EIAs might be required to make such determinations.

Social screening

The most obvious benefit that energy provides is social development.[26] Social welfare is invariably enhanced when electricity is provided to homes, schools, hospitals, and commercial and industrial establishments. When continuous and abundant electricity is available to a population, living standards rise considerably; services in education, are improved; and economic activity increases. Over the past century this has been the experience recorded in industrialised countries as they electrified their societies. For this reason, a population's access to electricity is often viewed as the key to modern social and economic development.

While it is clear that electricity provides benefits to society that are immediate, substantial, and far-reaching, the issue of maximising these benefits by selecting the most attractive power generation technology remains. Towards this end, positive social screens should seek projects characterised as/by:

◆ social acceptance of the technology

◆ a level and quality of service which meets end-user expectations

◆ the availability of continuous power supply

◆ a relatively low adoption cost to end-users

◆ a relatively low access cost to end-users

◆ minimising local health hazards

◆ encouraging local entrepreneurship and project-related side-industries

◆ providing a role for local residents in implementation and management of power facilities.

On the other hand, negative social screens should disqualify projects that seriously threaten the health and/or livelihood of local populations. They should also disqualify large-scale projects that have not been subject to local consultation and participation in project planning.

Economic screening

Ideally, many CDM projects will represent no-regrets options producing net economic benefits. Some have argued that such projects cannot be considered as additional since a host country would presumably implement them anyway on purely economic grounds.[27] If this were true, however, many no-regrets projects identifiable today would have already been implemented in developing countries years ago. This suggests that other factors such as imperfect markets, the lack of capital and technological capacity, and weak institutional infrastructure may be responsible for unexploited no-regrets projects in affected countries. Thus, many have argued that no-regrets projects remain valid CDM options as they would not likely be realised otherwise.[28] We would go one step further by recommending that only economically or commercially viable projects qualify for CDM, keeping in mind that a funding mechanism for non-commercial projects already exists, i.e., the UNFCCC Financial Mechanism.

[26] Energy as an Instrument for Socio-Economic Development, *José Goldemberg and Thomas Johansson, eds., (New York: UNDP, 1995) see overview by the editors*

[27] *Tsjalle van der Burg, "Economic Aspects," in* Joint Implementation to Curb Climate Change, *eds. Onno Kuik, Paul Peters, and Nico Schrijver, (Dordrecht: Kluwer, 1994).*

[28] *L. D. Danny Harvey and Elizabeth Bush, "Joint Implementation: An Effective Strategy for Global Warming," in* Environment *Vol. 39, No. 8 (1997).*

Positive economic screens should identify projects characterised as/by:

◆ providing local employment opportunities for construction, operations, and maintenance

◆ creating local ownership and income opportunities

◆ technology flexibility to meet changing economic conditions:
  • the potential to upgrade a facility's generating capacity in the future
  • the future possibility of co-firing or switching fuels in a facility
  • employing, or allowing future possibility for, co-generated heat and power applications
  • supporting both stand-alone and grid applications

◆ water and land requirements that can be met without conflicting with competing applications

◆ making the best use of, while not exhausting, local/national energy resources

◆ energy services that are commercialisable within the service area with full recovery of direct costs

◆ minimised distribution costs for generated power

◆ minimised transport costs for fuels and wastes

◆ ease of financial and engineering implementation

◆ ease of project replication

◆ increased local technology research, development, and production as national experience with the technology matures.

Sustainable development screens as guidelines

The sustainable development screens presented above are largely qualitative. Because project sustainability is intricately related to interactions between a prospective technology, a host country's geo-bio-physical matrix and its social and economic status, it is inappropriate to establish quantitative screens to be applied in all settings. Rather, screens should set qualitative guidelines to be used by a CDM certification body as it evaluates each project's sustainability. Such guidelines, when accompanied by technology and country specific data, can point to quantitative targets that evaluators may agree upon and apply.

PROJECT FINANCING

Demand and supply

Energy sector financing takes place today against a background of strong growth in world power markets. World demand for electricity is expected to double between 1990 and 2010, primarily due to high demand growth in developing countries, where it is expected to treble.[29] This rapid growth of power generation capacity in developing countries is accompanied by high capital requirements for energy infrastructure – extraction, transport, processing, production, and distribution – amounting to over US $100 billion annually.[30] Several sources of financing are tapped by developing countries to secure this needed capital. These include public sources: domestic investment, development assistance in the form of bilateral and multilateral loans and grants. Most recently, private sources have been increasing in importance: foreign direct investment and foreign private investment in the form of commercial debt and equity investments. Although private sources provided only one third of necessary energy sector financing just ten years ago, they account for over 80 per cent of today's larger market.[31]

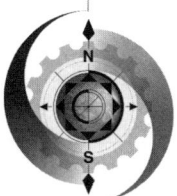

[29] World Economic and Social Survey, *United Nations, (New York: UN, 1994)*.

[30] Power and energy efficiency status report on the Banks Policy and IFC's Activities, *Joint World Bank IFC Seminar, The World Bank, (Washington: IBRD, 1994)*.

[31] Energy and Environment Strategy Approach Paper, *The World Bank, (Washington: IBRD, 1996)*.

As most of the expanded energy production taking place in developing countries relies on fossil fuel sources, externalities from energy sector activities impacting the local and regional environment, as well

> **The World Bank has estimated that the annual global market for all carbon offset exchanges could reach $8 billion by 2005 under commitment and trading conditions similar to those set forth in the Protocol.**

as the global climate system, are expected to increase significantly. The challenge of sustainable development is to reduce these impacts while maintaining needed energy service levels and ensuring that incentives for private investment – which dominates this market – are not diminished. The CDM is a mechanism that can help address this challenge.

Without negatively affecting a power project's expected returns, the CDM can generate financial resources to cover the incremental costs incurred when a climate-blind baseline project is modified so as to specifically reduce greenhouse gas emissions.[32] In the form of co-financing within a larger project finance context, CDM incremental cost financing will derive exclusively from Annex I project sponsors.[33] These sponsors seek to meet QELRCs with the CDM as well as other carbon offset exchange mechanisms permitted under the Protocol – bubbles, emissions trading, and Joint Implementation.[34] The World Bank has estimated that the annual global market for all carbon offset exchanges could reach $8 billion by 2005 under commitment and trading conditions similar to those set forth in the Protocol.[35] This is a large figure when compared with the roughly $300 million for climate change mitigation made available annually from Global Environment Facility (GEF). But how much of this financing will flow to CDM markets?

The magnitude of funding attracted to CDM will be influenced by various factors affecting demand and supply for CDM projects.[36] Project demand from sponsors will be characterised by such factors as:

- the level of QELRCs assumed by industrialised countries

- the strength of measures and regulation implemented in industrialised countries

- rules on supplementarity set forth in protocol negotiations

- how financial transactions are managed under the CDM

- relative availability and cost of CDM transactions, project co-financing, and insurance against project risks

- the cost and availability of domestic options

- the cost and availability of flexible options other than the CDM (emissions trading, Joint Implementation with other Annex I countries, and the formation of emission bubble agreements between Annex I countries).

Project supply from hosts will be characterised by such factors as:

- developing country capacity growth requirements

- other sources of finance available for developing country infrastructure investments

- developing country interest in pursuing the CDM

- developing country capacity to identify and market prospective projects.

---

[32] *Incremental costs are calculated based on cost differences between a CDM project and that of a baseline project providing equal service. Incremental costs must be negotiated between project sponsors and hosts.*

[33] *For an overview of project financing in the context of joint implementation, see: Brad Johnson, "Capital Formation and Project Finance," in* Regional Workshop on AIJ – Jakarta Indonesia, *(Washington: USIJI Secretariat, 1996).*

[34] *Through bubble agreements two or more Annex I parties share their aggregated QELRCs.*

[35] The Carbon Offset Investment Business and the Role of the World Bank, *Global Environment Division, (Washington: IBRD, 1997).*

[36] *Robert Hamwey and Andrea Baranzini,* How Big is the Total Carbon Offset Market After Kyoto?, *Working Paper, (International Academy of the Environment, Geneva: 1998), in preparation.*

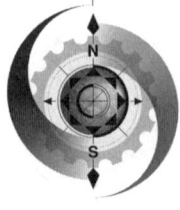

Although additional analytic work needs to be done to estimate the magnitude of these factors and their combined quantitative effect on future CDM markets, we can qualitatively examine how the manner by which financial transactions take place under the CDM might influence the size and growth of future CDM markets.

Pooled and direct approaches to CDM project financing

The CDM essentially has only two options available to govern how project financing will be transacted: (1) pooled investments to be globally managed and distributed by an oversight committee which could be the Executive Board, or (2) direct bilateral transactions between sponsor and host at the project level.

The multilateral option for CDM project financing would function in a similar manner to a mutual fund in financial markets. Annex I Party investor contributions would be pooled together and allocated into a portfolio of investments in CDM projects proposed by developing countries. Projects would have to be reviewed and accepted for investment by a central investment committee, possibly the Executive Board. Like a mutual fund, proceeds from the portfolio – carbon offsets – would be distributed among investors in proportion to their level of investment. The World Bank's Prototype Carbon Fund operates along these lines for the full range of carbon offset projects permitted under the Protocol.[37]

For the sponsor country investor, the multilateral option does have the advantage of spreading project risk over the entire portfolio and allowing investors to buy into the CDM at any level they desire. It could also reduce transaction costs for investors who could simply invest in a fund rather than research and transact individual projects. For the host country seller of CDM offsets, a multilateral option would decouple political considerations of bilateral partnerships they might wish to avoid – political and economic barriers, obligations, and responsibilities – from the CDM process. It would also provide host

countries with high investment risk profiles an opportunity to be awarded collective sponsor financing that individual sponsors would be unwilling to extend unilaterally.

However, multilateral review and acceptance of individual CDM projects could require comprehensive uniform application procedures, and inter-comparisons of multiple projects. Compared to freely negotiated bilateral deals, the process is likely to be protracted. Not unlike the GEF, the multilateral option might result in a slow and bureaucratic apparatus, unattractive to many potential project sponsors and hosts compared to a bilateral mechanism. It also reduces sponsor and host incentives to identify and develop high performance investment opportunities. For these reasons, the bilateral option might be a more attractive option for most sponsors and hosts.

By permitting countries and entrepreneurial project developers to uncover and market high return projects, the bilateral option would encourage competition and likely generate a larger and more efficient market. The bilateral option would treat each CDM project as a separate good, allowing highly competitive hosts to attain higher project volumes than in the multilateral option where caps might be present to ensure an equitable distribution of funds to all participating host countries. Similar to individual stock picking rather than mutual fund investing, it would allow sponsor countries to select what they believe will be the most profitable projects. It would also permit sponsors to focus on strategic regional markets where they have complementary economic interests – bilateral exchange or export development programmes.

However, the bilateral option may result in investments flowing only to those host countries with strong capacities to market projects and generate co-financing. In countries lacking such capacities, poorly promoted, yet equally attractive projects with low prospects for co-financing would be neglected. The multilateral option could establish collective funds to build national capacities in such countries. It could also assist in organising co-

[37] *See note 35.*

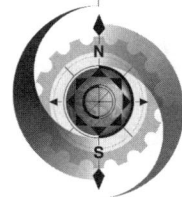

financing — where it is not accessible from private sources — by arranging grants, concessional loans, and non-commercial risk coverage through the World Bank Group.

Will a multilateral or bilateral financing mechanism be chosen for the CDM? In view of advantages and disadvantages present under both options, a hybrid model employing a mix of both options may be most appropriate. Sponsors and hosts alike could then utilise the option that best suits their evolving needs. ■

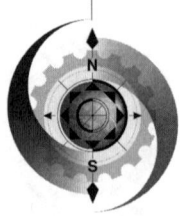

Chapter 11

ATTRACTING NORTHERN PRIVATE SECTOR INVESTMENT FOR GREENHOUSE GAS REDUCTION IN THE SOUTH

Björn Stigson, President
World Business Council for
   Sustainable Development (WBCSD)[1]
Geneva, Switzerland

Summary: A large proportion of international investments in emissions reductions will be made by businesses, which are significant emitters of greenhouse gas (GHG) in Annex I countries. Therefore, the Clean Development Mechanism (CDM) must be designed to accommodate business needs. This paper provides a private sector, or business, perspective on issues and options related to the design and operationalization of the CDM. Rules must be clear, transparent and fair, minimise transaction costs, reduce costs, assign accountability, and facilitate trading of emissions reductions. CDM rules that limit flexibility will restrict investment in emissions reductions in developing countries.

BACKGROUND

The World Business Council for Sustainable Development (WBCSD) believes that global climate change requires a global response, including a real partnership with developing countries. Under the United Nations Framework Convention on Climate Change (UNFCCC) and the Kyoto Protocol, the CDM provides one mechanism for building a partnership between businesses in the northern world and developing countries. It offers great potential benefits for both partners: for business, it represents an opportunity to lower greenhouse gas emissions at a reasonable cost, and for developing countries, it can facilitate the transfer of technology and know-how to contribute to sustainable development and poverty alleviation. Table 1 summarises several benefits from various perspectives.

Why is a business perspective important for designing and operationalizing the CDM? First, companies will be responsible for financing a large proportion of emissions reductions over the next 15 years. They will make investments where costs are lowest, and they have insights into how costs can be minimised to promote investment in developing countries. Second, experience shows that business-to-business partnerships are efficient means for transferring technologies for using cleaner fuels and fossil fuels more efficiently, reducing and re-using wastes, enhancing sinks, and improving watershed management to conserve biodiversity.

THE CHALLENGE

The WBCSD is optimistic about prospects for business action under the CDM. In 1996, WBCSD undertook a project called the International Business

---

[1] *With expert advice provided by Sid Embree, Consultant.*

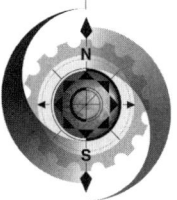

PLAYER	ADVANTAGES	DISADVANTAGES
Non-Annex I Countries	• Access to "cleaner" technology • Foreign direct investment • Jobs, new skills to workforce etc • Partnerships, joint ventures (JVs) etc. • Improved living standards • Improve access to energy • Biodiversity and community issues	• Could get bogged down in bureaucracy • Political sensitivities
Annex I countries	• Cost effective means to meet Kyoto commitments • Leverage in access to new markets • Show commitment to climate change issue • Step forward on engaging developing countries participation	• Bureaucracy and transaction costs may be high • Emissions trading may be an easier approach • Uncertainties surrounding many of the unresolved issues
Non-Annex I private sector entity	• May provide business opportunities in many sectors • Provide the possibility of partnerships and JVs with Annex I companies • Reduce energy costs	• Threat from Annex I companies taking domestic markets
Annex I private sector entity	• Depending on domestic regulation may be a cost effective option to take • Market opportunities • Partnerships and Joint Ventures • CO_2 business opportunities • Reputation and Public Relations benefits	• Uncertainty and unfamiliar nature of the new mechanism • "Hidden" costs • High transaction costs

Action on Climate Change (IBACC). An evaluation of the project found incentives for action and crediting were lacking in the pilot phase for Activities Implemented Jointly (AIJ), and business was not motivated to participate. The situation is different with the Kyoto Protocol. National commitments for quantified emission limitation or reduction (Annex B of the Protocol) will provide incentives for companies to seek low-cost emissions reduction investments, and the CDM allows for crediting after 2000. Further, Protocol Article 12.9 stipulates that private sector entities can be involved in the acquisition of certified emissions reductions (CERs), and Article 12.7

suggests a streamlined system for verification will be adopted. These are positive signals.

Nonetheless, some businesses are apprehensive that the CDM could evolve into a bureaucratic institution that will stifle investment. They fear the CDM could become an inefficient, perhaps political, mechanism that will limit greenhouse gas reduction investments in developing countries, or that restrictions will make such investments costly or unattractive relative to other possibilities. The challenge in designing the CDM is to ensure that it will facilitate investments in emissions reductions that are consistent with sustainable development.

THE WBCSD'S APPROACH TO THE CDM

Lessons from the International Business Action on Climate Change (IBACC)

WBCSD's experience with its IBACC project during the AIJ pilot phase offers lessons for designing a "private sector" friendly CDM.

The WBCSD believes that an enabling framework, with crediting, will create future value for greenhouse gas reductions that meet appropriate criteria. This value will stimulate demand for projects, which will, in turn, attract financing for GHG reductions. This financing will reduce risks associated with

international investments, particularly in developing countries.

In its July 1996 report to the Second Conference of the Parties (COP-2) to the UNFCCC, the WBCSD noted that very few AIJ projects would attract private sector investment. Rather, further development of emissions reduction projects would require national policies and an enabling framework for private sector participation, including:[2]

◆ Domestic greenhouse gas offset credit for implementing qualified GHG reduction projects. Crediting would catalyse action by business and create an asset that can be "banked" or traded and applied against emissions limitation commitments.

◆ Rules for project eligibility and procedures for recognition of eligible GHG emissions reductions arising from investments that provide environmental benefits, and are measurable and verifiable.

◆ Agreements among investor and host countries to facilitate emissions reduction investments.

◆ Incentives and mechanisms to reduce the transaction costs and risks associated with GHG emissions reduction projects.

◆ A framework for the period beyond the AIJ pilot phase, including an international system for trading GHG reductions.

The WBCSD also recommended continued efforts to increase awareness and build capacity among various participants in a successful market, including businesses, governments, project developers, and financial institutions.

Private sector decision making

The WBCSD's approach to the CDM assumes that Annex I Parties will allocate responsibility for emissions reductions for the first commitment period (2008 – 2012) among a significant proportion of greenhouse gas emitters in their jurisdictions. Once this occurs, these emitters will seek low- cost emissions reductions.

How does a company in an Annex I country identify opportunities for investing in emissions reductions? Early experience suggests that firms identify potential measures or projects at home and abroad, evaluate available options against several criteria, and decide where investments should be channelled.

In early 1998, many companies in Annex I countries began to examine the potential implications of the Kyoto Protocol on their businesses. These companies estimated their 1990 emissions, and projected their corporate emissions to the first commitment period (2008 – 2012). The resulting projection provides a general indication of the amount of emissions the company may be required to reduce over the next 10 to15 years – the company's "compliance gap." Once their compliance gap has been estimated, a firm will begin to identify measures and investments to reduce or eliminate its anticipated "gap." A typical "gap analysis" yields three potential target areas for investment that could be credited to a company based in an Annex I country:

◆ Reductions from adjustments to existing operations (e.g., improve energy efficiency, increase renewables). Companies will consider adjustments in operations in Annex I countries. Presumably, they will also consider adjustments to reduce emissions from developing country-based operations that could be credited to the parent firm.

◆ Reductions from changing strategic investment choices and re-orienting core businesses (e.g., new business in less GHG-intensive sectors; oil and gas company enters renewables business). Investments that reduce the overall GHG-intensity of an Annex I company could be made in Annex I and/or non-Annex I countries, and credited to the Annex I parent company.

---

[2] From the Progress report on International Business Action on Climate Change *prepared on behalf of the WBCSD, and presented to the Second Conference of the Parties to the Framework Convention on Climate Change, Bonn, July 1996.*

◆ Non-business related reductions (pure off-sets that are unrelated to core business or planned business). Offsets might be in Annex I and/or non-Annex I countries.

Firms may analyse several possible measures and projects against internal criteria before making an investment decision. Obviously, a company will seek lower-cost, rather than higher-cost, reductions. A company may favour investments that also improve its bottom line or longer-term business prospects. In fact, a company may be willing to pay more for emissions reductions that meet a variety of corporate objectives. Many firms agree that investments in offsets do not provide long-term value to a company's bottom line, although they can reduce a short-term liability and may improve corporate image.

> **Companies will be responsible for financing a large proportion of emissions reductions over the next 15 years. They will make investments where costs are lowest.**

Ultimately, a small number of satisfactory projects must compete with each other within the firm for financing. Projects compete with each other based on many factors that typically influence investment decisions, such as the need to minimise risks, the need to maximise shareholder value in the short and long terms, the need to minimise transactions costs, timing, and soundness of the regulatory environment.

These decision factors will influence whether companies pursue emissions reduction investments in developing countries or not. Any complicating administrative procedures will reduce the attractiveness of some options relative to others. The experience of trading of sulphur dioxide emissions (SO_2) "allowances" in the USA suggests that a significant proportion of trades take place between business units within the same company, rather than through relatively efficient market mechanisms for purchasing external reductions.

Companies are unlikely to pay more for CDM projects unless they are as easy to invest in as Annex B projects. Complex CDM procedures will reduce the appeal of non-Annex B projects. Therefore, the CDM must avoid bureaucracy

and provide flexibility for a range of investment decisions. An effective CDM should not involve multilateral institutions in projects, although there are roles in the development of rules and in system oversight.

A private sector interpretation of Article 12

The remainder of this paper suggests how the CDM could be designed. It will address governance, relevant institutions, funding, administration, and operations, as well as functions and responsibilities for oversight, setting standards for auditing and certification of reductions, and ensuring compliance. This section provides a private sector interpretation of Article 12, which defines the CDM. The next section defines a model for the CDM that would facilitate transfers of certified emissions reductions (CERs). The last section uses a case study to illustrate the model.

Further definition is required to operationalize the CDM. For business, the rules are still not clear. Businesses want governments and the Conference of the Parties serving as the meeting of the Parties to the Protocol (COP/MOP) to set rules so action can begin.

Article 12.2 indicates that the CDM should assist non-Annex I Parties to achieve sustainable development and contribute to the ultimate objective of the UNFCCC. From a business perspective, it appears logical that non-Annex I governments should describe their priorities for sustainable development in any national criteria that outline preferences for different types of emissions limitation projects (e.g., promote cleaner power generation; rational use of forests for purposes of sustainable socio-economic development). The remainder of Article 12.2 suggests that the CDM should also be used to assist Annex I Parties in achieving compliance with their commitments under Article 3. From a business point of view, this simply means that CERs (Article 12.10) can be used toward meeting Article 3 commitments.

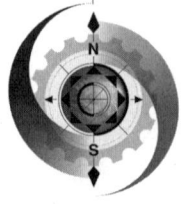

Article 12.3 (a) indicates non-Annex I Parties will benefit from project activities resulting in CERs. This implies that agreements governing relationships for financing projects and sharing benefits (including CERs) should be fair. This is standard business practice. Transactions and investment projects are rarely, if ever, agreed where the various parties come out worse than where they started – at least at the time that agreements are negotiated. To cover unanticipated risks that could result in unfair impacts on one or more parties over time, contracts may include provisions to revisit certain features of the deal.

Benefits to non-Annex I Parties can accrue in many different forms – technology, financial resources, CERs, employment, and so on. Government involvement in determining sharing of benefits makes transactions more complicated. Any *ex-ante* determination of how benefits, including credits, should be shared will influence pricing of CERs and reduce the scope for negotiating an acceptable arrangement among project participants. Such interference would reduce the appeal of CDM projects or of investing in countries where such determination has been made.

> **Business-to-business partnerships are efficient in transferring technologies for cleaner fuel use, reducing and re-using wastes, enhancing sinks, and improving watershed management conserve biodiversity.**

Article 12.3 (b) stipulates that CERs can be used to contribute to compliance with "part" of the commitments under Article 3. It also indicates that the issue of "what part" will be addressed by the Conference of Parties meeting as Parties to the Protocol (COP/MOP) will address. From a business perspective, the "part" should remain undefined. Why? First, defining a "part" will limit the flexibility of some businesses to seek a range of low-cost options for limiting emissions. In some instances, the choices are already limited by high cost, particularly in countries and/or sectors where efficiencies or use of renewables are already high. Second, defining a "part" will influence supply and demand, and therefore price. While some non-Annex I countries may prefer higher prices for reductions, high prices will

also encourage firms to look in Annex I countries for projects.

Most companies will not spend all of their emissions reduction investment funds on "offset" projects, or in countries where they do not have operations. Investments in CERs from offsets or outside of business or operations do not provide long-term benefits to the firm. Thus, while some companies may prefer to make substantial investments in low-cost offsets in developing countries, others may pursue only a small proportion of their needed reductions through CDM investments.

Thus, all of the above arguments for not defining "part" reflect business' perspectives on "supplementarity." Article 6 indicates that the acquisition of emission reduction units among Annex I Parties shall be "supplemental" to domestic actions for the purposes of meeting commitments under Article 3. Businesses would prefer to have the flexibility to invest in emissions reductions in Annex I or non-Annex I countries and would prefer to leave "supplemental" undefined, as well.

Article 12.4 suggests that the CDM should be subject to the authority and guidance of the MOP, and supervised by an Executive Board. The most appropriate Board would be a subsidiary body of the MOP, with administrative support provided by the secretariat for the UNFCCC and technical support/input from existing subsidiary bodies of the COP.

The objective of the Board must be to ensure objectivity and transparency. It would be responsible for seeking expert advice and:

◆ recommending to the MOP rules and modalities for participation in the CDM, standards and methodologies for CERs and for operational entities to be designated by the MOP

◆ ensuring transparency, efficiency, accountabil-

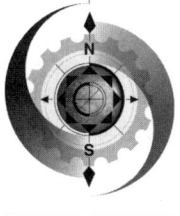

ISSUES&OPTIONS

The Clean
Development
Mechanism

ity through inde-
pendent auditing

◆ providing guidance
to the MOP on
participation

◆ an oversight func-
tion (e.g., random
audits of operational entities and CERs).

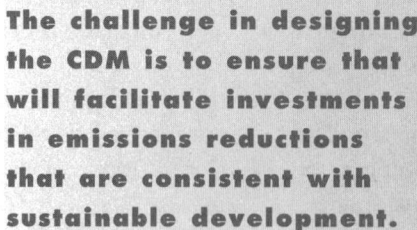

The challenge in designing the CDM is to ensure that will facilitate investments in emissions reductions that are consistent with sustainable development.

Article 12.5 indicates that emissions reductions (ERs) from each project activity shall be certified by "operational entities" to be "designated" by the MOP according to: voluntary participation; real, measurable, and long-term benefits related to mitigation of climate change; and reductions in emissions that are additional to any that would occur in the absence of the certified project activity. In the optimal situation, the Executive Board would recommend to the MOP professional standards/rules for designation (accreditation) of operational entities. These could be reviewed and adopted by the COP/MOP. Any "operational entities" that satisfy the rules and meet the standards would be designated or accredited by the MOP based on recommendations from the Executive Board.

The MOP should delegate responsibility for "designation" to the CDM Secretariat (or the Executive Board), which would become responsible for ensuring operational entities meet professional standards/rules set by the MOP. Such an accreditation process is applied in several sectors where professional, behavioural or activity-based standards or outcomes must be achieved to guarantee a minimum level of service or compliance. Parallels exist in financial accounting, engineering and environmental auditing. Recently, Costa Rica hired an independent auditing firm to certify carbon sequestered in its national park system. To take a conservative approach, the certifier (Société Générale de Surveillance - SGS) determined that 60 per cent of the carbon sequestered in the project area could be certified, with the remainder subject to risks that would have to be evaluated on an annual basis. If all or part of the remaining 40 per cent of carbon is sequestered in the future, SGS (or another certifier) would certify that the remaining portion has been sequestered.

Certification is an integral part of every-day transactions in commodities trading (to ensure quality, delivery as agreed), in goods shipping (to ensure goods are delivered according to contracts), in sustainable forestry operations, and elsewhere. In most cases, the buyer pays (directly or indirectly) for verification. Where certification is standard practice, the onus is placed on the accredited "operational entity" (certifier) for reporting whether standards and procedures are met and followed. Thus, for the CDM, the MOP could adopt standards or rules (recommended by the Executive Board and/or subsidiary bodies), with oversight provided by the Board of the CDM. In addition, clear penalties for non-compliance by Parties, operational entities and buyers and sellers of CERs must be developed, and the MOP should specify such penalties.

Business likes some rules, and finds **Article 12.5** relatively clear. To business, Article 12.5 (a) means that projects should only be pursued in countries that agree to participate in CDM activities. It also means that interested developing country Parties need to adopt simple, transparent rules and processes for accepting CDM projects. Article 12.5 (b) – real, measurable emissions reductions – is related to Article 12.5 (c), which requires that emissions reductions must be *additional* to any that would occur in the absence of certified project activity. This requires proof that CERs are not from "business-as-usual" project activities, since these cannot be certified by any operational entity.

The CDM Executive Board and/or the Secretariat, and/or UNFCCC Subsidiary Bodies, could assist the MOP to translate the Article 12.5 rules into methodologies for preparing baselines and estimating emissions reductions, and recommend these to the MOP for adoption. Article 12.5 would be enforced by participants in individual CDM projects. It would also be enforced through verification by designated "operational entities." This assumes that the MOP has adopted methodologies defining what is and is not "business-as-usual", and that

governments in participating non-Annex I countries have elaborated criteria for what kinds of CDM projects they will or will not accept.

Article 12.6 says the CDM shall assist in arranging funding of certified project activities as necessary. This means that, once project activities have been certified, the CDM could (but need not) provide assistance to "sellers" of CERs to locate funding for project activities related to creating the CERs. Given that several actors already assist project developers to locate funding for emissions reduction projects, the CDM should not be obligated to play this role. Currently, business rarely looks to multilateral institutions to identify projects for investing in emissions reductions. Rather, it seeks investments through more business-oriented channels. To the extent that the CDM does provide assistance to arrange funding, the MOP and Executive Board must avoid any conflict of interest between certification activities and marketing of CERs.

> **Such factors as the need to minimise risks, maximise shareholder value, and minimise transactions cost will influence whether companies pursue emissions reduction investments in development countries, as will timing and the soundness of the regulatory environment.**

Article 12.7 indicates that the MOP must elaborate modalities and procedures for auditing and verification of project activities. Highly complex modalities and procedures will discourage private sector investment in CDM projects. Nonetheless, rules are needed – at several levels:

First, rules should describe what Parties must do if they wish to voluntarily engage in CDM projects. At a minimum, Parties must establish a focal point for approval of CDM activities and adopt criteria specifying the types of CDM projects that are consistent with sustainable development (Article 12.2).

Second, Article 12.7 indicates that auditing and verification of project activities will be independent. This means that "operational entities" should be responsible for independent auditing and verification (e.g., applying methodologies for preparing baselines and

estimating emissions reductions). Auditing and verification should be performed according to rules and standards set by the MOP, and paid for by investors in CERs. Operational entities must meet criteria that assure the MOP and buyers and sellers of CERs that CERs are real, measurable, and verifiable and that they are not "business-as-usual." The CDM's Executive Board could recommend to the MOP the attributes of appropriate operational entities.

The modalities and procedures will address the procedures and credentials for designation (accreditation) by the MOP (or a delegated authority), the rules for certifying ERs, the role of the EB in supervising (Article 12.4) the process, and the rules, standards and procedures needed to ensure transparency, efficiency and accountability. Several models can be examined to develop rules for accreditation and certification; there are more than 100 private standards organisations and more than 500 accredited certifiers throughout the world. Lloyd's Register, a British company, is regularly assessed by 13 accreditation bodies that provide oversight for compliance with standards in various sectors.

Article 12.8 indicates that a "share" of the "proceeds from certified project activities" will be used to cover administrative expenses. This means that a small proportion of costs should be paid to the CDM for administration. The share should be determined on the basis of the amount of CERs being processed via the CDM rather than the actual proceeds from project activities ("proceeds" is subject to multiple interpretations). Any processing fee could discourage CDM transactions, since it will increase the marginal costs of CERs from developing countries. Therefore, the fee should be comparable to those charged in other trading businesses – a very small percentage to cover costs for registration and reporting transfers of CERs to the Parties and the MOP.

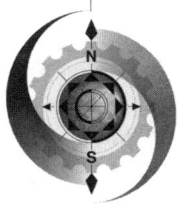

A small fee is justified for value-added services. With independent auditing and verification, certification services will be paid for by investors and provided by "operational entities". This leaves a small, but reasonable, set of potential responsibilities for the Executive Board and secretariat: recommending auditing, verification, and certification procedures to the MOP; operationalizing procedures adopted by the MOP; and processing information on CERs. Processing requirements should be limited to ensuring that rules, standards and procedures established by the MOP are met, the spirit of Article 12 is complied with, maintaining a data base on CER transfers, and confirming transactions of CERs for participating Parties and for the MOP. The lower the fee, the more likely the CDM will process a larger number of transactions. A higher fee will stifle the number of transactions.

Article 12.8 also indicates that a share of proceeds will be used to assist developing country Parties that are particularly vulnerable to the adverse effects of climate change to meet the costs of adaptation. This "condition" has the potential to substantially limit private sector investment in CDM activities. Investors are concerned that this provision will increase the cost of CER project investments and reduce the efficiency of CER processing.

It is reasonable to assume that Article 12.8 will *not* be the only source of assistance to vulnerable developing country Parties. Therefore, only a *very small* "share of the proceeds" would be appropriate. This small share could be channelled, according to guidance provided by the MOP, into other

> **Several models can be examined to develop rules for accreditation and certification; there are more than 100 private standards organisations and more than 500 accredited certifiers throughout the world.**

much larger initiatives aimed at assisting vulnerable developing country Parties.

Article 12.9 confirms that the private sector can engage in CDM activities through *direct investment* in projects. To business, "operational entities" can be private sector entities, as long as they satisfy the modalities and procedures for auditing, verification, and certification established by the MOP.

Finally, **Article 12.10** indicates that CERs obtained during the period from the year 2000 up to the beginning of the first commitment period can be used in achieving compliance in the first commitment period. This means "banking" of CERs from projects processed by the CDM is allowed after the year 2000 so that they can be used toward meeting commitments in the first commitment period. This does not preclude CDM activities from continuing during the first commitment period.

A private sector-friendly model: WBCSD's vision of the CDM

Based on the "interpretation" presented in the previous section, a model is proposed for the CDM. This model, defined within the constraints of Article 12, would encourage private sector investment in non-Annex I Parties consistent with their stated national policies and priorities for sustainable development. It will describe how the various elements of Article 12 can be operationalized to meet host country *and* private sector needs. The final section will use a hypothetical project to illustrate how this model would work.

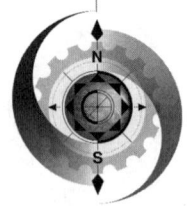

CASE STUDY: PROCESSING REDUCTIONS FROM A CDM PROJECT

A hypothetical project will illustrate how the model proposed on the previous page would function. The example shows how the CDM would process and transfer CERs from an emissions reduction project in a non-Annex I country to an Annex I country. It explains the respective responsibilities and functions of

various institutions and entities.

Before any CERs can be processed by the CDM, certain rules and standards must be adopted and put into place. These are:

◆ Indications by Parties that they wish to

voluntarily participate in CDM project activities (Article 12.5 (a)), including designating a national focal point to provide information on which project types contribute to sustainable development – Article 12.2 *(requires action by Parties, and probably direction from MOP)*.

◆ Methodologies for preparing and estimating baselines, and determining "additional" emissions reductions (Article 12.5 (b) and (c)). Methodologies are needed for different types of projects in different sectors (e.g., energy efficiency and fuel switching in the energy sector; afforestation and forest protection in the forestry sector), and they should create a minimum standard of acceptability for all CERs *(requires action by COP Subsidiary Bodies, CDM Executive Board, MOP)*.

◆ Minimum rules and standards for designated operational entities, including qualifications, reporting procedures and oversight by the CDM Executive Board *(requires action by CDM Executive Board, MOP)*.

◆ Designation of operational entities *(requires action by the MOP and CDM Executive Board)*.

◆ Rules for ensuring compliance and enforcement of minimum standards and rules, including penalties for non-compliance by operational entities (requires action by CDM Executive Board, MOP).[3]

◆ Determination of "share of proceeds" for administrative costs, etc. *(requires action by MOP)*.

Once these rules and standards are formally adopted, CDM project activities may officially proceed. Before they are formally adopted, business would prefer interim arrangements in order to gain experience and to contribute to the development of rules and procedures.

A straightforward fuel-switching project will illustrate how the model would work. Assume that it is the year 2000. In this hypothetical case, a power generating company (POWER) based in Canada has decided to invest in a sugar plantation and refinery expansion (SUGAR) in Peru. POWER's investment will enable SUGAR to use sugar cane waste (bagasse) to produce electricity and steam. With this system, SUGAR will reduce its consumption of fossil fuels (electricity generated from oil and purchased from the local Power Company).

POWER has selected the investment in SUGAR because it is consistent with its internal criteria for reducing POWER's future greenhouse gases and meeting anticipated GHG limitation requirements to be assigned by the Government for the first commitment period. For example, POWER's management will only agree to investments in emissions reductions if they are in the power sector, and in politically stable countries where POWER anticipates future business opportunities. POWER is relieved that the CDM is evolving into a streamlined, efficient mechanism with simple rules, transparent decision making and operations, no interference in project activities and a low fee for processing CERs. While the methodologies for preparing and estimating baselines and determining "additional" emissions reductions seem complicated, POWER is confident that designated operational entities have the qualifications and experience to apply them according to the rules established by the MOP and CDM Executive Board.

Before deciding to invest in SUGAR's fuel switching project, POWER investigated whether Peru would approve the proposed GHG reduction investment. In this case, Peru's (hypothetical) criteria indicate that renewable energy projects are acceptable, and that projects must yield real, measurable reductions that would not have occurred in the absence of the investment. Before deciding to invest in Peru, POWER had compared Peru's criteria with those of other countries. Peru's criteria were straightforward and easy to understand. Canada's (hypothetical) criteria indicated that all CERs transferred to Canada should comply with the rules and standards adopted by the MOP and CDM Executive

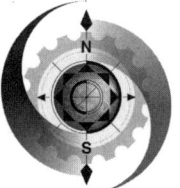

ISSUES&OPTIONS
The Clean
Development
Mechanism

---

[3] *The MOP must also eventually address non-compliance with the Kyoto Protocol by Parties participating in CDM activities. This issue is beyond the scope of the paper.*

[4] *In this hypothetical case, the MOP agreed the "share" would be between 0.5 per cent and 3 per cent of the financial value of CERs, with 0.5 per cent applying to the largest transactions and 3 per cent applying to the smallest. A sliding scale was used: 0.5 per cent for CER transactions of 10 million tons of CO2 or more (0.5 x 10,000,000 = $50,000); 1 per cent for transactions between 1 and 10 million tons of CO2 equivalent (.01 x 1,000,000 = $10,000); 2 per cent for transactions of 100,000 to 1 million tons of CO2 equivalent (.02 x 100,000 = $2,000); and 3 per cent for transactions of less than 100,000 tons of CO2 equivalent (.03 x 50,000 = $1,500).*

Board and use methodologies to be applied by designated operational entities.

Also before deciding to invest in SUGAR's project, POWER hired a consultant to perform a preliminary analysis of the potential GHG reductions that would result compared to the business-as-usual baseline situation. The consultant estimated that reductions would be substantial, and compared the estimates with those from other proposed projects.

Once POWER was satisfied that SUGAR presented an excellent emissions reduction opportunity relative to others available internally and elsewhere, POWER entered into negotiations with SUGAR to co-finance the fuel switching project and agreed on a "benefits-sharing" arrangement that was mutually acceptable to POWER and SUGAR. The arrangement took into account benefits such as reduced electricity expenses for SUGAR, emissions reductions, local employment and other factors. In this case, SUGAR was not interested to own any future CERs because it would benefit from reduced costs for electricity and waste disposal. POWER and SUGAR then proceeded to implement their joint project. As a courtesy, they advised their respective governments of their intention to transfer CERs after they have been certified by one or more designated operational entities.

The emissions reduction investment project is implemented in late 2000 and early 2001. The emissions reductions will occur for several years, according to the methodologies for determining baselines and estimating reductions adopted by the MOP.

It is now early 2002. POWER and SUGAR agree that emissions reductions actually achieved during the first year of the project should be measured and certified. Therefore, POWER issues a "request for proposals" from designated operational entities (OEs). After several proposals are submitted to POWER, POWER and SUGAR review them. They decide to hire OE No. 67 to certify the reductions since it has been designated as an OE, has significant experience with biomass power projects, and has strong internal quality assurance procedures.

OE No. 67 assesses the greenhouse gas reductions from the SUGAR project. It uses the method-

ologies adopted by the MOP (e.g., recommended by the CDM Executive Board, secretariat and COP Subsidiary Bodies) to ensure compliance with Article 12.5, as well as Peru's criteria for voluntary participation in CDM projects. Once OE No. 67 is satisfied that a specific amount of emissions reductions have occurred, it issues a certificate with its conclusions to POWER and SUGAR. The certificate indicates that the project has resulted in real, measurable reductions equivalent to 10,000 tons of CO_2 during the first year.

POWER submits the certificate to the CDM administrative secretariat (within the secretariat of the UNFCCC). Accompanying the certificate is a cheque for $300.00 to cover administrative costs and to assist vulnerable developing country Parties. This is equivalent to 3 per cent of the proceeds from certified project activities in financial terms (10,000 tons x .03).

The CDM administrative secretariat will record the CERs that are being transferred from Peru to Canada. POWER and SUGAR also forward the certificate to their respective governments so that they can credit and debit the CERs accordingly and report on these in their national communications. The CERs will be accounted as reductions during the first budget period.

POWER and SUGAR agree to wait until 2004 before the next certification of reductions. In 2004, they hire OE No. 86 to certify reductions. OE No. 86 certifies that 24,000 tons of CO_2 were avoided during the previous two years. POWER submits the certificate to the CDM administrative secretariat for processing, with a cheque for $720 (24,000 tons x .03). This process continues until the end of the agreed lifetime of the project.

The EB and CDM secretariat will audit, on a random basis, both CERs and OEs, according to rules and standards adopted by the MOP. In 2006, OE No. 67 is audited for its performance in certifying reductions from another project. In addition, POWER's reported CERs for 2005 are audited. The CDM Executive Board and secretariat conduct audits by hiring external OEs. POWER and SUGAR are relieved when OE No. 67 and their CERs from 2005 are found to be in conformance with rules and procedures of the MOP and CDM. ∎

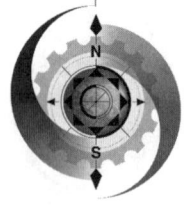

ISSUES&OPTIONS

The Clean
Development
Mechanism

SUSTAINABLE DEVELOPMENT AND GREENHOUSE GAS REDUCTION

Paul Hassing[1]
Netherlands Development Assistance
and Matthew S. Mendis[2]
Alternative Energy Development Inc., USA

Summary: This paper analyses fundamental differences for sustainable development associated with different types of greenhouse gas (GHG) offset projects. Agriculture, land use and forestry projects, if designed only for GHG offset benefits, tend to support sustainable development only marginally Nor do energy and industry sector GHG offset projects support long-term sustainable development. Renewable energy, energy efficiency, improved industrial processes and waste management initiatives show more promise in this regard.

A number of factors critical to the successful implementation of GHG offset projects are also examined; specifically, the role of stakeholders, the legal and institutional framework, and the financial requirements of GHG offset projects. The paper briefly outlines a strategy for trading of GHG offsets. It proposes a preliminary structure for operating the CDM while incorporating the services of government, NGOs and the private sector. It concludes with a list of a number of measures that could be adopted by the CDM to help promote GHG offsets for sustainable development.

INTRODUCTION

The recently negotiated Kyoto Protocol allows for the trading of greenhouse gas (GHG) offsets and for Joint Implementation between Annex I Parties.[3] The Protocol also makes provisions for the trading of GHG offsets from non-Annex I Parties[4] to Annex I Parties within the context of a Clean Development Mechanism (CDM). It does not, however, provide the details of how the trading mechanisms, Joint Implementation or CDM will operate and what exactly qualifies for trading. The details of the GHG offset trading mechanisms are left for consideration at the next meeting of the Conference of Parties scheduled for November 1998 in Buenos Aires. This paper analyses some of the issues that will be taken up at that time, with the purpose of showing how different ways of implementing GHG trading can have very different impacts on sustainable development.

Market failures and solutions

The atmosphere presents a classic case of a global common: all have access to it and no one has ownership of it. As a result, the global atmosphere has been

---

[1] *The author is a Dutch National and the head of the Division of Climate, Energy and Environment Technology (DML/KM) Netherlands Development Assistance (NEDA) in the Ministry of Foreign Affairs. The opinions expressed in this paper are the personal views of the author and do not necessarily reflect the position of NEDA.*

[2] *The author is a Malaysian national and president of Alternative Energy Development, Inc. (AED) located in the USA.*

[3] *The Annex I Parties include the OECD countries and the Eastern European countries with economies in transition.*

[4] *Principally the developing countries.*

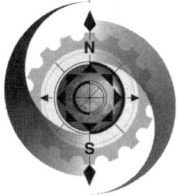

ISSUES&OPTIONS

The Clean
Development
Mechanism

underpriced (in fact, given no value), and used indiscriminately. To date, the economic benefits of reducing anthropogenic greenhouse gases or, alternately, the real costs of increasing greenhouse gases are not known. In economic terms, the damage function for greenhouse gases is undefined. Under these circumstances, it is fair to state that the market has failed to protect the global climate and reduce harmful greenhouse gases.

When markets fail to allocate resources efficiently, policy interventions often have been used to limit damage to the commons. National air and water pollution control regulations are now in place in many developed and developing countries. Pollutants, such as sulfur dioxide (SO_2), nitrogen oxides (NO_x), particulates and others of immediate local or national concern, have all been regulated. The regulations vary from outright bans, as in the case of lead in gasoline, to limits on allowable levels, as in the case of SO_2, NO_x and particulates. The Kyoto Protocol is the second attempt to legally limit the pollutants that are threatening the stability of the global climate. The Montreal Protocol for limiting chlorofluorocarbons (CFCs) was the first.

Market solution

Experience shows that when emissions of pollutants are regulated by limits, a cost-effective way of achieving these limits can occur within a framework of "emissions trading." The emissions trading approach was first implemented in the United States in 1976 to limit air pollution under the Clean Air Act. The fundamental principle of emissions trading is that the location of emissions and specific actions employed to reduce emissions are not important. What matters is that society is better off when emitters are free to pursue least-cost options for reducing emissions. Additionally, emissions trading is based on the idea that polluters responsible for reducing their emissions, rather than regulators, have the greatest incentive to minimise costs and, therefore, will seek new and innovative methods to reduce emissions, if given the opportunity. Finally, by creating a market for emission reductions, regulators can leverage the profit-seeking motives of the private sector to channel investments and

resources needed to meet environmental targets and social needs. This is a particularly important point, as compliance with environmental standards (or targets) generally requires significant initial investments, which the private sector is usually unwilling or unable to accommodate easily.

Trading mandate of the Kyoto Protocol

Two conditions are necessary to create an effective market for emission (in this case, GHG) offsets. The first is standards that limit GHG emissions at the national level. The second is a system for accepting, measuring, validating and trading emission offsets as an alternative to mandated uniform reductions of emissions from all sources. The Kyoto Protocol establishes both of these criteria, first by setting emission limits for Annex I countries and second by allowing for the trading of "emission reduction units" between Annex I Parties (Article 6). In addition, the Kyoto Protocol, in Article 12, establishes the CDM to allow for trading of emission offsets from non-Annex I Parties to Annex I Parties.

The trading of emission reduction units or greenhouse gas offsets represent a cost-effective, flexible and market-based means for achieving overall targets for reductions in GHG emissions. In recognition of this effective market tool, the Conference of Parties (COP) to the United Nations Framework Convention on Climate Change (UNFCCC) incorporated the principle of emissions offset trading in the recently adopted Kyoto Protocol. Specifically, Article 6 of the Kyoto Protocol allows for emissions offset trading between Annex I Parties while Article 12 defines the Clean Development Mechanism (CDM) to facilitate trading of GHG emission offsets from non-Annex I Parties to Annex I Parties. The trading of emission offsets between Annex I Parties allows the Annex I Parties to jointly comply with the limitations of their GHG emissions as established in Annex B of the Kyoto Protocol. The trading of emissions offsets from the non-Annex I Parties to the Annex I Parties is specifically to assist the non-Annex I Parties to "achieve sustainable development while contributing to

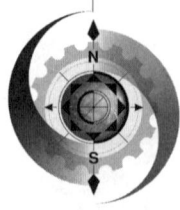

the ultimate objective of the Convention.[5] Additionally, it is intended to assist Parties included in Annex I in achieving compliance with their quantified emissions limitation and reduction commitments under Article 3."

Since the location or origin of GHG emissions is not important to the mitigation of global climate change, economic efficiency would dictate that the lowest cost options for reducing such emissions should be pursued. This can be achieved by the open and free intra-national and international trading of GHG offsets.

> **Fossil fuel consumption also accounts for the largest share of the national GHG emissions from most developing countries and is the fastest growing sector for GHG emissions in all cases.**

Additionally, the open trading of GHG offsets will trigger the large investments needed to deploy new and more efficient technologies to help realise overall reductions in GHG emissions. The Kyoto Protocol clearly recognises and has adopted this principle to allow for trading between Annex I Parties and also from non-Annex I Parties to Annex I Parties.

In both Article 6 and Article 12 of the Kyoto Protocol, two key criteria are associated with the principle of emissions offset trading: (a) additionality; and (b) certification. The additionality criteria specifies that only the reduction in emissions, either by mitigation of sources or enhancement of sinks, that result from activities that would not otherwise occur in a "baseline" situation are considered eligible for offset trading. The certification criteria specifies that the claimed offsets are "real, measurable and will result in long-term benefits related to the mitigation of climate change."

Article 12.3(b) clearly states that Annex I Parties "may use the certified emission reductions ... to contribute to compliance with part of their quantified emission limitation and reduction commitments." The combination of these covenants in the Kyoto Protocol establishes the foundations for a GHG offset trading market.

ASSESSMENT OF GHG OFFSETS

Sources and sinks of GHG emissions

In order to assess the potential for various types of GHG offsets, one must first have an understanding of the primary GHG sources and sinks. The Intergovernmental Panel on Climate Change (IPCC) classifies all GHG sources and sinks into the seven principal categories:[6] These are briefly described in Table 1.

The primary causes of GHG emissions from the IPCC's principal categories are quite varied. A summary of the primary causes associated with each sector is presented in Table 2. The primary global source of anthropogenic GHGs, however, is the production, conversion and use of fossil fuels. Greenhouse gases from fossil fuel-related activities accounted for 73 per cent of total global GHG emissions in 1991.[7] More important, in most Organisation for Economic Co-operation and Development (OECD) countries, over 90 per cent of their GHG emissions are attributable to their fossil fuel consumption. Furthermore, fossil fuel consumption also accounts for the largest share of the national GHG emissions from most developing countries and is the fastest growing sector for GHG emissions in all cases. In many developing countries, GHG emissions from agriculture, land use change and forestry are also significant but growing at a much slower pace in comparison to the GHG emissions from their energy sector. In some countries, the forestry sector emissions,

---

[5] Intergovernmental Panel on Climate Change: Greenhouse Gas Inventory Reporting Instructions - Volume I, *1995.*

[6] Intergovernmental Panel on Climate Change: Greenhouse Gas Inventory Reporting Instructions - Volume I, *1995.*

[7] *Carbon Dioxide Information Analysis Center, Environmental Sciences Division, Oak Ridge National Laboratory, 1993.*

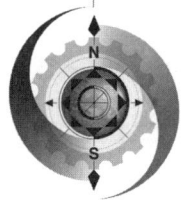

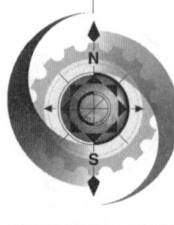

Table 1. Principal categories for GHG sources and sinks

SECTORS	DESCRIPTION OF ACTIVITIES INCLUDED*
Energy	Total emissions of all GHGs from energy activities (fuel combustion as well as fugitive fuel emissions).
Industrial processes	Total emissions from industrial processes where GHGs are the by-product of various production processes. Emissions exclude GHGs from the combustion of energy used during the production process (reported in 1 above).
Solvent and other product use	This category pertains mainly to non-methane volatile organic compounds (NMVOCs) emissions resulting from the use of solvents and other products containing volatile organic compounds.
Agriculture	All anthropogenic emissions from this sector, except for fuel combustion emissions which are covered in 1 above.
Land use change and forestry	Total emissions and removals from forest and land use change activities.
Waste	Total emissions from waste management.
Other	Any other anthropogenic source or sink not referred to above.

* All activities are limited to anthropogenic and related emissions and removals.

after years of exploitation, have now stabilised and is even a negative source (i.e., sink) due to reforestation and forestry management efforts. As a result, the continuing growths of GHG emissions from the energy sector are the primary concern for most developing countries.

The most dramatic growth of GHG emissions is expected to come from the energy sector of the developing countries. This is principally due to the fact that these countries at present have relatively low energy consumption rates and per capita GDPs. Their development plans

Table 2. Primary causes of GHG emissions by sector

SECTORS	PRIMARY CAUSES OF GHG EMISSIONS
Energy	From the production, conversion, transportation and use of fossil fuels (coal, oil and natural gas). This is the single most important source of GHG emissions in most developed countries, accounting for over 90 per cent of total national GHG emissions annually. The principal emissions are CO_2 and CH_4 and some N_2O. The principal source is the combustion of fossil fuels for electricity production, heat, motive power and stationary shaft power. Fugitive emissions from fossil fuel production, conversion and transportation are also significant contributors.
Industrial processes	Principally, CO_2 emissions from cement production, lime manufacture and limestone use. Also some N_2O production from nitric and adipic acid production.
Solvent and other product use	From the use of solvents and other chemical products that principally result in NMVOCs. This source accounts for a relatively minor (usually less than one per cent) fraction of total national GHG emissions.
Agriculture	These are principally methane emissions from enteric fermentation in domestic livestock, manure management, rice cultivation. Also N_2O emissions from use of fertilisers and agricultural waste burning.
Land use change and forestry	This sector is potentially both a source and a sink for GHGs. GHGs are emitted or stored through land use changes and forest management activities such as deforestation, land clearing, reforestation, draining of wetlands, clearing for urban or agricultural development, etc.
Waste	GHG emissions from this sector principally result from the decay of waste disposed in landfills, municipal wastewater treatment and combustion or open burning of waste materials. Landfills are the principal source of GHG emissions in this sector.
Other	Any other anthropogenic source or sink not referred to above.

Table 3. GHG offset options by IPCC sector

SECTORS	GENERALISED GHG OFFSET OPTIONS
Energy	• Switch from fossil fuels to "clean fuels" and renewable energy. • Increase efficient production, conversion and use of fossil fuels. • Capture and use fugitive emissions from fossil fuel chain.
Industrial processes	• Improve efficiency of production technology. • Introduce alternative materials and processes.
Solvent and other product use	• Substitute with GHG neutral substances. • Use products more efficiently.
Agriculture	• Improve livestock/feed management. • Improve manure management. • Modify rice cultivation practices. • Adopt low-methane rice cultivars. • Switch from nitrogen to organic fertilisers. • Eliminate open burning of agricultural wastes.
Land use change and forestry	• Protect/conserve/preserve forests and wetlands. • Increase efficiency of forest management. • Practice reforestation and afforestation. • Enhance forest regeneration. • Improve agroforestry practices. • Improve soil and grassland management.
Waste	• Reduce and recycle wastes. • Capture methane from waste disposal and wastewater treatment. • Eliminate open burning of waste.
Other	• Reduce, modify or eliminate practice.

are specifically targeted at increasing per capita GDP and in the process also increasing their per capita energy consumption. As a result, total GHG emissions from the developing countries are expected to surpass those of the OECD countries some time in the beginning of the new century. This dramatic increase will derive mostly from the large increase in fossil fuel consumption that is projected for the developing countries.

Taxonomy of GHG offsets

A taxonomy of GHG offsets is briefly presented to clarify the implications of different types of GHG offsets on sustainable development. This taxonomy is by no means exhaustive but is presented to be illustrative of the sustainable development issues that are associated with different categories of GHG offsets. GHG offsets can be derived from two principal actions: (1) preventing or reducing GHG emissions; which can be done in the sectors listed above and (2) preserving or increasing GHG sinks, which applies only to the land use

change and forestry sectors. Table 3 presents a generalised list of the GHG offset options by IPCC sector.

Assessing GHG offset trading potential

Within each of the generalised GHG offset options presented in Table 3 is a wide range of specific GHG offset options. For example, switching from fossil fuels to clean fuels comprises adopting hydropower, wind energy, solar energy, bioenergy, nuclear power, and ocean thermal energy. Similarly, increasing efficiency of forestry management can include productive use of forest wastes, increasing density of forest biomass, reducing loss of forest cover, among other things. Each of the specific GHG offset options have unique characteristics regarding costs, availability, reliability, safety and other relevant factors. In-depth treatment of all these factors is beyond the scope of this paper. The objective of this paper is to determine which of the generalised GHG offset options provide the best prospects for: (a) GHG offset

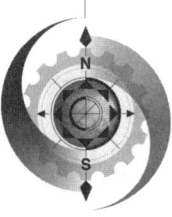

ISSUES&OPTIONS

The Clean
Development
Mechanism

trading; (b) contributing to sustainable development; and (c) significantly reducing GHG emissions or increasing GHG sinks.

Real, measurable and certifiable offsets

Three principal criteria for GHG offsets to qualify for trading are stipulated by the Kyoto Protocol. Emission reductions resulting from each project activity shall be certified on the basis of three criteria:

◆ Voluntary participation approved by each Party involved

◆ Real, measurable and long-term benefits related to the mitigation of climate change

◆ Reduction in emissions that are additional to any that would occur in the absence of the certified project activity.

The first criteria, that of voluntary participation approved by each Party is not expected to be a major barrier to GHG offset trading. The pilot program of "Activities Implemented Jointly" (AIJ) has clearly demonstrated the willingness of both developed and developing country Parties to explore this eventual possibility. However, the last two criteria are particularly important, as it is not necessarily simple or straightforward to verify these criteria for all of the generalised GHG options listed in Table 3.

The "real, measurable and long-term benefits" are much more difficult to quantify in the case of the agriculture, land use and forestry activities than for activities in the other sectors. In agriculture, land use and forestry sector activities, benefits are not as easily measured and are much more variable than is the case for the energy, industry and waste sector activities, where units of GHG offsets produced can be metered and accounted for with great detail and accuracy. Long-term benefits to the mitigation of climate change are also not specifically assured in the case of many agriculture, land use and forestry sector activities. The output of GHG offsets can vary significantly over time and

must be constantly monitored to substantiate their values. There are no solid assurances that sinks (particularly forests) will remain in place indefinitely, and, in principal, they are limited in supply. Similarly, modified agricultural and forestry practices present such highly variable results that it is extremely difficult and potentially expensive to certify their actual GHG offsets and benefits.

Assuring that projects will result in "reduction of emissions that are additional" is also more difficult for agriculture, land use and forestry sector projects than for projects in the other sectors. Determining the additionality of a project requires clearly defining a baseline. Given the recent trends for reforestation and commercial tree plantations such as in Thailand, Malaysia, India, the Philippines, China, Costa Rica and several other developing countries, it is difficult to defend a baseline in which deforestation is slated to continue unchecked, without reforestation being part of a "baseline" national forestry action plan. Accepting that deforestation is part of a "national baseline" runs the risk of rewarding countries for supporting policies that are clearly not in their basic national development interests. Similarly, improvements in agricultural productivity are leading many countries to abandon unsustainable agricultural practices and to reduce dependence on chemical fertilisers. Thus the baseline in this sector is also changing in the direction of reduced GHG emissions.

Potential for sustainable development

One of the key criteria of the proposed CDM is "to assist Parties not included in Annex I in achieving sustainable development." The term "sustainable development" is defined as a form of development or progress that "meets the needs of the present without compromising the ability of future generations to meet their own needs."[8] The methods and approaches for sustainable development have been broadly debated over the past decade in all quarters of the world community. It is important to note that the World Commission on Environment and

---

[8] *Source: World Commission on Environment and Development (WCED),* Our Common Future, *Oxford, Oxford University Press, 1987.*

Development (WCED) report did not define sustainable development exclusively for the developing countries, but also for the developed countries. Therefore, within the context of the CDM,

> It is important to note that the WCED report did not define sustainable development exclusively for the developing countries but also for the developed countries.

the sustainable development criteria should be viewed as a two-way street. That is, the Annex I Parties should simultaneously pursue sustainable development within their own economies and, in the process, transfer their acquired technology and know-how to the developing countries to help them also achieve the goal of sustainable development.

GHG offset projects that propose to assist non-Annex I Parties achieve sustainable development should be derived from successfully proven efforts and not from efforts that are in need of an experimental platform. Within this context, many energy efficiency, industrial process improvements, some renewable energy and most waste to energy options are ready for application on a large scale. Alternately, some forestry and land use GHG offset projects that principally lock up productive use of resources from future generations clearly do not meet the criteria of sustainable development. Similarly, if modifying rice cultivation, adopting low-methane rice cultivars or changing livestock feed and management practices result in increased costs without increased productivity, then it is unlikely that these practices can meet the sustainable development criterion. In many cases, introducing these "high-tech" agricultural processes also ignores more traditional and sustainable agricultural practices and fails in the long term by causing social and economic damage.

Potential for significant GHG mitigation

An additional stated criterion of the proposed CDM is "to assist Parties not included in Annex I ... in contributing to the ultimate objective of the Convention" (i.e., stabilisation of global GHG concentrations). This means that projects undertaken within the CDM should have the potential to catalyse significant

and long-term GHG mitigation benefits. This could occur when such projects help remove barriers, reduce future costs or facilitate replication so that subsequent GHG offset efforts are cost-effective, can be implemented without the continued assistance of the CDM and ultimately become the baseline or normal practice.

GHG offset options in the energy sector have the most potential for significant GHG mitigation and long-term benefit. This is because GHG emissions from the energy sector are rapidly increasing in most developing countries and are, in many instances, the most significant source of GHG emissions. Energy sector GHG emissions already account for over 90 per cent of total emissions from most OECD countries. In most developing countries, energy sector GHG emissions are presently dominating or are projected to soon dominate their national GHG emissions inventory. As a result, GHG offset options in the energy sector provide the most likely source for sustained and significant GHG offset options. Additionally, investments made in energy sector infrastructure today have long-term implications on energy consumption patterns for the future. The opportunities and benefits for redirecting the investments in this sector for more sustainable options are significant. On the other hand, the opportunity for redirecting investments in the developing countries for mitigation options in the land use change and forestry sectors are not as significant. The land use change and forestry sector options are also limited by physical, social and economic factors and by competing uses for scarce (land) resources.

Comparison of GHG offset options

Table 4 presents a comparison of the generalised GHG offset options against the criteria for GHG offset trading is suggested for the CDM in Article 12 of the Kyoto Protocol. The comparison is based on a subjective assessment

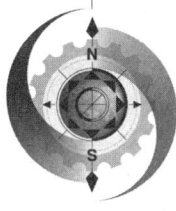

Table 4. Comparison of the potential of GHG offset options for the CDM

GHG OFFSET OPTIONS	Real, measurable and certifiable	Assist in sustainable development	Potential for significant mitigation
Energy sector			
• Switch from fossil fuels to clean fuels	H	H	H
• Efficient use of fossil fuels	H	H	H
• Capture fugitive fossil fuel emissions	H	H	H
Industrial processes			
• Improve production efficiency	H	H	H
• Use alternative materials and processes	H	H	M
Solvent and other product use			
• Substitute with GHG neutral substances	H	L	L
• Use products more efficiently	H	M	L
Agriculture sector			
• Improve livestock/feed management	L	M	L
• Improve manure management	L	H	L
• Modify rice cultivation practices	L	L	M-H
• Adopt low-methane rice cultivars	L	L	M-H
• Switch from nitrogen based fertilisers	L	H	L
• Eliminate open burning of agri-wastes	L	M	L
Land use change and forestry			
• Protect/conserve forests and wetlands	L	H	M
• Increase efficiency of forest management	L	M	M
• Reforestation and afforestation	L	M	M-H
• Enhance forest regeneration	L	M	M
• Improve agroforestry practices	L	M	M
Waste sector			
• Reduce and recycle wastes	H	H	L-M
• Capture methane from waste disposal	H	M	L-M
• Eliminate open burning of waste	H	M	L-M
Other			
• Reduce, modify or eliminate practice	U	U	U

H = High probability of meeting the criteria   **L** = Low probability of meeting the criteria
M = Medium probability of meeting the criteria   **U** = Unknown probability of meeting the criteria

of the probability of the various GHG offset options being able to meet the three key criteria discussed in previous three sections. The comparison clearly demonstrates that the energy sector GHG offset options best meet all the criteria proposed by the CDM for carbon offset trading.

IMPLEMENTING GHG OFFSET PROJECTS

Role of stakeholders

One of the most important elements associated with the successful implementation of GHG offset projects is the role of stakeholders in the process. The impact on and the accountability of stakeholders must be carefully considered in the design of any project to ensure that affected parties are not adversely impacted. At the same time, responsible parties are legally bound to deliver on their commitments. As an example, a bagasse co-generation project designed to offset diesel consumption for power generation will have several affected and responsible parties. The responsible parties may include growers who receive surplus bagasse fiber for sale; the rural poor who receive the surplus fiber for use as a supplemental fuel; and the supplier of the diesel fuel that will be displaced. They may include growers who must supply the raw sugarcane, millers who must convert their mills and boilers to co-generate electricity and the utility company that must agree to buy electricity that is delivered into its grid. In an agriculture project, the stakeholders could include the farmers who carry out the targeted project, the buyers of the farm outputs and the consumers of the farm products. Similarly, in a forestry project, the stakeholders could include national and local governments, landowners, forest dwellers, adjacent communities and hosts of other interested parties.

The number of key stakeholders will vary from sector to sector and, more specifically, from project to project. In general, agriculture, land use and forestry sector projects will have larger numbers of key stakeholders than energy and industry sector projects. This single factor can make designing, implementing and operating agriculture and forestry projects more complicated, costly and risky in comparison to energy and industry sector projects. Projects with multiple and varied stakeholders, each with different functions and concerns, are much more difficult to design and implement success-fully. Projects with limited stakeholders and similar objective functions are easier to design and implement. Energy and industry sector projects fall into this later category.

> **Projects with multiple and varied stakeholders, each with different functions and concerns, are much more difficult to design and implement successfully.**

Legal and institutional framework

All affected Parties should be willing or able to deal with the changed circumstances brought about by the project. If they are not, problems can undermine the ultimate success of the project. More important, responsible Parties must be legally bound to meet their responsibilities – such as delivering raw materials and purchasing project outputs at agreed prices over pre-determined periods.

One of the key outputs of a GHG offset project – and a key part of the cost-benefit equation – is the GHG offset itself. Securing legally binding GHG offset supply and purchase agreements along with all other project related supply and purchase agreements can help secure the financing for any project. Again, because of the nature of GHG offset projects, it should be more straightforward to secure legally binding agreements for energy and industry sector projects than for agriculture, land use and forestry sector projects. In the former, the GHG offsets produced can be easily tied to the other measurable physical outputs of the project (e.g., kilowatt-hours of electricity or tons of cement produced). In the case of agriculture, land use and forestry sector projects, the GHG offsets produced are more difficult to measure accurately as they are based on highly variable biological processes.

The institutional framework is equally important for the success of a GHG offset project. As GHG offsets will require certification and validation, it is critical to have established institutional standards, data, measurement procedures, access to project sites and enforcement of agreed practices. In a project where the output of GHG offsets can be independently verified by the delivery of physically measured units, the institutional framework is less important, though the independent verification of delivered units is still necessary. Energy, industry and waste sector GHG offset projects represent projects in this category. Where the output of GHG offsets cannot be directly measured and must be estimated, the institutional framework becomes critical, as the possibility for error, disagreement and disputes increases significantly. Agriculture, land use and forestry sector projects tend to fall into this category as their levels of output are highly variable.

Financial needs

The ability to secure financing for GHG offset projects will be a critical factor in the imple-

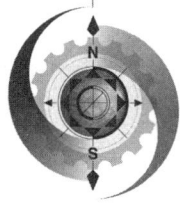

mentation of these projects. The financing needs for GHG offset projects can vary significantly – from relatively small sums to secure land rights or capitalise efficiency improvements to large sums needed to establish reforestation programs or institute infrastructure changes. Financing needs must balance project capital and operating costs against cash flow, debt service and return on investment (ROI). It is difficult to generalise the financing needs of GHG offset projects. Clearly, projects with higher expected ROIs – assuming that risks are manageable – are more attractive for financing than those with lower ROIs. However, two key distinctions can help identify GHG offset projects that are more attractive for financing. The first is projects in which the revenues from the GHG offsets contribute only marginally to their overall financial viability. Given the unknown market value for GHG offsets at this stage, projects that do not depend solely on GHG offset sales for revenues are better prospects than those that do. The second distinction is the length of time before a positive cash flow is achieved. The longer the gestation period before a positive cash flow, the higher the financial risks. Some GHG offset

> **In the case of agriculture, land use and forestry sector projects, the GHG offsets produced are more difficult to accurately measure as they are based on highly variable biological processes.**

projects, such as those in the forestry sector, may require a substantial period (more than ten years) before turning a positive cash flow. In these cases, the financiers of the project bear greater risks than in cases where positive cash flows can be realised in one to three years from date of financial closure.

GHG offset risks

Several forms of risks are associated with all projects. In addition to the normal set of project risks, GHG offset projects encompass a number of others. Two risks, specific to GHG offset projects, are worth exploring: (1) the uncertain market value for GHG offsets; and (2) the possibility that changing baselines could invalidate the additionality of future GHG offsets.

The issue of uncertain market value for GHG offsets was briefly discussed in the section above in relation to financing of GHG offset projects. The markets for GHG offsets are just emerging and not yet formalised. Principally experimentation and speculation drive the market. A wide range of values exists for GHG

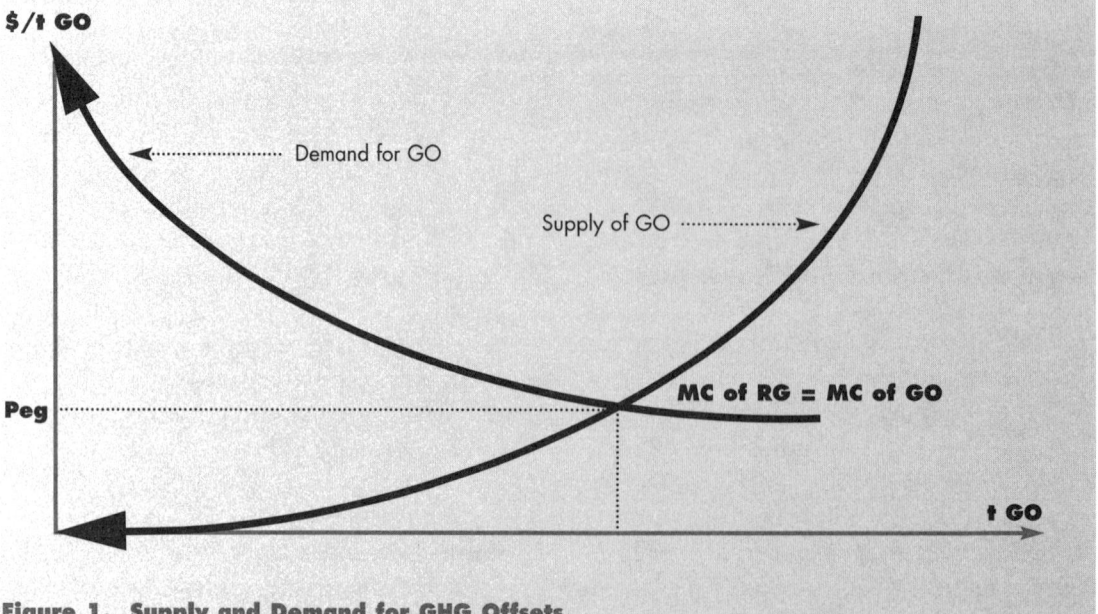

Figure 1. Supply and Demand for GHG Offsets
RG = Reducing GHGs   **MC** = Marginal Costs   **GO** = GHG Offsets   **Peq** = Equilibrium Price   **t** = tons

offsets, from less than US$1 per ton of carbon equivalent (TCE) to over US$50 per TCE. It is not clear in which direction the market value for GHG offsets will gravitate. However, as shown in Figure 1, the equilibrium price for GHG offsets will gravitate toward the point at which the marginal cost for reducing GHG emissions is equal to the marginal cost of producing GHG offsets.

Minimising the risk of uncertain market prices for GHG offsets requires selecting GHG offset projects·in which the revenues from offset sales are a small component of total revenues. In this way, uncertainties or fluctuations in GHG offset market prices will only have a minimal impact on the financial viability of the project. Forestry projects designed to serve solely as carbon sinks are an example of GHG offset projects that are fully exposed to the risks associated with uncertain market prices for GHG offsets.

For some projects, changing conditions can affect the baseline they started with and invalidate the additionality they anticipated. Rapidly evolving technologies can bring fluctuations in cost, and shifting economic conditions can also have unpredictable effects. In these circumstances, for example, the declining costs of a GHG offset technology, such as renewable energy, could eventually make a GHG offset option more cost-effective than the baseline GHG-producing option. In this case, the GHG offset option would replace the old baseline option. The net result would be that the GHG offset option would no longer qualify for GHG offset certification under the additionality criteria.

To mitigate the "changing baseline" risk, the additionality of future GHG offsets should be "grand-fathered" or guaranteed at the time of project financial closure. This is an important as project financing is based on the ability to secure project costs and revenues over the life of a project and not just for short periods. Additionally, a decision to institute a GHG offset project, especially in the energy and industry sector, may result in displacing an investment in a GHG producing project. If not displaced, the committed investment in the GHG producing project will give rise to future GHG emissions over the entire life of the GHG producing project. The fact that the GHG offset project may become more cost effective at a future point in time does not negate the value of displacing future GHG emissions at an earlier date.

STRATEGY FOR TRADING GHG OFFSETS

Establishing a market framework

Two major components are necessary for an effective market framework for trading GHG offsets within the CDM. The first is clear and effective GHG Offset Validation Services (GOVS) – internationally recognised administrative services that validate and certify tradable GHG offsets and thereby give them marketable value. The second is to catalyse the development and investment in GHG offset projects. This will most effectively be accomplished through robust GHG Offset Trading Services (GOTS). The specific elements of each component are briefly outlined below.

The GHG offset validation services (GOVS)

The specific elements of a CDM offset validation service are:

◆ International GHG Emissions Registry – a COP-appointed or approved agency that establishes and applies the rules for GHG offset trading, tracks and registers national GHG emissions (e.g., inventories) of Annex I Parties, validates the additionality of proposed GHG offsets in non-Annex I Parties, and certifies and registers national transfers of GHG offsets

◆ National GHG Emissions Registries – nationally appointed agencies that establish and monitor national GHG emission reduction programs and certify and register audited GHG offsets

◆ GHG Emission/Offset Auditors – independent professional/accounting organisations or individuals who provide GHG emission and offset auditing and validating services for a fee.

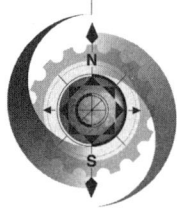

ISSUES&OPTIONS

The Clean
Development
Mechanism

The GHG offset trading services (GOTS)

The specific elements of a CDM offset trading service are:

- GHG Emitters – private and public sector entities, in Annex 1 countries, that own and operate primary activities associated with GHG emissions;

- GHG Offset Suppliers – private and public sector entities or partnerships, in developing countries, that develop, own and operate GHG offset projects/activities;

- GHG Offset Brokers – independent organisations or individuals that trade/broker GHG offsets between suppliers/sellers and emitters/buyers.

A graphical representation of the institutional framework for GHG offset market within the CDM is presented in Figure 2. The key elements of this institutional framework include:

- The International GHG Emissions Registry (TIGER)

- The National GHG Emissions Registry (TNGER)

- GHG Emission/Offset Auditors

- GHG Emitters

- GHG Offset Suppliers

- GHG Offset Brokers.

A hypothetical example of a GHG offset market transaction is presented in Text Box 1.

Operation of the GHG offset market

The effective operation of the GHG offset market within the CDM requires a clear and transparent set of rules. In order for any internationally traded GHG reduction to become a credible, tradable asset, it must meet accounting criteria adopted by the COP and applied by the CDM's International GHG Emissions Registry (TIGER). These criteria must be selected and designed to ensure that all GHG offsets traded internationally are real, surplus, measurable, auditable, and certifiable. "Real" implies that they are true reductions in actual emissions, net of any consequential increase in actual emissions resulting from shifting demand. A real reduction must be properly measured, recorded and reported.

An emissions reduction is surplus if, at a minimum, it exceeds emission requirements mandated by other laws or regulations; that is, the reduction is not being relied upon to

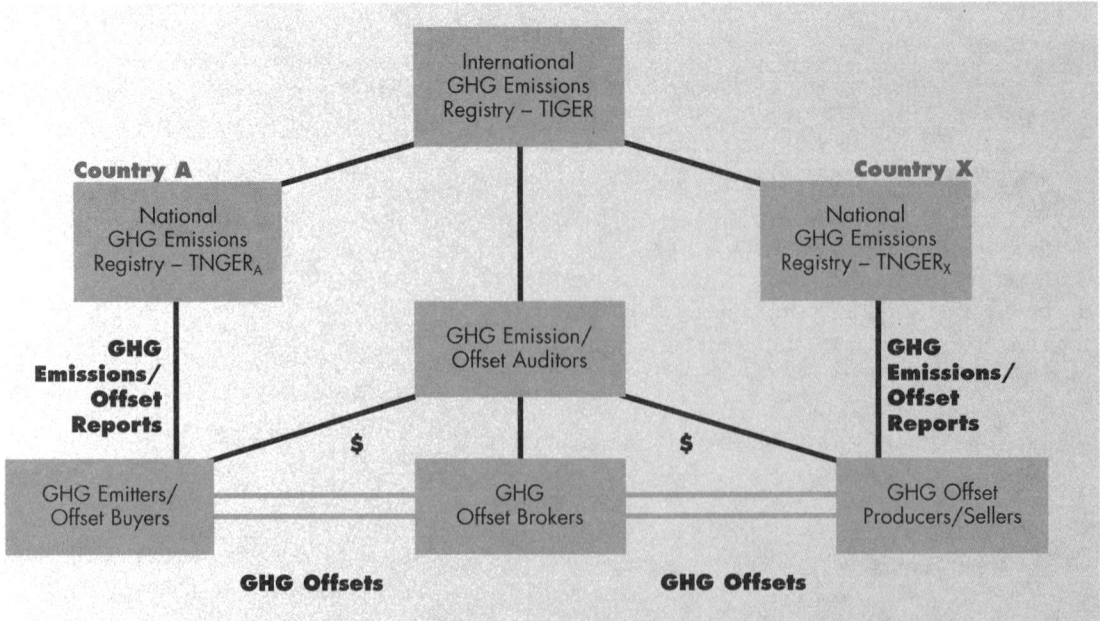

Figure 2. Institutional Framework for GHG Offset Market within the CDM

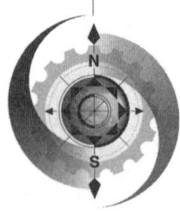

Box 1. Hypothetical example of a CDM GHG offset market trade

(The following is presented for illustrative purposes only and does not represent any commitments, implied or otherwise, by the countries mentioned in this illustrative example.)

In 2002, according to regulations implemented by the Government of the Netherlands to comply with provisions of the Kyoto Protocol, Dutch POWER generating company has a requirement to reduce its carbon emissions. It will cost POWER more than $30 to reduce every additional ton of carbon beyond the reductions it has already achieved in its plants. POWER is aware that there are cheaper options available for reducing carbon emissions internationally, and decides to consult with carbon brokers to obtain information on carbon offset investment opportunities. The Netherlands has joined the Kyoto Protocol's CDM, which is for Parties that are capable of registering, certifying and reporting offsets traded at the international level. Thus, POWER can invest in international carbon offsets in other countries, such as Malaysia, that have also joined the CDM.

Broker 1 can supply verified carbon offsets from a Dutch firm for $20/ton. Broker 2 can supply carbon offsets from Malaysia for $8 per ton of carbon reduced, plus a fee to hire a professional auditor and to cover the costs of broker services, for a total of $9 per ton. POWER decides to investigate the Malaysian offsets. POWER pays Broker 2 to have the offsets audited in order to confirm that they are real, surplus and additional reductions. Broker 2 hires a private auditing firm, Auditor, which verifies that the Malaysian offsets are in compliance with carbon offset credit rules adopted by the CDM. With such an audit, POWER is assured that the offsets will be certified for international trade, according to rules established by the CDM and agreed to by both the Malaysian and Dutch governments. POWER therefore pays Broker 2 $9 per ton. Broker 2 submits the audit to the Malaysian government for registration and certification. Once the carbon offsets credits are registered and certified by the Malaysian government, POWER submits the certificate to the Dutch government for registration and certification and the results of these transactions are then registered with the appropriate authority designated by the CDM.

This example is not unrealistic. The market is already being used for international trades to buy and sell low-cost emissions reductions. However, very few trades are taking place at present because trades for offsets created prior to 2000 will not be recognised. The incentives to reduce emissions will be adopted when the provisions of the Kyoto Protocol are implemented. Thus, all that will be needed are the rules. These should be developed and adopted by the COP-appointed International Regulator and CDM as soon as possible in order to ensure the widest range of low-cost options.

comply with another law or regulation (in the host country or by another offset buyer). Measurable means the rate and total amount of a reduction is quantifiable in a reliable and verifiable manner. An auditable carbon offset is one that a third party can measure and verify in order to confirm that the emissions reductions are real and surplus.[9] Finally, certification confirms that an offset has been included in the national registry, can be traded, and will be reported to the COP. Both Parties involved in a CDM offset trade must certify that GHG offsets are registered, eligible for trade and reported to the COP.

The CDM's TIGER must develop generic rules for offset accounting to ensure that offsets are real and surplus. The initial reporting criteria adopted by the COP may be sufficient for this purpose. The rules will be applied by independent accounting or auditing firms. TIGER will provide an oversight role, similar to that played by securities exchange commissions or financial accounting standards boards, to ensure that audited reports meet minimum standards. They will set the rules for creating offsets and sanctions. In addition, TIGER will serve as the central international clearinghouse

and recording agency for GHG offset trades. TIGER will deal directly with the National GHG Emissions Registries in carrying out the recording and reporting functions.

By relying on approved international auditors and the National GHG Emissions Registries, TIGER will not be involved in the detailed assessments and field work required for approving or reviewing all offset applications, nor will it be involved in the details of the international transactions and trades of approved offsets. However, it will be informed and will record all trades, in real time, and keep track of international trades in terms of debits and credits against national emissions inventories. TIGER, however, may undertake random audits to ensure that accepted standards of accounting are met and to maintain a "threat" to ensure that audits undertaken by private entities comply with the rules. Those found not to be in compliance with TIGER standards would lose their accreditation.

TIGER, in consultation with the national regulatory agencies, must determine how auditing firms and other entities will become eligible for undertaking audits. For example,

---

[9] *The third party should not have a stake in the creation or sale of the offset.*

these firms could be trained and certified by TIGER, or the market could decide by directing GHG buyers and sellers to use accountants that have a history/track record of performing credible, professional audits. A market-based approach would rely on the second option (where demand will be low for poor accounting firms since their offsets cannot be certified for inclusion in government registries). National governments may also hire private firms to carry out some of the functions related to certification.

Participating in the offset trading system

In a functioning market, it is most likely that offsets will be created and sold by a range of private, non-government organisations and government actors. These offsets can be audited by independent certified auditors, purchased by net GHG emitters or brokers and speculators, and certified by national agencies – all according to rules set by the CDM (as discussed in the previous section). However, differences in national policies, levels of development, and economic structures mean that the quality and reliability of emission offsets created in one country will not necessarily be "equal" to those created in other countries. Therefore, in order to create a "level playing field" that ensures a minimum acceptable quality and reliability, the CDM must devise a system to ensure that internationally traded offsets are created, audited, certified, credited and reported within a transparent national framework. Such a national framework must be able to signal the CDM that it is ready and willing to play by the CDM's rules. One signal could be joining the CDM and abiding to its prescribed rules.

Membership in the CDM would be voluntary. However, members of the CDM would follow established rules for registering, certifying, and reporting offsets and offset trades. The CDM, with COP guidance, will set these rules to ensure credibility. The rules would state that:

◆ All offsets to be traded must be audited and validated to be additional and registered in the national registry and CDM.

◆ All offsets to be traded internationally must be certified by the host government where the offset was created.

◆ All offsets to be credited internationally must be registered and certified by the government of the buyer, and reported immediately to the CDM's TIGER.

◆ The national registry must be capable of maintaining the basic required information on the offsets, including an offset tracking number.

◆ The government is accountable for maintaining the additionality and credibility of all certified offsets.

Once the rules for participation in offset creation and trading have been adopted, the market can rapidly evolve at both the national and international levels. A majority of the GHG offset buying, trading, auditing, and certifying activities can be cost-effectively performed for a fee by the private sector in established boards of trade or stock markets. The seekers, or buyers, of GHG offsets will pay for many of the transaction costs, if transactions plus offset costs are lower than available compliance measures in their home countries.

Currently, few offset seekers/buyers seem willing to pay for offset project development costs. The risks associated with an unknown process appear too high. Therefore, some governments may wish to financially support the CDM to kick-start offset trading by funding the project development costs in order to create an initial pipeline of creditable projects and to signal their interest in engaging in international GHG offset trading. Whether this is a high priority would depend on the national policies and incentive structures adopted in Annex I countries to limit GHG emissions.

Promoting sustainable development

To meet the objective of assisting the non-Annex I Parties in achieving sustainable development, the CDM should incorporate a system of incentives to encourage the development and trade of GHG offsets that are beneficial for sustainable development. Such options include renewable energy, energy efficiency, improved industrial processes, reducing and recycling wastes and a number of other options. While

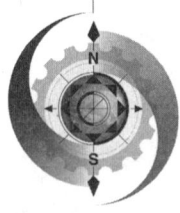

ISSUES&OPTIONS
The Clean
Development
Mechanism

the proposed strategy for trading of GHG offsets is to rely on market forces, it is important for the CDM to apply its leverage to encourage and catalyse GHG offsets that support sustainable development. There are a number of possible financial and administrative instruments the CDM could consider, such as:

◆ Validation and certification of only those GHG offsets that have a clear and demonstrable positive impact on sustainable development. While this measure may be effective for promoting sustainable development options, it would inhibit achievement of least-cost GHG mitigation.

◆ Attaching an additional premium to the CDM certification costs of GHG offsets that do not meet a minimum "sustainable development criteria." This option would, in effect, tax GHG offsets that are not fully supportive of sustainable development. For example, some projects that claim GHG offsets by switching from coal to oil or to "clean coal" are able to meet the additionality criteria. However, they are not fully supportive of sustainable development objectives. The premium earned by the CDM could be used to help identify, develop and implement GHG offset options that do meet the sustainable development criteria.

◆ Discounting the GHG offset value of those offsets that do not meet the sustainable development criteria. While the impact of this measure would be similar to that of a premium certification charge, no net revenues for the CDM would be generated in the process. The effect of discounting "non-sustainable GHG offsets" would be to make them more expensive to potential buyers. This will simultaneously make "sustainable GHG offsets" more attractive.

◆ Limiting the period into the future that "non-sustainable GHG offsets" would be certified by the CDM. This measure would also cause the effective cost of "non-sustainable GHG offsets" to rise, but would be revenue-neutral for the CDM.

◆ Placing quotas on the amount of "non-sustainable GHG offsets" that could be traded in a given period. This measure would have to be based on some prior knowledge of the anticipated level of trading in order to be effective. If quotas are able to limit the supply of lower cost non-sustainable GHG offsets, it would allow the higher-cost sustainable GHG offsets to enter the market and would in effect increase the price for GHG offsets by shifting the supply curve up.

The above is a sampling of measures that could be adopted by the CDM if it is to meet its objective of assisting the non-Annex I Parties in achieving sustainable development in the process of GHG offset trading. However, significantly more study and analysis of the effectiveness of these measures are needed.

CONCLUSIONS

This paper has demonstrated the fundamental differences for sustainable development associated with different types of GHG offsets. It has shown that many of the GHG offsets in the agriculture, land use and forestry sectors, if designed only for GHG offset benefits, are only marginally supportive of sustainable development. Similarly, energy and industry sector GHG offset projects that continue their reliance on fossil fuels are also not supportive of long-term sustainable development. On the other hand, renewable energy, energy efficiency, improved industrial processes and waste management initiatives can provide GHG offsets that are supportive of sustainable development. This is also the case for some well-defined multi-purpose agriculture, land use and forestry sector projects.

This paper has identified a number of critical factors associated with the implementation of GHG offset projects. Specifically, it has shown that the role of stakeholders, the legal and institutional framework, and the financial

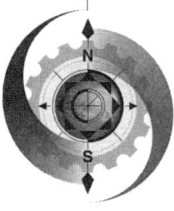

ISSUES&OPTIONS
The Clean
Development
Mechanism

requirements of GHG offset projects are important. Furthermore, it has demonstrated that agriculture, forestry and land use sector projects may be more difficult to implement, validate and certify in comparison to energy, industry and waste sector projects. These distinctions increase the risks associated with GHG offset projects in the agriculture, forestry and land use sectors.

The paper briefly outlines a strategy for trading of GHG offsets. It proposes a preliminary structure for operating the CDM while incorporating the services of government, NGOs and the private sector. It concludes with a list of a number of measures that could be adopted by the CDM to help promote GHG offsets for sustainable development. ■

Chapter 13

FOREST AND LAND USE PROJECTS

**Paige Brown and Nancy Kete,
with Robert Livernash
World Resources Institute
Washington, DC**

Summary: The Clean Development Mechanism (CDM), as outlined in Article 12 of the Kyoto Protocol, is now closer to an idea than an operational entity. To what extent forest and land use projects will be addressed by the CDM is one of the many issues still undecided. This paper poses partial responses to a range of objections about including forestry and land use projects under the CDM, and considers a number of unresolved questions. Fully resolving many of these issues will require further research. Clearly, however, the Protocol's impact on biodiversity, as well as climate, will be maximised by including a wide range of land use projects, including forest management and preservation, and provided that credible guidelines for monitoring and verification are in place.

The CDM arose from a Brazilian proposal for a "Clean Development Fund." It was originally intended to serve two purposes: a) provide an incentive for developed (Annex I) countries to comply with the Convention; and b) provide a source of revenue for developing countries to implement the Protocol (by assessing financial penalties against those Annex I Parties that exceeded their assigned emission amounts).

In its final form as Article 12 of the Kyoto Protocol, the Clean Development Mechanism (CDM) gained acceptance by dropping any role in compliance enforcement. Instead, the CDM borrows from arrangements under the "Activities Implemented Jointly" (AIJ) pilot phase to reduce greenhouse gas emissions or sequester carbon, which includes national programs such as Costa Rica's national "Certified Tradable Offset" program and the United States Initiative on Joint Implementation. Because it has originated from a developing country proposal, and incorporates several new design principles proposed by Southern delegations, the CDM is expected to enjoy greater support than did Joint Implementation.

The skeletal text of Article 12 is now closer to an idea than an operational entity. Highly innovative, it has the potential to meet the needs of both developing and industrialised countries. If properly constructed, it may offer Annex I nations lower-cost, more flexible options in meeting emissions constraints, while providing a source of capital for the financing of clean, energy-efficient economic development and for projects to reduce deforestation and forest degradation in non-Annex I countries.

The United Nations Framework Convention on Climate Change (UNFCCC) commits all Parties, Annex I and non-Annex I, to promote sustainable management and conservation of forests and other ecosystems that serve as sinks of greenhouse gases.[1] However, the question of how to implement this

---

[1] *United Nations,* United Nations Framework Convention on Climate Change, Article 4(d). *(United Nations, New York, 1992). Available online at: http://www.unfccc.de/fccc/conv/conv.htm.*

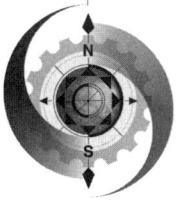

commitment remains unclear in the Kyoto Protocol. The CDM provides the best opportunity in the Protocol to promote and fund lower-emission resource use and management patterns driving greenhouse gas emissions in developing countries. It has the potential to fund "techno-logical leapfrogging" that would enable developing countries to bypass the inefficient choices made by industrialised countries. While most examples of leapfrogging center on the energy sector, such as building the most efficient and up-to-date power plants, the forest and land use sector also offers technology transfer opportunities that can both decrease emissions and improve environmental performance. Some examples include improving agricultural productivity through transfer of irrigation or management practices, increasing milling efficiency, improving silvicultural practices, or sustainable forest management techniques.

Through such carbon sequestration activities, the CDM has the potential to stop the loss of biological diversity, protect critical watersheds, and accelerate the reforestation of degraded forests. If constructed to deliver credible greenhouse gas reductions, it can provide needed financial resources to developing countries for the sustainable use and conservation of their forests.

Rapid, human-caused climate change is likely to result in a significant loss of biodiversity. It is likely to alter regional precipitation and temperature, affecting the range and species composition of ecosystems, perhaps more rapidly than species will be able to adapt.[2] Though forest-based CDM projects may offer both biodiversity and climate benefits, it is important to underscore the need to prevent or slow human-caused climate change with its potentially severe negative impacts on biodiversity. Nations should ratify and implement the Kyoto Protocol and the UNFCCC.

THE CDM AND FORESTS

The Protocol acknowledges the dual role of forests in climate change. Forests have an enormous ability to sequester – or store – carbon that would otherwise be released into the atmosphere. That is why protecting, restoring and improving the management of forest can help slow climate change. Conversely, forest conversion contributes to the problem by adding carbon dioxide to the atmosphere. Deforestation is estimated to account for 30 per cent of the atmospheric build-up of carbon dioxide, the most prevalent greenhouse gas, and future projections show large emissions from deforestation.[3]

The international community is about to make momentous choices about what is included and what is left out in the global approach to mitigate climate change. One of the biggest choices is how much of a role forest and land use change projects will have under the CDM. Forests and land use changes are addressed in the following Articles.

Parties disagree over the role of forest and land use change projects under the CDM. Several countries claim that, because forests and land use change are not explicitly mentioned in the Protocol text on the mechanism, they are therefore not included. Others insist that, since there are no explicit limits placed on the mechanism, any and all forest and land use projects are eligible. The matter will clearly have to be decided by negotiators.

This paper sorts through issues relating to forest and land use change projects under the CDM. It considers remaining unresolved issues, and poses partial responses to a range of objections facing the inclusion of forest and

[2] *Working Group II. 1996. Impacts, Adaptations and Mitigation of Climate Change: Scientific-Technical Analyses. Contribution of Working Group II to the Second Assessment Report of the Intergovernmental Panel on Climate Change. R.T. Watson, M. C. Zinyowera, R.H. Moss, eds. Cambridge University Press. United States of America.*

[3] *Austin, D., J. Goldemberg, and G. Parker. Contributions to Climate Change: What are We Trying to Measure? In Press. World Resources Institute. Washington, D.C.*

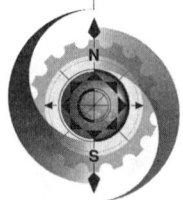

land use change projects under the CDM in order to clarify and separate them. Fully resolving most of these issues will both require further research and constructing the CDM with sufficiently stringent monitoring and verification procedures.

The World Resources Institute's (WRI's) past research on carbon reduction opportunities indicates that, with the correct incentives and controls, such efforts can deliver quantifiable climate benefits as well as help meet development and environmental objectives.

If forest and land use projects are to emerge as significant factors in the greenhouse gas reduction effort, three areas of concern must be satisfactorily resolved:

◆ unintended negative consequences
◆ project eligibility
◆ measurement, tracking, and certification.

Forest and Land Use Change Under the Kyoto Protocol

ARTICLE	RELEVANCE TO LAND USE CHANGE AND FORESTS
Article 3	*Domestic Greenhouse Emissions by Industrialised Countries.* Defines which domestic emissions should be inventoried by industrialised countries during the 2008-2012 commitment period. The Protocol currently requires tracking greenhouse gas removals and emissions from human-induced afforestation, reforestation, and deforestation that has occurred since 1990. However, the Article states that later Conference of the Parties may include additional activities such as forest harvest and management.
Article 12	*Clean Development Mechanism(CDM).* Allows industrialised countries to meet "part" of their emission limits and reduction commitments via certified emission reductions accruing from project activities in developing countries. There is no explicit mention of land use change and forest projects, making it unclear what range of projects will be allowed.

UNINTENDED NEGATIVE CONSEQUENCES

This first category concerns ways in which forest and land use change projects may have unintended negative consequences. They may fail to sequester the estimated amount of greenhouse gases, or they may be misused.

Issue: Forest projects will distract countries from the real business of reducing energy-related emissions.

Some national governments and environmental organisations oppose fully including forest and land use emissions and reductions because they do not want the focus of the negotiations to shift from fossil fuel to forest sector emissions. They believe this would allow developed countries to avoid making difficult changes in fossil fuel

consumption by investing in cheap projects to maintain rainforests. If this proved to be the case, the Protocol's ability to induce the development of new climate-friendly technology in the industrial sector would be diminished.

How much of a difference can promoting sinks through land use change and forest management projects make? A significant amount, but hardly enough to allow nations to completely bypass the industrial sector. By 2050, land use and forest options from all regions, including temperate and boreal, can reduce or sequester about 12-15 per cent of cumulative fossil fuel emissions over the same period.[4] In the Unites States, domestic forest options could remove or conserve about three per cent of the needed reductions over the commitment period,[5] thus

[4] *Ibid.*

[5] *Using data extrapolated from graphs on pages 785, 7867, we estimated that between 2008-2012, approximately 80.4 million tons of carbon can be sequestered or conserved within the United States. Then using projections from* International Energy Outlook 1998, *for the years 2008-2012, we estimate that to reach the 7 percent reduction from reference case projections, the U.S. must reduce its carbon emissions by 2,388.49 million tons. The percentage may in fact be optimistic as the emissions only estimate carbon, thus omitting emissions from the other six greenhouse gases. Department of Energy. 1998.* International Energy Outlook 1998. With Projections Through 2020. *Energy Information Administration. DOE/EIA-0484 (98). April. Table A9 Pg. 142.Washington DC.*

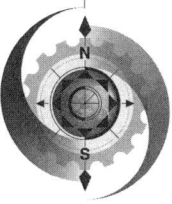

the U.S. cannot rely solely on the forest and land use sector. Given the physical limits, the concern that forest and land use projects will distract developed nations from the goal of reducing industrial fossil fuel use seems overstated.

On the other hand, emissions from deforestation are a significant part of the cause of climate change. Deforestation in tropical countries currently contributes an estimated 20 per cent of global carbon dioxide annual emissions. If the CDM were to summarily exclude efforts to avoid deforestation, a critical tool to combat climate change and biodiversity loss would be lost, since a large percentage of developing country emissions comes from deforestation.

Issue: Forest options could become a loophole. Governments could try to claim "credit" for activities they would have done anyway, regardless of the Protocol.

Importantly, this issue is not confined to forest and land use change projects, but can also affect energy-sector projects under the CDM. In either case, a recipient government or other agency could claim an incorrect "reference" scenario (that is, the likely course of future development in an area if projects were not implemented). For example, a country may claim that an area of forest would have been converted to agricultural use, when it is not, in actuality, in danger of being converted. In that instance, CDM funds could be used to protect the area and an investor would gain unearned greenhouse gas reduction credits. Similarly, in the energy sector, a recipient country may obtain funding from an Annex-I entity to switch an electrical power station from high-emission coal to low-emission natural gas. However, the municipality may have already been planning such a fuel switch for public health reasons, and again, unearned credits could be gained. In both sectors, the CDM must establish guidelines requiring proof of prevailing management practices, trends, and

existing legal requirements, all of which must be surpassed by the CDM project. Barriers to improving practices in the absence of CDM unds should be identified as well.

Issue: The potential exists for negative environmental impacts of some forest and land use carbon storage strategies, such as the conversion of natural forests into fast-growing plantations.

The CDM must incorporate guidelines preventing negative impacts, even if the net result is positive for climate change. Consider, for instance, the conversion of wetlands to agricultural uses. Less methane – and thus fewer emissions – are produced. But the conversion destroys a natural ecosystem. The Protocol calls for an Executive Board and entities that will certify project activities, presumably concentrating on greenhouse gas reductions. However, social and environmental criteria should serve, at a minimum, as a screen for projects. Many public institutions involving international trade regimes employ such environmental screens, such as the U.S.-based Overseas Private Investment Corporation, which provides risk insurance to overseas investors.

Issue: The potential exists for negative social impacts of some forest and land use carbon storage projects, if property rights are contested or unclear.

Because property and usage rights for forest resources are unclear or contested in many parts of the world, social screens an important part of a CDM regime.[6] Over the past 150 years, much of the world's tropical forests were brought under state ownership, sometimes without regard for the customary rights of local or forest dwelling communities.[7] The state often lacks the ability to enforce its ownership rights, leading to an "open access" situation

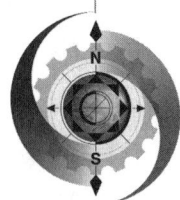

---

[6] Dudley, N., D. Gilmour, and J.P. Jeanrenaud. 1996. Forests for Life. The WWF/IUCN Forest Policy Book. World Wildlife Fund and IUCN/The World Conservation Union. February. Switzerland.

[7] Panayotou, T. and P. S. Ashton. 1992. Not by Timber Alone: The Economics and Ecology for Sustaining Tropical Forests. Island Press. Washington DC.

in which many different users exploit forest resources without legally recognised rights.[8]

If the CDM introduces new financing for forest and land use activities, competition for control over forest resources may intensify as various users compete for access to the new financial flows. These factors make it especially important that CDM projects be screened and designed to avoid

> **The CDM has the potential to fund "technological leapfrogging" that would enable developing countries to bypass the inefficient choices made by industrialised countries.**

negative social impacts. Project negotiation and design should involve not only state governments or private entities, but also local users. In many cases, contracting with host government entities for projects will not be sufficient; it may also be necessary or preferable to negotiate and contract directly with local and indigenous users of the project area.

PROJECT ELIGIBILITY

While some criteria for eligibility under the CDM are clearly specified, others, particularly those related to land use and forest projects, are not so clear cut.

Issue: Some countries opposed a broad inclusion of forest and land use activities, citing national sovereignty issues and a desire to separate forest management issues from the climate convention.

Article 12 specifies that participation in the CDM is voluntary and must be approved by each Party involved, meaning investor and host countries, thus national sovereignty is protected.

The Protocol instructs the Conference of the Parties to determine what kinds of project activities will be allowed under the CDM to meet part of developed country greenhouse gas reduction commitments. Some countries argue that the activities specified in Article 3.3 — which limits land use change and forest activities to removals and emissions from afforestation, reforestation, and deforestation — are the only land use change and forest activities to be allowed under the CDM. Conservation and forest management projects appear to be in jeopardy of exclusion, given the rules under Article 3.3, even when the evidence suggests

that such projects can potentially result in reliable climate, biodiversity, and social benefits.

The current pilot phase of AIJ extends to the end of 1999, and additional greenhouse gas offset projects continue to be funded. If future investors anticipate that the CDM will be restricted to tree planting, investors may avoid projects linking conservation to community

development, which could yield substantial environmental and social benefits, such as the Rio Bravo and CARE/Guatemala projects, as described in Box 1.

Issue: Should forest management and harvesting projects be eligible?

Projects that promote sustainable forest management or reduced impact logging can clearly improve carbon storage and potentially offer additional environmental benefits, such as reduced erosion and improved wildlife habitat.[9] A current example of reduced-impact logging, desc-ribed in Box 1, is underway in Malaysia.

Some of these projects have been carefully monitored for their carbon gains and losses. Past research on logging practices and the use of control plots for reference cases make it

[8] *Ostrom, Elinor. 1994.* Rules, Games, and Common-pool Resources. *Elinor Ostrom, Roy Gardner, and James Walker; with Arun Agrawal. Ann Arbor : University of Michigan Press, 1994.*

[9] *Pinard, M. A. And F. E. Putz. "Retaining Forest Biomass by Reducing Logging Damage." Biotropica. Vol. 28. No. 3.*

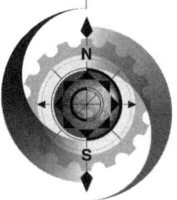

Box 2. Forest and Land Use Change Carbon Sequestration Projects

REDUCED IMPACT LOGGING IN SABAH, MALAYSIA

In August 1992, New England Electric Systems of Massachusetts, a coal-burning utility, decided to provide funds to Innoprise Corp., of Sabah, Malaysia, a timber concession holder, to implement reduced-impact logging guidelines for 1,400 hectares of Innoprise's 1-million hectare concession (Pinard 1996). The project emphasises staff training to use existing technology and machinery in an environmentally sensitive way and to increase supervision of harvesting operations. The harvesting guidelines include specifications for creating buffer zones for streams and roads, developing a formal harvesting plan, cutting climber vines before harvesting, planning and marking skid trails, marking trees for future harvests, and undertaking directional felling of marked trees to residual damage to surrounding forest.

The project's potential benefits include reduced damage to the residual forest; decreased erosion, carbon emissions, and land degradation; increased capacity for future timber production; increased biodiversity; decreased incidence of fire; reduced weed infestations; and increased long-term ecological and economic productivity.

THE CARFIX SUSTAINABLE FOREST MANAGEMENT PROJECT

The CARFIX project is located in central Costa Rica in the buffer zone of Braulio Carillo National Park, a World Biosphere Preserve. The project activities include forest preservation, regeneration, reforestation, sustainable forest management, and reduced-impact logging with the aim of stopping forest conversion and increasing cover. (United States Initiative on Joint Implementation 1998) The project activities will replace income from marginal agricultural activities with income from carbon sequestration and sustainable forestry.

The project is expected to create a biological corridor between parks, reduce soil erosion and water degradation.

THE RIO BRAVO CARBON SEQUESTRATION PROJECT

A project in Belize, the Rio Bravo Carbon Sequestration Project, funded by multiple utilities and implemented by the Programme for Belize and the Nature Conservancy, may be excluded if current rules are not changed. The project purchased endangered forest and is developing a sustainable forest management component that will provide income to local people and increase the amount of carbon sequestered (Programme for Belize 1994). Over its lifetime, the project is estimated to sequester slightly over one million tons of carbon.

CARE/GUATEMALA AGROFORESTRY PROJECT

One project located in Guatemala and proposed and implemented by CARE had several components, including creating community woodlots, implementing agroforestry practices, terracing vulnerable slopes, thus improving agricultural productivity, and providing training for community forest fire brigades (Brown 1997). WRI calculated that the project would sequester an estimated 11.2 million tons of carbon over 40 years, through net addition to the standing inventory of biomass carbon, retention of standing forests as a result of demand displacement via woodlots and agroforestry projects, protection of some carbon in soils, and retention of some standing forests because of community fire brigades.

References

Brown, P., B. Cabarle, and R. Livernash. 1997. *Carbon Counts: Estimating Climate Change Mitigation in Forestry Projects.* World Resources Institute. September.

Pinard, M.A. and F.E. Putz. "Retaining Forest Biomass by Reducing Logging Damage", Biotropica. Vol. 28, no. 3. 1996.

Programme for Belize, The Nature Conservancy, and Wisconsin Electric Power Company. 1994. The Rio Bravo Conservation and Management Area Belize. Carbon Sequestration Pilot Project Proposal. Submitted fore consideration under the United States Initiative on Joint Implementation. November.

United States Initiative on Joint Implementation. 1998. Activities Implemented Jointly: Second Report to the Secretariat of the United Nations Framework Convention on Climate Change. Accomplishments and Descriptions of Projects Accepted Under the U.S. Initiative on Joint Implementation. Volume 2. EPA 236-R-97-003.

relatively easy to estimate the net carbon sequestered. Currently, six pilot-phase carbon projects involve sustainable forest management or reduced-impact logging. Before deciding whether to include such projects in the future, the Conference of the Parties should, at the minimum, investigate their efficacy and overall environmental impacts under the current AIJ pilot phase. Emerging institutions, such as the Forest Stewardship Council, and their efforts offer opportunities and lessons for monitoring and verifying improved forest management.[10]

To avoid rewarding poor logging practices by paying for improvements over a low baseline, minimum reference case practices should be established. The minimum reference case should consist of basic standards for harvesting practices and only avoided emissions due to improvement over these standards would be creditable. Without these minimum standards, the most destructive harvest operations would yield greater carbon credits due to a lower baseline than less destructive operations. These minimum baselines should at least be equal to, or above, the existing laws of the host country.

---

[10] *Forest Stewardship Council. 1995.* Manual for Evaluation and Accreditation of Certification Bodies. *Oaxaca, Mexico.*

If such efforts were allowed under the CDM, then sustainable forest management may become more profitable in developing countries than clearing forest for cattle production, especially if income from carbon sequestration were part of the cost/benefit equation.[11]

> The international community is about to make momentous choices about what is included and what is left out in the global approach to mitigate climate change. One of the biggest choices is how much of a role forest and land use change projects will have under the CDM.

commercial timber operations, so they may be less efficient. One study of tropical timber harvests found that a maximum of 25 per cent of individual tree biomass became sawn timber, meaning that the carbon previously stored in 75 per cent of the tree, the soil, and other biota returns to the atmosphere. Further, most timber products are not long-lived, as a very small percentage of harvested wood goes into furniture or buildings, most becoming pulp, paper, or short-lived products such as pallets that are used several times and then discarded.

Issue: Should the CDM allow projects to track carbon stored in wood products?

Research by WRI and others indicates that carbon storage in wood products is relatively small and often temporary. Tracking and crediting such storage has limited potential to mitigate climate change.

Improving milling efficiency or timber production through silvicultural methods clearly increases carbon storage. However, too great an emphasis on carbon storage in wood products could lead to the incorrect conclusion that increasing harvest area or intensity will lead to greater carbon sequestration.[12]

WRI evaluated the net carbon sequestration potential of five forestry and land use projects, some of which included storing carbon in wood products as part of their strategy.[13] Of the projects examined, the average amount of carbon in wood products as a percentage of total carbon sequestered was 1.5 per cent, the maximum being 2 per cent. However, these projects involved community forestry, not

Furthermore, wood products are extracted through a greenhouse gas emitting activity – logging. In Russia, it is estimated that 33 Tera grams (Tg) of carbon per year is stored in wood products, while 115 Tg is released from logging. Clearly, increasing harvests to enhance carbon storage is a losing strategy.[14] Especially as measurement methods improve, carbon in wood products can play a role in carbon offsets, but should not be used as an excuse to increase harvest area or intensity.

Issue: Should forest conservation projects be eligible?

Conservation, or avoided deforestation, offers the greatest confluence of climate and biodiversity benefits and presents significant emission reduction opportunities.[15] However, some seek to specifically exclude conservation projects.

[11] *FUNDECOR. 1995. CARFIX Project Proposal for the Edison Electric Institute. Costa Rica.*

[12] *United States House of Representatives. 1997. House Resolution 151. Regarding Management of National Forests to Reduce Greenhouse Gases. October 21.*

[13] *World Resources Institute. 1994. Forestry as a Response to Global Warming. A Workshop Report. World Resources Institute. Washington, D.C.*

[14] *Kolchugina, T. P. and T. S. Vinson. 1995. "Role of Russian Forests in the Global Carbon Balance." Ambio Vol. 24. No. 5. August.*

[15] *Mark C. Trexler and Christine Haugen,* Keeping It Green: Tropical Forestry Opportunities for Mitigating Climate Change *(Washington D.C.: World Resources Institute, 1995).*
     Brown, P., B. Cabarle, and R. Livernash. Carbon Counts: Estimating Climate Change Mitigation in Forestry Projects. World Resources Institute. September.
     Cairns, Carbon Sequestration, Biological Diversity, *and Sustainable Development.*
     Robert N. Stavins, The Costs of Carbon Sequestration: A Revealed Preference Approach, *CSIA Discussion Paper 95-06 (Kennedy School of Government, Harvard University, 1995).*
     Harmon, M.E. and W.K. Ferrell, and J.F. Franklin. 1990. "Effects on Carbon Storage of Conversion of Old-Growth Forests to Young Forests." Science. February 9. Pg. 699.

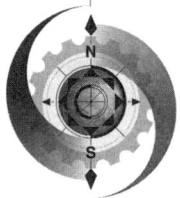

ISSUES&OPTIONS

The Clean Development Mechanism

Their opposition is based on concerns that: a) it is too difficult to determine whether deforestation would have occurred in the absence of carbon offset activities; and b) on the moral hazard that recipient countries might untruthfully claim a forest area is endangered to obtain carbon offset funds.

However, under appropriate CDM guidelines, conservation projects can result in reliable greenhouse gas reductions. First, the "without mitigation" or "reference" case must be confirmed, using local deforestation trends. Second, the underlying causes of these trends must be established.

Establishing a reference scenario will require evidence of an imminent threat to the standing forest in the absence of actions. The project activities should seek to address and counter the threats leading to land use change, by providing alternate income sources, such as land purchase or payments, or substitutes for the alternate use of the forest land. For example, if fuelwood gathering is contributing to deforestation, one aspect of the project should seek to provide alternate household fuel sources.

Under such conditions, the project should combine enforcement of protected areas with alternatives to forest conversion. The Rio Bravo project in Belize combined forest protection with income from sustainable forest management to replace farming. In other cases, though not all, the value of carbon sequestration may be able to provide an income stream that competes with the value of forest conversion, such as the CARFIX project in Costa Rica.

Issue: Should projects involving the improvement of agricultural productivity be eligible?

Increasing agricultural productivity in developing countries can stabilise the agricultural frontier, thus slowing deforestation. Early carbon sequestration offset projects included increasing agricultural productivity as a component.[16] The connection between deforestation and agricultural land demand makes improving agricultural productivity an important strategy for reducing greenhouse gas emissions from non-Annex I countries.

The problem is that the connection between maintaining forest cover and increasing agricultural productivity is indirect, even if it is well understood.[17] If possible, the CDM guidelines should be constructed to allow projects that seek to increase agricultural productivity in conjunction with forest protection. An example of such a project, CARE/Guatemala, is described in Box 1.

MEASUREMENT, TRACKING, AND CERTIFICATION

Quantifying and verifying greenhouse gas reductions from the forest sector can be problematic, especially compared to the energy sector. The key scientific and technical issues included establishing a reference case, leakage, permanence of reductions, and measurement accuracy.

Issue: Establishing a reference case

Determining the reference, or business-as-usual case, requires estimating what would have happened in the absence of greenhouse gas reduction efforts. The reference case will be a challenge for energy as well as forest sector projects.

The reference case is the foundation for determining net greenhouse gas reductions and emissions. In many cases, prevailing forest and land use practices and conversion trends are well understood and can be documented. Some projects, such as the reduced impact logging project in Malaysia and the more recent AIJ

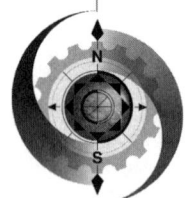

ISSUES&OPTIONS
The Clean
Development
Mechanism

[16] *Brown, P., B. Carbarle, and B. Livernash. 1997.* Carbon Counts: Estimating Climate Change Mitigation in Forestry Projects. *World Resources Institute. September.*
Faeth, P., C. Cort, R. Livernash. 1994. Evaluating the Carbon Sequestration Benefits of Forestry Projects in Developing Countries. *World Resources Institute. Washington, D.C.*
[17] *United Nations Environment Program. 1995.* Global Biodiversity Assessment. *Great Britain. Cambridge University Press. Pg. 891*

project "Noel Kempff", in Bolivia, established control areas similar to the project site, which allow a direct comparison of "with-mitigation" and "without-mitigation" activities.[18]

Determining the business-as-usual reference case for both sectors requires an understanding of barriers to improvement over time, to ensure that mitigation efforts are not overstated. Parallel barriers exist between the two sectors. For example, cost is a barrier both in switching from inexpensive coal to natural gas within the energy sector and in moving from conventional logging to sustainable forest management in the forest sector. In both sectors, high, up-front costs may be a barrier, even if, in the long run, the project's benefits ultimately outweighs the costs. Switching from conventional light bulbs to compact fluorescents involves higher initial costs, but uses less energy and saves money in the long run. Similarly, farmers may be unable to move from conventional agriculture to agroforestry because the up-front costs for the trees are prohibitive. In these cases, funding from greenhouse gas mitigation could help overcome the barriers.

In some cases, determining the reference case may be more problematic. For example, a reforestation project may have difficulty proving why the area would not have regrown under a business-as-usual case. Or, there may be clear data and evidence of deforestation, but determining the cause and the appropriate response may be more difficult. For example, if farmers are moving into the area and converting forest to agriculture, the reference case may be based on immigration fuelled by government policies. Or, the deforestation could be related to poor agricultural practices, or suggest other causes, all of which could impact the reference case.

Recent and continued improvements in the monitoring and inventorying of regional

and global land use cover and change, that incorporates on the ground measurements, will help to develop reference cases. The first global maps showing existing land cover have already been produced from satellite data.[19] These maps can provide the basis for tracking future land use changes.

Issue: Leakage

Leakage is the unexpected loss of anticipated greenhouse gas reductions due to the displacement of activities leading to carbon emissions. It is a potential problem in carbon offset projects. For example, in some cases, a reduced-impact logging project may lower timber output, causing increased harvests in another area. Because of this displacement of the emitting activity, total greenhouse gas benefits will be lower than expected.

WRI research indicates that in many cases leakage can be anticipated and avoided by properly designing projects or net carbon estimates can be revised, incorporating leakage effects if they occur.[20] The leakage risk assessment is primarily based on whether the project activities displace the emitting activity or provide an alternate use or income source for the forest. These risk assessments should be codified within the CDM certification systems so that leakage-prone projects can be identified and avoided. Early research from WRI and project implementation experience, such as that of the Nature Conservancy, offers some initial suggestions for project-level guidelines and leakage avoidance.[21]

Issue: Permanence of reductions

Some also question the permanence of reductions. Natural ecosystems are inherently dynamic, so sequestered carbon may not be

[18] *Ibid.*

[19] *Mission to Planet Earth. Remarks by William Townsend, Acting Associate Administrator. September 17, 1997. Earth Science Enterprise Website. http://www.hq.nasa.gov/office/mtpe/what_news/97accomps.htm*

[20] *Brown, P., B. Carbarle, and B. Livernash. 1997. Carbon Counts: Estimating Climate Change Mitigation in Forestry Projects. World Resources Institute. September.*

[21] *Ibid. United States Initiative on Joint Implementation. 1998. Activities Implemented Jointly: Second Report to the Secretariat of the United Nations Framework Convention on Climate Change. Accomplishments and Descriptions of Projects Accepted under the U.S. Initiative on Joint Implementation. Volume 2. EPA 236-R-97-003. This report describes the measures taken by AIJ project implementors to avoid and guard against leakage of greenhouse gas benefits.*

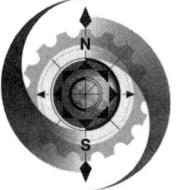

held forever. Weather, climate change itself, pests, disease, or fire can all reverse efforts to reduce or sequester greenhouse gas emissions. The carbon contract can also be reversed and the trees cut, thus losing carbon gains. However, although carbon stored in biota may be "temporary," some old-growth forests and grasslands have held their carbon for hundreds and even thousands of years.

To address the impermanence of forest sector reductions, greenhouse gas offsets credits could be "discounted" at some fixed ratio such that buyers are required to purchase a greater amount of "credits" than they ultimately own. This requirement would create a buffer of credits, so that if one project fails or is reversed, then the additional, "buffer" reductions will cover the losses. Such an approach would also generate added funds for sustainable development projects.

A recent example illustrates a trend towards a portfolio approach where greenhouses gas reductions come from a pool of projects rather than individual ones. Costa Rica recently established Certifiable Tradable Offsets, where they bundle certified carbon sequestration activities under one of two national umbrellas – the Protected Areas Project and the Private Forestry Project. The portfolio approach to sequestration could mean that the failure of one mitigation project will be made up by the buffer, especially if portfolios are required to hold a greater amount of reductions than are traded or sold.

Issue: Measurement accuracy

Finally, some question whether carbon losses and gains from vegetation and soils due to land use and management strategies can be accurately estimated. At the project level, measurement uncertainty is overstated. The Intergovernmental Panel on Climate Change (IPCC) reports a high confidence in site-level estimates of net carbon conserved or sequestered under particular management schemes.[22] It defines high confidence as a high degree of consensus among the report's authors based on "substantial" evidence.[23] Thus, project-based efforts, if well monitored, could yield measurable carbon losses and gains due to project activities.

The main hurdle facing accurate carbon accounting is the cost of obtaining the measurements. Any project or effort can be monitored and measured closely, but increasing accuracy increases costs. This is true as well for energy sector offsets.[24] While there continues to be uncertainty regarding soil carbon, most pilot offset projects have not included soil in their net carbon estimates.

PENDING DECISIONS

The decisions relating to forests and land use change have yet to be finalised, so it is still possible to capture potential biodiversity and climate benefits. While more research is needed to fully understand the calculation of greenhouse gas benefits, significant progress has been made. Concerns about accurately quantifying greenhouse gas reductions and emissions can in large part be solved by sharpening the IPCC methodology guidelines, establishing national-level inventory methods, instituting procedures for independent

verification required under Article 12, and utilising existing technology and data on forest cover and land use change.

The IPCC has been tasked by the Subsidiary Body for Scientific and Technological Advice (SBSTA) to prepare a special report on key forest and land use change issues to be completed in mid 2000. The special report will investigate defining terms, which, if any, emissions from additional land use activities should be counted under the Protocol, and whether Article 3, that

[22] *Working Group II, 1996.*

[23] *Working Group II. 1996.*

[24] *Trexler and Associates, 1998.* The Role of Forestry Climate Mitigation Strategy. *Draft Workshop Report.*

Box 2. Sources of Greenhouse Gas Emissions

Among the principal greenhouse gases, carbon dioxide is estimated to account for about 64 per cent of all greenhouse warming. To date, most of the policy emphasis related to greenhouse gas reductions has focused on industrial emissions of fossil fuels. Though they are unquestionably the largest component, this emphasis tends to overlook the significant contribution of deforestation and other land use changes to the atmospheric build up of carbon dioxide. As noted in the text, since the 1800's forest conversion has contributed approximately 30 per cent of the accumulated carbon dioxide in the atmosphere (Austin, 1998). Since the vast majority of those land use emissions have come from the developing world, narrowing the options to address deforestation under the CDM will inhibit the ability of developing countries to limit current and future emissions.

References

Austin, D., J. Goldemberg, and G. Parker. Contributions to Climate Change: What are we Trying to Measure? In Press. World Resources Institute. Washington, D.C.

addresses domestic activities, should apply to the CDM. Forest, biodiversity, and development experts need to participate in the IPCC process and other fora, such as the upcoming Conference of the Parties and advisory meetings to communicate more widely what is known about land use change and forest trends, and how and where they can be influenced for the betterment of climate and biodiversity.

If the Convention delegates allow a broad range of projects and activities under the CDM, new systems and technologies will be required to accurately monitor and verify regional forest and land use change trends. a significant contribution in itself. While the CDM will require monitoring and verification systems, to include forest and land use change projects, systems that can track regional and local changes in land use must be put in place. The system should combine the use of remote sensing technologies with ground truthing, which would serve both those concerned

generally with the loss and degradation of forests and the accompanying greenhouse gas emissions. Many projects under the AIJ pilot phase are employing such techniques in their monitoring and verification protocols. If governments or certification agencies employed and installed regional monitoring systems, then costs are likely to decrease.[25] The US National Aeronautics and Space Administration (NASA) is currently testing and developing technologies combining *in situ* measurements with current and planned satellite systems that will be able to inventory global land cover and land use change with the goal of providing policy-relevant data at the regional scale.[26]

Such a system could identify forest areas subject to conversion and degradation, or candidate areas for restoration. A subset of the threatened forests could then become candidates for CDM projects – if the drivers leading to conversion could be substituted with lower-impact, lower-emitting activities. For example, in Costa Rica sustainable forest management, rather than relatively low-productivity cattle ranching, is replacing forest conversion.

The associated monitoring and verification costs should be considered integral to the project, not as unnecessary transaction costs to be eliminated. To realise the potential biodiversity and climate benefits of the CDM, appropriate project guidelines, as well as auditing and verification systems are needed. Putting them into place is a better approach than restricting the types of forest and land use activities that are eligible.

Most importantly, by coupling credible CDM guidelines for verification, accountability, and monitoring with a broad inclusion of forests and land use change – including avoided deforestation and forest management – the Protocol can maximise impact on both biodiversity and climate. ∎

---

[25] *For example, the Rio Bravo Carbon Sequestration pilot project is using air photography, control sites, and satellite imagery. Similarly, ECOLAND, a forest preservation project in Costa Rica is using satellite and photographic imaging in conjunction with contracting a local eco-tourist group to undertake on-the-ground monitoring. CARFIX project implementors will undertake triennial remote sensing, annual forest growth measurements, with LANDSAT imagery. United States Initiative on Joint Implementation. 1998. Activities Implemented Jointly: Second Report to the Secretariat of the United Nations Framework Convention on Climate Change. Accomplishments and Descriptions of Projects Accepted under the U.S. Initiative on Joint Implementation. Volume 2. EPA 236-R-97-003.*

[26] *Mission to Planet Earth Science Research Plan. Land-Cover and Land Use Change Strategy. NASA Website: http://www.hq.nasa.gov/office/mtpe/draftsciplan/mtpe-srp.htm*

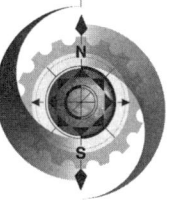

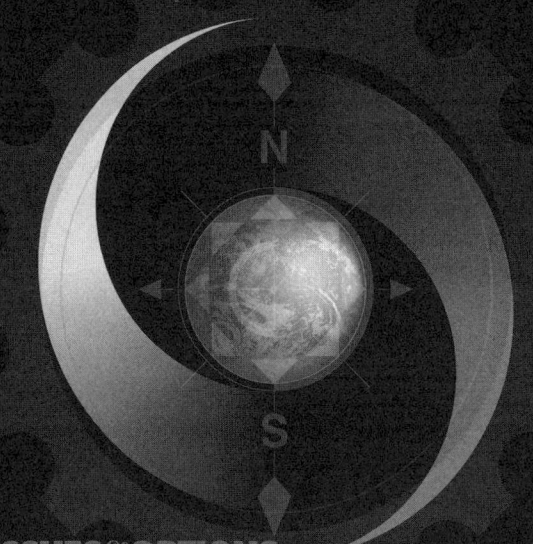

ISSUES&OPTIONS
The Clean Development Mechanism

Annexes

NOTES ON THE EDITOR AND CONTRIBUTORS

Annexes

Editor:

José Goldemberg - Professor at the University of São Paulo for Instituto de Eletroténica e Energia in São Paulo, Brazil.

Contributors:

Paige Brown - Research Analyst with the Climate, Energy and Pollution Program at the World Resources Institute and was a participant at COP-3.

Benjamin Dessus - Head of Ecodev Programme at the Centre National de la Recherche Scientifique (CNRS) in Meudon, France, Chairman of the Scientific and Technical Advisory Panel of the Fonds Français pour l'Environnement Mondial (FFEM), and member of the French Delegation to COP-3.

Raúl A. Estrada-Oyuela - Ambassador, Argentina, Chairman of the Committee of the Whole during the Third Conference of the Parties to the United Nations Framework Convention (COP-3).

Alessandra Goria works with the Fondazione ENI Enrico Mattei, Milan, Italy.

Robert Hamwey - Associate Professor for Climate Change at the International Academy of the Environment (IAE) in Geneva, Switzerland. His research at IAE has focused on energy consumption, technology transfer, and international policy mechanisms and he has been active in UNFCCC Sessions since 1993.

Paul Hassing - Head of the Division of Climate, Energy and Environment Technology of Netherlands Development Assistance in the Ministry of Foreign Affairs. Active in the UNFCCC process.

Stephen Humphreys - Research Fellow with the Energy Programme at Environment and Development Action in the Third World (ENDA-TM), Dakar, Senegal.

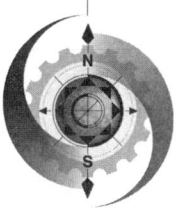

ISSUES&OPTIONS
The Clean
Development
Mechanism

Josef Janssen works with the Fondazione ENI Enrico Mattei, Milan, Italy.

Nancy Kete - Director of the Climate, Energy and Pollution Program at the World Resources Institute. Dr. Kete has been very active in the UNFCCC process.

Robert Livernash - Former Senior Editor for the World Resources Report, World Resources Institute.

Luiz Gylvan Meira Filho - President of the Brazilian Space Agency in Brasilia, Brazil, member of Brazilian Delegation to COP-3 and Chairman of contact Group that negotiated the inclusion of the Clean Development Mechanism.

Matthew S. Mendis - President of Alternative Energy Development Inc. (AED) in USA and Project Leader for the Asia Least-Cost Greenhouse Gas Abatement Strategy (ALGAS) Project being executed by the Asian Development Bank.

Mark Mwandosya - Professor at the Centre for Energy, Environment Science and Technology (CEEST) in Dar-es-Salaam Tanzania, member of the Tanzanian Delegation to COP-3, Chairman of the Group of 77 and China at the time of COP-3.

Rajendra K. Pachauri - President of the Tata Energy Research Institute (TERI) in New Delhi, India. Observer at COP-3.

Theodore Panayotou - Fellow of Harvard Institute for International Development in Cambridge, Massachusetts where he is Director of the International Environment Programme.

Domenico Siniscalco works with the Fondazione ENI Enrico Mattei, Milan, Italy.

Youba Sokona - Deputy Executive Secretary of ENDA-TM and Head of the Energy Programme at ENDA-TM, Dakar, Senegal. Observer at COP-3.

Björn Stigson - President of World Business Council for Sustainable Development (WBCSD) in Geneva, Switzerland. The WBCSD had a strong presence at COP-3 in Kyoto, brining a business view to the negotiations especially on issues such as flexible mechanisms, voluntary agreements and technology transfer.

Francisco Szekely - Professor and the Director of the International Academy of the Environment (IAE) in Geneva, Switzerland.

Jean-Philippe Thomas - Senior Research Coordinator for the Energy Programme at ENDA-TM, Dakar, Senegal.

Farhana Yamin - Director of the Foundation for International Environmental Law and Development (FIELD) who runs FIELD's climate change programme in London, UK. Ms. Yamin has participated in the UNFCCC process as Legal Advisor to Samoa.

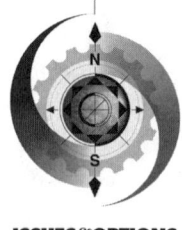

ARTICLE 12 OF THE KYOTO PROTOCOL

Annexes

1. A clean development mechanism is hereby defined.

2. The purpose of the clean development mechanism shall be to assist Parties not included in Annex I in achieving sustainable development and in contributing to the ultimate objective of the Convention, and to assist Parties included in Annex I in achieving compliance with their quantified emission limitation and reduction commitments under Article 3.

3. Under the clean development mechanism:

    (a) Parties not included in Annex I will benefit from project activities resulting in certified emission reductions, and

    (b) Parties included in Annex I may use the certified emission reductions accruing from such project activities to contribute to compliance with part of their quantified emission limitation and reduction commitments under Article 3, as determined by the Conference of the Parties serving as the meeting of the Parties to this Protocol.

3. The clean development mechanism shall be subject to the authority and guidance of the Conference of the Parties serving as the meeting of the Parties to this Protocol and be supervised by an executive board of the clean development mechanism.

5   Emission reductions resulting from each project activity shall be certified by operational entities to be designated by the Conference of the Parties serving as the meeting of the Parties to this Protocol, on the basis of:

    (a) Voluntary participation approved by each Party involved;

    (b) Real, measurable, and long-term benefits related to the mitigation of climate change; and

    (c) Reductions in emissions that are additional to any that would occur in the absence of the certified project activity.

6. The clean development mechanism shall assist in arranging funding of certified project activities as necessary.

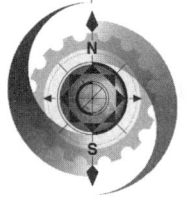

ISSUES&OPTIONS

The Clean
Development
Mechanism

7. The Conference of the Parties serving as the meeting of the Parties to this Protocol shall, at its first session, elaborate modalities and procedures with the objective of ensuring transparency, efficiency and accountability through independent auditing and verification of project activities.

8. The Conference of the Parties serving as the meeting of the Parties to this Protocol shall ensure that a share of the proceeds from certified project activities is used to cover administrative expenses as well as to assist developing country Parties that are particularly vulnerable to the adverse effects of climate change to meet the costs of adaptation.

9. Participation under the clean development mechanism, including in activities mentioned in paragraph 3(a) above and in the acquisition of certified emission reductions, may involve private and/or public entities, and is to be subject to whatever guidance may be provided by the executive board of the clean development mechanism.

10. Certified emission reductions obtained during the period from the year 2000 up to the beginning of the first commitment period can be used to assist in achieving compliance in the first commitment period.

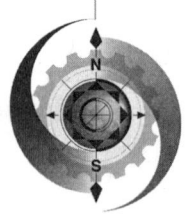